Cognitive Behavior Therapy for Depressed Adolescents

Cognitive Behavior Therapy for Depressed Adolescents provides clinicians, clinical supervisors, and researchers with a comprehensive understanding of etiological pathways as well as current CBT approaches for treating affected adolescents. Chapters guide readers from preparations for the first session and clinical assessment to termination and relapse prevention, and each chapter includes session transcripts to provide a more concrete sense of what it looks like to implement particular CBT techniques with depressed teens. In-depth discussions of unique challenges posed by working with depressed teens, as well as ways to address these issues, also are provided.

Randy P. Auerbach, PhD, ABPP, is a board-certified clinical psychologist and an assistant professor in the department of psychiatry at Harvard Medical School. At McLean Hospital, he is the director of clinical research for the division of child and adolescent psychiatry.

Christian A. Webb, PhD, is an instructor in the department of psychiatry at Harvard Medical School and an assistant neuroscientist at McLean Hospital.

Jeremy G. Stewart, PhD, is a postdoctoral fellow at McLean Hospital and a research fellow in psychology in the department of psychiatry at Harvard Medical School.

Cognitive Behavior Therapy for Depressed Adolescents
A Practical Guide to Management and Treatment

Randy P. Auerbach
Christian A. Webb
Jeremy G. Stewart

NEW YORK AND LONDON

First published 2016
by Routledge
711 Third Avenue, New York, NY 10017

and by Routledge
2 Park Square, Milton Park, Abingdon, Oxon, OX14 4RN

Routledge is an imprint of the Taylor & Francis Group, an informa business

© 2016 Randy P. Auerbach, Christian A. Webb, and Jeremy G. Stewart

The right of Randy P. Auerbach, Christian A. Webb, and Jeremy G. Stewart to be identified as the authors of this Work has been asserted by them in accordance with sections 77 and 78 of the Copyright, Designs and Patents Act 1988.

All rights reserved. No part of this book may be reprinted or reproduced or utilized in any form or by any electronic, mechanical, or other means, now known or hereafter invented, including photocopying and recording, or in any information storage or retrieval system, without permission in writing from the publishers.

Trademark notice: Product or corporate names may be trademarks or registered trademarks, and are used only for identification and explanation without intent to infringe.

Library of Congress Cataloging in Publication Data
Auerbach, Randy P.
Cognitive behavior therapy for depressed adolescents : a practical guide to management and treatment / Randy P. Auerbach, Christian A. Webb, Jeremy G. Stewart.
pages cm
Includes bibliographical references and index.
Depression in adolescence—Treatment. 2. Cognitive therapy for teenagers. I. Webb, Christian A. II. Stewart, Jeremy G. III. Title.
RJ506.D4A92 2016
616.85'2700835—dc23
2015029367

ISBN: 978-1-138-81613-8 (hbk)
ISBN: 978-1-138-81614-5 (pbk)
ISBN: 978-1-315-74630-2 (ebk)

Typeset in Baskerville
by Swales & Willis Ltd, Exeter, Devon, UK

Contents

About the Authors   viii
Acknowledgments   x

1 Introduction   1
Epidemiology 1
DSM-5: Definitions and Subtypes 3
Cognitive Behavior Therapy 5
Goals for the Book 7
Intended Audience 8
Effective Use of the Book 8
Summary 9

2 Models of Depression   10
Life Stress and Adolescent Depression 10
Behavioral Models of Depression 16
Social Cognitive Learning Models of Depression 18
Cognitive Theories of Depression 19
Information-Processing Models of Depression 24
Summary 29

3 Assessment   30
Assessment Goals 30
Diagnostic Interviews 32
Self-Report Questionnaires 35
Observational Methods 37
Third-Party Reports 38
Suicide and Self-Harm Risk Assessment 39
Summary: An Ounce of Prevention is Worth a Pound of Cure 41

4 Setting the Stage — 43
Psychoeducation 44
Collaborative Empiricism and Guided Discovery 48
Therapeutic Alliance 49
Alliance-Interfering Behaviors 55
Motivational Interviewing 59
Summary 65

5 Starting — 66
Major Elements of Early Sessions 66
The Anatomy of Session 1 79
Session Content and Structure: Session 2 and Beyond 84
Behavioral Activation Strategies 86
Summary 95

6 Working — 96
Identifying Negative Automatic Thoughts 96
Suggested Strategies to Elicit Negative Automatic Thoughts 97
The Bottom Line 104
Challenging Negative Automatic Thoughts 105
Suggested Strategies for Challenging Negative Automatic Thoughts 105
Between-Session Homework 112
Core Beliefs and Intermediate Beliefs 113
Communication Styles and Cognitions 116
Problem-Solving 123
Summary 130

7 Maintaining Gains and Relapse Prevention — 131
Preparing for Treatment Termination 131
Reassessing Treatment Goals 132
Post-Treatment Competency in CBT Skills 134
Anticipating and Addressing Depression Triggers 137
Addressing Residual Symptoms 138
Addressing Underlying Vulnerability Factors 141
Additional Treatment 142
Parental Depression 142
Booster Sessions 144
Mindfulness-Based Interventions for Relapse Prevention 145
Summary 158

8 Therapeutic Challenges and Comprehensive Care — 160
Family Involvement in Treatment 160
Cultural Considerations 164
Sleep 174
Comorbidity 178
Pharmacotherapy 185
Summary 187

9 Addressing Suicidality — 188
Assessing Suicidality 188
Treatment of Suicidality 199
Summary 203

10 Innovations and Future Directions in CBT — 205
Computer- and Internet-Based Interventions 205
Mobile Depression Interventions (Smartphones and Applications) 210
Providing CBT via Videoconferencing 215
Summary 216

References — 217
Index — 243

About the Authors

Randy P. Auerbach, PhD, ABPP, is a board-certified clinical psychologist and an assistant professor in the Department of Psychiatry at Harvard Medical School. At McLean Hospital, he is the director of clinical research for the Division of Child and Adolescent Psychiatry as well as the director of the Child and Adolescent Mood Disorders Laboratory. Dr. Auerbach's program of research is aimed at identifying psychosocial, behavioral, and neurobiological factors that render certain children, adolescents, and young adults vulnerable to experience depressive symptoms and episodes, and the research also examines factors that contribute to successful cognitive behavioral therapy (CBT) interventions. This work is funded by grants from the National Institute of Mental Health, the Klingenstein Third Generation Foundation, the Dana Foundation, and several private foundations, and to date, it has resulted in over 50 published scientific papers and book chapters. Dr. Auerbach is the recipient of a number of awards, including the David Shakow Early Career Award for Distinguished Scientific Contributions in Clinical Psychology and the Society for Clinical Child and Adolescent Psychology Early Career Award.

Christian A. Webb, PhD, is an instructor in the Department of Psychiatry at Harvard Medical School and an assistant neuroscientist at McLean Hospital. Dr. Webb's primary area of research investigates the underlying psychosocial and neural mechanisms of symptom improvement in treatments for depression, with a particular focus on CBT. He also conducts research on the causes of depression, as well as studies low-cost, internet-based interventions for depression. He has received several awards for his research, including awards from the Anxiety and Depression Association of America, the Beck Institute for Cognitive Behavioral Therapy, the Canadian Psychological Association, and the Association for Behavioral and Cognitive Therapies. Dr. Webb's research has been supported through grants from the National Institute of Mental Health, the Social Sciences and Humanities Research Council of Canada, and the Klingenstein Third Generation Foundation.

Jeremy G. Stewart, PhD, is a postdoctoral research fellow at McLean Hospital and a research fellow in psychology in the Department of Psychiatry at Harvard Medical School. He completed his PhD in clinical psychology at Queen's University in Kingston, Ontario, Canada, which included a predoctoral internship at McLean Hospital. Dr. Stewart has devoted his career to better understanding factors that contribute to the development and maintenance of major depressive disorder in adolescents, with particular attention to the role of adverse experiences and stressful life events. Currently, Dr. Stewart is investigating the complex interplay among environmental, behavioral, and neural factors in predicting suicide risk in depressed adolescents. His research has been supported through awards from the Canadian Institutes of Health Research, the Natural Sciences and Engineering Research Council, and the Ontario Ministry of Training, Colleges and Universities.

Acknowledgments

My parents, Russell and Elyse Auerbach, have provided limitless support, and my wife, Tiffany Chantra, has showered me with warmth, laughter, and love, giving me the strength and courage to pursue that which seems out of reach. My mentorship team across the McGill, McLean, and Harvard community has nurtured my development as a clinical researcher and therapist, providing boundless opportunities to excel in the professional arena. Finally, I am indebted to the adolescents and families with whom I worked, as I learned invaluable lessons from all of you.

Randy P. Auerbach

To John Hunt: I am forever indebted to you for sparking my love of learning and teaching me to challenge fundamental assumptions. To my parents, Anthony and Micheline Webb: your sage advice and unwavering support over the years have provided me with immeasurable guidance and encouragement. To Renata: your love, laughter, and boundless *joie de vivre* inspire me each and every day. Finally, thank you to my many research and clinical mentors and colleagues, in particular at Penn and McLean Hospital: I am immensely grateful for your mentorship, wisdom, and the countless opportunities you have provided me.

Christian A. Webb

To my parents, Kent and Marianne Stewart: your patience and unconditional support throughout my education and training have allowed me to pursue my aspirations (and achieve some of them). To my wife, Stephanie Boyer: I am forever grateful for your generosity, warmth, and love. Your talents as a clinician and scientist continue to inspire my own work. To Kate Harkness: thank you for the opportunities you gave me, for fostering my creativity and for modeling an approach to clinical psychological science that I strive to emulate. To Michela David: thank you for sharing your substantial wisdom and skill and for approaching my CBT training with empathy and humor. Your teachings echo through the pages of this book. Finally, thank you to the exceptional group of clinical and research mentors at both Queen's University and McLean Hospital that have supported and shaped my career, providing me with the necessary tools, inspiration, and opportunity to succeed.

Jeremy G. Stewart

1 Introduction

The prevalence of major depressive disorder (MDD) surges in adolescence and is associated with a range of negative downstream emotional, behavioral, interpersonal, and socioeconomic consequences (Greden, 2001; Greenberg et al., 2003). Despite relatively effective treatment options for depression in adolescence, the average length of a depressive episode is about 6 months and approximately 40–70% experience a recurrent episode within 5 years of the initial diagnosis (Avenevoli, Swendsen, He, Burstein, & Merikangas, 2015; Rao et al., 1996). Taken together, depression is both recurrent and debilitating, and, perhaps not surprisingly, it is one of the leading causes of disability and premature death worldwide (Kessler, 2012). Therefore, providing effective treatment for depressed adolescents, earlier in the disease course, is paramount.

Epidemiology

The most comprehensive epidemiological study completed on adolescent depression has been the National Comorbidity Study – Adolescent (NCS-A) Supplement. This project has amassed invaluable information about adolescent psychopathology, particularly as it relates to prevalence, age of onset, course, comorbidity, and treatment (e.g., Avenevoli et al., 2015; Nock et al., 2013). The study includes a large, ethnically diverse sample of adolescents ages 13–18 years ($n \sim 10,000$), and reports on clinical data (survey and interviews) collected over a span of 4 years (2001–2004).

Lifetime and 12-Month Prevalence

Our most recent estimates show that depression is a common and widespread problem. In school-aged children, prevalence rates range from 1% to 2% (for review, see Avenevoli, Knight, Kessler, & Merikangas, 2008); however, there is a dramatic increase during adolescence. Specifically, data from the NCS-A suggest that, by the end of adolescence,

11% of teens will have experienced at least one major depressive episode (MDE), and moreover, 7.5% of adolescents met criteria for MDD in the previous year. Compared to males, female adolescents have a two- to threefold greater likelihood of experiencing MDD and are at four times greater risk for experiencing severe MDD. Similar effects are found when examining trends in age, as older adolescents are at twofold greater risk for MDD and a fourfold greater risk of reporting severe MDD relative to younger teens (Avenevoli et al., 2015). As a whole, these findings echo previous work that has shown that relatively older female adolescents are at greatest risk for experiencing MDD (Hankin, Mermelstein, & Roesch, 2007).

Twelve-Month Comorbidity

Depression rarely occurs in isolation, and results from the NCS-A suggest that approximately 64% of youth reporting MDD experience comorbid mental health disorders. Youth with MDD have a four times greater likelihood of reporting anxiety and behavioral disorders, and this comorbidity is associated with more severe depressive symptoms. Surprisingly, the pattern of comorbidity does not vary as a function of gender. This may reflect the fact that, among depressed youth the prevalence of oppositional defiant disorder, conduct disorder, and substance use disorders does not differ in males versus females (Avenevoli et al., 2015).

Socioeconomic Status, Race, and Ethnicity

In contrast to adults where depressive disorders are associated with a lower socioeconomic status (SES) (Kessler et al., 2003), reports in youth have been inconsistent (see Merikangas & Knight, 2009). Specifically, in a meta-analysis including 310 studies of youth, Twenge and Nolen-Hoeksema (2002) found no association between SES and depression. Nonetheless, in studies targeting the most impoverished individuals, a modest to moderate inverse association was found between SES and depression (Costello et al., 1996; Gilman, Kawachi, Fitzmaurice, & Buka, 2003).

There is limited research on racial and ethnic differences among depressed youth. Preliminary epidemiological investigations have not found between-group differences in the incidence of MDD among Caucasian and African American (Costello et al., 1998) or Native American (Costello, Farmer, Angold, Burns, & Erkanli, 1997) youth. Research examining differences in depressive symptoms has, however, indicated that Hispanic youth report modestly greater symptom severity relative to Caucasian and African American youth (Twenge & Nolen-Hoeksema, 2002). An important caveat to these findings is that the studies included relatively small samples, and therefore should be interpreted with caution.

Suicidality

Depression is intimately connected to suicidality; however, whereas depressive symptoms are predictive of increased suicidal ideation and a greater number of suicide plans, symptom severity is a weaker predictor of attempts (Nock, 2009). Twelve-month prevalence estimates from the NCS-A suggest that approximately 11% of depressed adolescents made an attempt, and this rate was nearly twofold greater among those with severe symptoms (~21%). Moreover, and strikingly, 75% of depressed adolescents make a suicide attempt in their lifetime (Nock et al., 2013).

DSM-5: Definitions and Subtypes

According to the *Diagnostic and Statistical Manual of Mental Disorders, Fifth Edition* (DSM-5: American Psychiatric Association, 2013) a MDE requires a patient to report five or more symptoms over a period of at least 2 weeks. At a minimum, patients must report depressed mood (or irritability in youth) and/or loss of interest or pleasure (i.e., anhedonia). Additional depressive symptoms include: weight change (i.e., 5% increase or decrease in body weight), sleep disturbance (insomnia or hypersomnia), psychomotor agitation or retardation, fatigue, feelings of worthlessness and/or excessive guilt, concentration difficulties, and recurrent thoughts of death.

To better define different *stages* of the MDE, consensus teams have agreed on definitions for the following terms: *episode, remission, response, recovery, relapse*, and *recurrence* (see Boland & Keller, 2009; Frank et al., 1991; for review, see Monroe & Harkness, 2011). Whereas an *episode* is operationalized as manifesting a set number of symptoms for a specific period of time, *remission* marks the end of a depressive episode when a person is either in *partial* or *full remission*. *Partial remission* is characterized by more than a minimal presentation of symptoms, but typically there is a reduction in the number and intensity of symptoms compared to within the episode. Conversely, when a patient is in *full remission*, he or she no longer meets diagnostic criteria for the disorder; however, it is not atypical for these individuals to experience some minimal symptoms. At its core, *remission* is an absence (or reduction) of symptoms; however, it does not assume that an intervention has been delivered. A *response*, by contrast, suggests that a course of treatment (e.g., psychotherapy, pharmacotherapy) has been applied, and that the depressive symptoms attenuated (e.g., >50% reduction) *as a result* of the intervention. *Recovery* connotes sustained improvement for roughly 4 months or that the underlying depressive episode has been resolved, and in most instances, a depressive episode is unlikely to surface in the near future. The difference between *relapse* and *recurrence* is important. A *relapse* is the return of a depressive episode after remission but before recovery, whereas *recurrence* refers to a new episode following recovery.

An important clinical distinction in diagnosing MDD in youth versus adults is the presence of irritability. Irritability is considered a cardinal symptom of depression among children and adolescents, and in fact, it is widely believed to be among the most frequently reported symptoms of moderate MDD in adolescents (see Crowe, Ward, Dunnachie, & Roberts, 2006). While adults often endorse irritability during subclinical and clinical depressive episodes, irritability in the absence of either sadness or anhedonia is not sufficient for a diagnosis of MDD. Similar to depressive episodes with strong anhedonic features (see Auerbach, Admon, & Pizzagalli, 2014; Loas, 1996), some research suggests that prominent irritability may reflect a subtype of MDD (Perlis et al., 2005). Specifically, Perlis and colleagues assert that irritability, as a feature of MDD, is cause for concern given that it may be associated with more severe symptoms, compromised functioning, and suicidality.

Persistent Depressive Disorder

An important change introduced in DSM-5 was merging chronic MDD and dysthymic disorder into persistent depressive disorder (PDD). PDD is characterized by depressive mood nearly all day, every day, for a period of at least 2 years. This depressive mood is accompanied by the presence of at least two of the following symptoms: appetite disturbance, sleep problems, low energy or fatigue, low self-worth, inattention/indecision, and hopelessness. If at any time an adolescent meets criteria for MDD (i.e., satisfying at least 5/9 symptoms, as described above), then a diagnosis of MDD is given in place of PDD. PDD also may be associated with anxious, atypical, and psychotic features.

Melancholia

A subtype of MDD that has received a great deal of clinical and research attention is melancholia (e.g., Curry et al., 2006). Melancholia requires the presence of anhedonia or lack of mood reactivity and at least three of the following symptoms: depressed mood, weight/appetite loss, psychomotor agitation/retardation, excessive guilt, and worse mood in the morning. Melancholia is believed to be biologically based, and studies have linked this subtype to hypothalamic–pituitary–adrenal axis overactivity as well as genetic factors (see Dinan & Scott, 2005; Kendler et al., 1996).

Specifiers

Although less frequently diagnosed, two cyclical subtypes of depression include seasonal affective disorder (SAD) and premenstrual mood disorder (PMD). Blazer, Kessler, and Swartz (1998) found that approximately 1% of the population satisfy diagnostic criteria for SAD, and identified cases were more typical in winter months and more prevalent in northern versus southern latitudes (Blazer et al., 1998). Pearlstein and Stone (1998) indicated that mood changes occurring during the menstrual cycle are common; however, only 4–6% of women experience PMD (Sveindottir & Backstrom, 2000). A critical feature of PMD is the unequivocal recurrent onset–offset pattern of five or more depressive symptoms occurring in the majority of menstrual cycles for at least 1 year.

Additionally, the DSM-5 describes other specifiers such as recurrent brief depression, short-duration depressive episode (4–13 days), and depressive episode with insufficient symptoms. The empirical literature on these specifiers is sparse, but each connotes a shorter episode duration (i.e., recurrent brief depression, short-duration depressive episode) or subthreshold characteristics (i.e., depressive episode with insufficient characteristics).

Symptom Clusters

The manifestation of depressive symptoms is enormously heterogeneous, and consequently, the *experience* of MDD varies substantially from patient to patient. Importantly, there are preliminary data on how treatment may differentially impact symptom clusters. For example, Fournier and colleagues (2013) found that both antidepressant medication and cognitive behavior therapy (CBT) led to a greater reduction in cognitive- and suicide-related symptoms as compared to the placebo. Further, CBT was particularly effective in reducing atypical-vegetative symptoms (i.e., hypersomnia and weight gain) as compared to both antidepressant medication and the placebo. In contrast, Stewart and Harkness (2012) reported no differences; the authors concluded that antidepressant medication and CBT did not differentially impact cognitive versus somatic symptoms of depression. However, Harkness and Stewart (2009) reported that depressive symptom clusters may lead to the generation of different types of stressful life events. Whereas cognitive-affective symptoms led to higher levels of interpersonal-oriented events (e.g., conflicts with peers and parents), somatic symptoms generated more independent, or fateful life events (e.g., physical illness). As learning to effectively respond to, and cope with, life stressors is a central goal of CBT, attending to these differences may be of critical import when working collaboratively with youth.

Cognitive Behavior Therapy

CBT is the most empirically supported psychotherapeutic intervention for adolescent MDD (Spence & Reineke, 2003; Spirito, Esposito-Smythers,

6 *Introduction*

Wolff, & Uhl, 2011). Generally speaking, CBT provides a short-term (12–18 sessions), structured approach to systematically and strategically target dysfunctional interrelationships among thoughts, emotions, and behaviors (Figure 1.1). Patients learn about how negative cognitions and depressogenic information processing biases shape emotional experiences, particularly as this may relate to thoughts about the self, world, and future (i.e., the negative cognitive triad; Table 1.1). According to the cognitive behavioral model, *negative automatic thoughts* trigger negative emotions (e.g., sadness, anger, anxiety) and associated behaviors (e.g., isolating, self-harm). CBT helps patients identify patterns of distorted or biased thoughts, and teaches them skills to challenge these cognitions as a means of reducing emotional distress and maladaptive behaviors.

In addition to identifying and challenging depressogenic cognitions, CBT highlights the importance of *behavioral activation.* Depressed youth often isolate and avoid previously enjoyed activities (e.g., spending time with friends; playing sports), and consequently, a therapist uses a stepwise approach to help teens gradually re-engage with key sources of reinforcement and reward in their environment. Re-engaging is essential, as it also

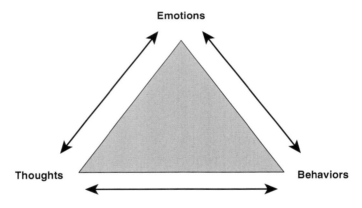

Figure 1.1 CBT Triangle: Thoughts, Emotions, and Behaviors

Table 1.1 Cognitive Triad

Domains	Definition	Example Negative Automatic Thought
Self	Self is worthless	I am unlovable
World	World is unjust	My parents and classmates don't want to spend time with me because I am unlovable
Future	Future is hopeless	I'll always be alone because I am unlovable

provides a testing ground to evaluate entrenched distorted patterns of thinking (e.g., Why bother going out? I won't have fun anyway), and the opportunity to experience pleasure.

Together, interventions aimed at challenging negative cognitions and reducing maladaptive behaviors are the bedrock for effective CBT. The therapy encourages an active and engaged adolescent patient, and, critically, necessitates an adaptable and flexible therapist. For patients who engage in treatment and persist with the exercises, optimal outcomes often ensue.

Goals for the Book

Before preparing this book, we brainstormed about the ideal components to include. After many hours of discussion, we decided it was important for readers to have essential information at their fingertips to target many important aspects of depression in adolescence. In the spirit of this aim, we sought to create a veritable *one-stop shopping* experience, including passages addressing the scope of problem (e.g., epidemiological data), background on prevailing models of depression (e.g., social-cognitive models), assessment (e.g., clinical interviews, narrow-band severity indicators), and treatment across all phases (i.e., early, middle, termination, and booster sessions). Although there are many books on CBT for depression (e.g., Beck, 1995, 2011; Friedberg & McClure, 2002), many are targeted toward younger people (i.e., children) or, most often, written with adult patients in mind. These books describe the array of cognitive and behavioral techniques available in CBT. Our goal is not to repeat the procedures and approaches detailed, but rather, to describe how to adapt CBT for adolescents. Given the unique developmental features of adolescence, we believe that tailoring one's approach may contribute to more effective outcomes. Adolescents are entangled in one of the most interesting and dynamic phases of human development, and it is a period rife with growth, discovery, angst, and uncertainty. Teens speak a language that is stridently different than that of children and adults. Thus, when administering CBT to depressed adolescents, it is essential to bear in mind these many differences and to tailor interventions and one's communication style accordingly. This book may serve as a *Rosetta Stone* for deciphering depressed adolescents, and by consequence, navigating potential pitfalls and obstacles that occur throughout treatment. Make no mistake, providing effective treatment for depressed adolescents is undeniably challenging, and at the same time, working with adolescents also may be among the most rewarding experiences. With all adolescents, there is a unique opportunity to guide them back on to a healthier developmental trajectory, which may have profound consequences across their lifespan.

Intended Audience

First and foremost, the book is intended for therapists – defined broadly. CBT is the most widely used psychotherapeutic approach for depression and is delivered across an array of clinical contexts. We envision our readership to be any allied mental health professional working with depressed youth, including, but not limited to, psychiatrists, psychologists, social workers, clinical counselors, and nurses. The information and techniques described throughout the book bring together the most recent research advances in our understanding of etiological mechanisms that contribute to the onset and maintenance of depression, as well as procedures and strategies for effective psychotherapy with teens. In this way, the book is equally appropriate for students, early-career clinicians, and seasoned therapists. For students, it will provide a *foot in the door* to starting therapy with depressed teenagers and, thus, may be used as an introductory guide. It provides accessible guidance on how to structure and organize sessions. Additionally, it includes sample dialogues which will afford reassurance that the resistance so often encountered in the early going of therapy is not a byproduct of inexperience, but rather, the natural consequence of sitting with an adolescent who may be struggling through this pivotal developmental transition. With respect to early-career and more experienced therapists, the book integrates and updates information on CBT for depression. As noted earlier, it will provide ready access to the latest advances in CBT, as well as describe more nuanced ways to manage challenging cases (e.g., comorbidity, suicidality). Furthermore, we incorporate discussions of emerging technologies for targeting depression in the 21st century (e.g., smartphone applications, internet-based CBT).

In addition to its practical and pragmatic use for mental health professionals, the book is written in an accessible, reader-focused manner, which we believe makes it suitable for both parents and adolescents to read prior to beginning therapy or during the CBT course. Indeed, many of the chapters, particularly those focusing on the background of MDD, may dispel myths about depression and answer questions about the nature of treatment. As we emphasize in our description of setting the stage for effective CBT, psychoeducation plays a key role. The book provides background on the causes, correlates, and consequences of depression, and moreover, describes the process and nature of CBT. When used as a resource for patients and their parents, this book may therefore help alleviate anxieties and clarify questions regarding treatment.

Effective Use of the Book

There is no *right* way to use this book. For some, it may be most helpful to read from cover to cover, which will provide an overview on depression in adolescence and treatment guidelines. However, more commonly, therapists may *read as they go*. Specifically, it may be helpful to revisit the book before sessions as a way to refresh one's memory on etiological models of depression (Chapter 2), and prior to beginning treatment, review different ways to assess depression and related constructs (Chapter 3). The book also will guide readers through early (Chapters 4 and 5), middle (Chapter 6), and late (Chapter 7) stages of treatment. And, critically, it will provide an important overview on how to address common challenges that arise in therapy (Chapters 8 and 9) as well as more recent CBT innovations (Chapter 10).

Dialogues

The book presents a series of exemplar exchanges between patients and therapists. While these exchanges are representative, they do not reflect a specific session with any patient. Rather, they are an amalgamation of many exchanges across patients over time. They are included to invoke the spirit of what therapists often experience in their work with youth. The inclusion of these passages is intended to model *the good, the bad, and the ugly*, and further, urge therapists to revisit how to approach challenging therapeutic exchanges.

Summary

Treating depression in adolescence is challenging. Whether you are a new or experienced therapist, we believe this book will serve as a strong starting point to demystify the process of CBT and will serve as a guide when approaching complex and challenging cases. With alarming prevalence rates for depression and suicidality in adolescents, broad-based dissemination of effective treatment such as CBT is critical.

2 Models of Depression

Crafting a concise and useful review of the many models that describe how MDD develops in adolescents is a monumental task. As an author, it is easy to slip into many of the thinking styles that one is writing about; there are certainly periods where it seems that working through a chapter is devoid of positive reinforcement (*behavioral* models); moments of low perceived self-efficacy (*social cognitive learning* models); times where setbacks or mistakes are viewed as internal (this is all my fault) and stable (I'm never going to get this right) (*cognitive* models); or instances wherein one's attention is drawn towards the weakest sections of drafts and away from parts that are done well (*information-processing* models). This illustrates an important strength of the etiological models of adolescent depression that we review below: at their hearts, they are intuitive. As clinicians, we are charged with harnessing intuitiveness and connecting with the processes that bring about our patients' psychiatric symptoms (perhaps by even recognizing them in ourselves). At the same time, it is crucial to recognize that our patients' experiences of these processes are categorically more intense, which may contribute to profound disruptions in their psychosocial functioning.

A strong foundation in the dominant models describing factors that confer vulnerability to depression can aid clinicians in connecting with and understanding their patients. Below, we provide a non-exhaustive review of etiological models most relevant to cognitive behavioral interventions for adolescents, with the hope that this information is useful for developing practical case conceptualizations and treatment plans.

Life Stress and Adolescent Depression

Adolescence is a period marked by normative shifts in many areas of day-to-day life, including schooling and home life, as well as peer and romantic relationships. For example, at school, adolescents must adjust to a heavier and more difficult workload, while also balancing the increased opportunities to pursue specific interests that high school may afford (e.g., clubs, teams). At home, adolescents strive for greater autonomy and independence, and these needs often put them at odds with their parents, creating increased tension and conflict. On average, teens are interacting with same-aged peers for more than twice the number of hours they spend with their families (Barnes, Hoffman, Welte, Farrell, & Dintcheff, 2007). On the one hand, the closeness and intimacy of peer relationships are major sources of social support (Furman & Buhrmester, 1992); however, conflict within these relationships is common and is linked to increases in internalizing symptoms over time (La Greca & Harrison, 2005).

Given the changes that occur in the adolescent years, do teens experience a corresponding increase in stressful life events (SLEs)? The empirical literature suggests that this is indeed the case. For example, in a sample of youth drawn from a community outpatient clinic, Rudolph and Hammen (1999) found that adolescents reported greater levels of stress, assessed using a detailed contextual interview, compared to preadolescents. Furthermore, Garber, Keiley, and Martin (2002) conducted annual interview assessments on a large sample of youth, beginning when they were in grade 6 through to grade 11. The authors found that the total number of SLEs that youth reported increased linearly over the course of the study. As we discussed in Chapter 1, incidence rates of MDD rise dramatically in adolescence, and given concurrent increases in SLEs, coupled with the strong association between stress and depressive symptoms, research has paid substantial attention to the role that stress plays in the development of depression in teens.

Nearly four decades since George Brown and his colleagues conducted their seminal studies (e.g., Brown & Harris, 1978), the association between severe SLEs and the development of MDD is among the most robust and consistently replicated findings in depression research. SLEs classified as severe are acute, pernicious experiences that have an enduring negative impact on the individual. Severe SLEs often involve serious threats or damage to central relationships and roles (e.g., student) and/or major negative changes in life circumstances (e.g., financial, housing, health). In a review of the literature on life stress and depression, Dr. Kate Harkness at Queen's University (Kingston, Ontario, Canada) summarized the results of several early studies on adult patients with MDD and non-depressed control participants. Across these studies, 62–93% of patients reported at least one severe SLE in the 3 months prior to the onset of their depressive episode; in contrast, only 25–39% of the non-depressed controls reported severe SLEs in a comparison period (see Harkness, 2008). Consistent with these adult studies, Williamson et al. (1998) found that 62% of depressed adolescent outpatients reported a severe event in the year prior to their episode versus only 27% of non-depressed adolescents. Furthermore, depressed adolescents report a greater total *number* of SLEs prior to episode onset than non-depressed adolescents during a similar time period (Harkness, Bruce, & Lumley, 2006; Shih, Eberhart, Hammen, & Brennan, 2006).

The link between SLEs and MDD in adolescents also has been confirmed in a handful of longitudinal investigations. Several large community studies have repeatedly administered self-report measures of both SLEs and depressive symptoms at regular follow-up intervals over multiple months (Auerbach, Bigda-Peyton, Eberhart, Webb, & Ho, 2011; Auerbach, Ho, & Kim, 2014; Hankin, 2008) and years (Carter, Garber, Ciesla, & Cole, 2006; Cole, Nolen-Hoeksema, Girgus, & Paul, 2006) and found a prospective association between stress and subsequent increases in depressive symptoms among adolescents. Although fewer in number than studies focused on depressive symptoms, some investigations have shown that self-reported stress is associated with the onset of episodes of MDD among adolescents over periods of 1 (Lewinsohn, Joiner, & Rohde, 2001) and 3 (Burton, Stice, & Seeley, 2004) years. Finally, using an interview-based measure of stress, Carter and Garber (2011) reported that interpersonal SLEs (e.g., termination of a close friendship), but not achievement SLEs (e.g., failing a course at school) were associated with episodes of MDD over a 6-year longitudinal investigation. Taken together, these studies demonstrate a consistent association between stress and later depression in adolescents across both self-report and interview-based assessments of these constructs.

Life Stress Domain

In recent years there has been a growing awareness that not all *domains* of life stress may be equally important to understanding the development of MDD. The most commonly used nomenclature for SLEs groups acute stress into "dependent" (i.e., at least partly influenced by the characteristics or behaviors of the respondent) and "independent" (i.e., fateful and outside of the person's control) events. For example, failing a grade at school would be classified as a dependent event, while a parent being diagnosed with a serious medical illness would be an independent event. Importantly, dependent events can be further divided into interpersonal (e.g., a major argument with a close friend; a break-up of a romantic relationship) and non-interpersonal (e.g., being fired from a part-time job).

A specific type of dependent life event called *targeted rejection* (Slavich, Thornton, Torres, Monroe, & Gotlib, 2009) may be particularly linked to depression outcomes. Targeted rejection SLEs are events that involve a single person and whose core feature is an active and intentional breaking of important social bonds (e.g., being "dumped" by a boyfriend or girlfriend). One large-scale study of adults found that targeted rejection events increased the risk for subsequent MDD by nearly 22-fold, which was more than twice the increased risk associated with the death of a loved one (Kendler, Hettema, Butera, Gardner, & Prescott, 2003). Furthermore, adults reporting targeted rejection events developed new episodes of MDD three times faster than patients who experienced equivalently severe non-targeted rejection events (e.g., death of a loved one; initiating a romantic break-up; parent diagnosed with a serious medical illness; Slavich et al., 2009). Although no research to date has examined interview-assessed targeted rejection events in adolescent samples, a growing body of evidence suggests that adolescents are more *sensitive* to interpersonal forms of rejection than either adults or children. First, adolescents report higher trait rejection sensitivity than children and young adults (Hafen, Spilker, Chango, Marston, & Allen, 2014) and also exhibit heightened neuroendocrine and autonomic nervous system (e.g., heart rate, blood pressure) reactivity to peer rejection compared to children (Stroud et al., 2009). Second, data from functional neuroimaging studies suggest that adolescents may respond to negative and positive social feedback with heightened recruitment of socioaffective neural circuitry compared to children and adults (Somerville, 2013). Relatedly, adolescents respond to negative social feedback with a larger reduction of self-reported mood and increase in anxiety relative to adults (Sebastian, Viding, Williams, & Blakemore, 2010). Considering these data on how adolescents process rejection-related information, particularly in the interpersonal domain, it stands to reason that targeted rejection events may be especially relevant to the development of MDD in adolescence.

Understandably, the theoretical and empirical literature on stress and depression in adolescents has leaned considerably towards investigating dependent, interpersonal SLEs. However, as researchers and clinicians, it is critical not to lose sight of the importance of stress that may be outside of adolescents' control (i.e., independent SLEs). One ambitious study examined interview-assessed life events that individuals 13–65 years old reported 6 months prior to the onset of their depressive episodes. The authors found that adolescents (ages 13–17) reported a higher percentage of other-focused (e.g., father hospitalized for kidney stones) and independent (e.g., mother gets laid off from her job) events prior to their episodes than any other age cohort, despite having generally lower rates of other types of life events (Harkness et al., 2010). As the authors note, these results suggest that many of the stressful features of adolescents' environments are out of their control, which may clash with the normative drive for autonomy and independence that characterizes adolescence. These factors may create fertile ground for the development of depressive symptoms in many cases.

Stress Sensitization

Although the majority of individuals (62–93%) who develop MDD report a severe SLE prior to their episode, only a small fraction of all people who experience even major negative life events will develop MDD. As we describe below, *diathesis-stress* models of MDD suggest that some individuals possess traits that make them more likely than others to develop depression following acute SLEs. In addition, a compelling avenue of research suggests that stress itself may render individuals more vulnerable to the depressogenic effects of later stress. Specifically, *stress sensitization theory* posits that stressful environmental and/or physiological experiences produce *memory traces* in the brain that prime the stress response system. Ultimately, primed individuals have a lower threshold for stress necessary to initiate future depression (Monroe & Harkness, 2005; Post, 1992). The stress sensitization model was initially applied to depression recurrence; the basic hypothesis was that first episodes of depression would be preceded by more severe SLEs than recurrences. This hypothesis has been confirmed in adult samples (Kendler, Thornton, & Gardner, 2000; Monroe, Slavich, Torres, & Gotlib, 2007), as well as in studies of adolescents (Stroud, Davila, Hammen, & Vrshek-Schallhorn, 2011).

However, a lifetime history of MDD is not the only factor that may sensitize adolescents to the impact of later SLEs. Child abuse, neglect, and other forms of childhood adversity are robustly associated with the presence of a range of internalizing and externalizing psychopathology, including depression (Green et al., 2010). One important extension of research on stress and recurrence is to examine whether childhood adversity may operate in a manner consistent with stress sensitization theory. Studies of adult women have demonstrated that a history of childhood sexual abuse (Kendler, Kuhn, & Prescott, 2004) and general early adversity (e.g., parental separation; Hammen, Henry, & Daley, 2000) sensitized participants to later acute SLEs. Additionally, the general stress sensitization effects of childhood adversities have been replicated in adolescent samples (Harkness et al., 2006; Rudolph & Flynn, 2007).

Nonetheless, there are a number of open questions regarding which types of adversity are most relevant to stress sensitization, and to which types of life events individuals actually become sensitized. For example, Harkness and her colleagues (2006) found that childhood maltreatment sensitized adolescents to independent SLEs, but *not* to dependent SLEs. In contrast, a recent study reported that adolescents with a history of MDD showed a stress sensitization effect to dependent, but not independent, life stress, as indexed by prospective associations between self-reported dependent SLEs and increases in depressive symptoms (Technow, Hazel, Abela, & Hankin, 2015). In addition, an interesting study raised the possibility that those experiencing certain types of childhood adversity may be specifically sensitized to later life events with the same theme as the previous adversity. Specifically, Slavich, Monroe, and Gotlib (2011) found that adults who reported early parental loss or separation (e.g., death of parent; parental abandonment following divorce) showed stress sensitization to loss events (e.g., death of a loved one; dissolution of a close friendship or romantic relationship) but not to other types of SLEs. To our knowledge, no comparable analysis has been conducted in an adolescent sample. Additional research is required to unpack the complex association between previous stress and the degree of sensitization adolescents show to proximal SLEs.

Clinical Implications

In the sections above, we presented research that implicates severe life stress in the development of adolescent depression. Along with acting as the trigger of many depressive episodes, an adolescent's environment also colors the clinical presentation we see in our offices and the course the illness may take. Studies of adults using interview-based measures of life stress have found that individuals who report severe SLEs prior to MDD onset have more severe depressive symptoms than those who do not report these events (Monroe, Harkness, Simons, & Thase, 2001; Muscatell, Slavich, Monroe, & Gotlib, 2009). Additionally, major contextually assessed SLEs (Monroe et al., 2001), as well as life stress in general (Liu & Miller, 2014), are associated with suicidal ideation and behaviors. Furthermore, ongoing life stress may be detrimental to treatment outcomes. For example, a randomized controlled trial of adults with MDD treated with either medications or CBT showed that those who experienced a severe SLE during treatment had a lower rate of remission than those who did not, but only if they were in the medication group (Bulmash, Harkness, Stewart, & Bagby, 2009). These findings underscore the potential stress inoculation properties of effectively delivered CBT, emphasizing the importance for practitioners to actively assess recent SLEs (see Chapter 3) and to address ongoing environmental stress directly when working with depressed adolescents.

Summary

Decades of research have confirmed that acute SLEs often precede the development of MDD, both in adolescents and adults. More recently, clinical scientists have sought to develop a more fine-grained understanding of this association by exploring which *types* of stress may be particularly toxic and which *individuals* may be particularly sensitive to stress based on their prior experiences (i.e., previous depressive episodes; childhood maltreatment). In the Cognitive Theories of Depression section below, we build from the general theme that certain individuals may be more susceptible to the depressogenic effects of life stress than others. Specifically, we will describe how maladaptive ways of appraising and processing environmental stress place adolescents possessing these characteristics at risk for developing MDD in the face of SLEs.

Behavioral Models of Depression

In general, behavioral models operate under the assumption that depression is the product of behavior–environment associations in a person's life that evolve over time. These models pay particular attention to the *contingencies* (i.e., if–then relationships) that exist between a person's behavior and the resulting consequences within the environments in which these behaviors occur. For example, an adolescent putting off doing her homework after school (behavior) may result in having to do the assignment very quickly before class (consequence), handing in a lower-quality paper (consequence), and receiving a lower grade for her work (consequence).

Guided by ideas drawn from early behaviorism (e.g., Skinner, 1957), Ferster (1973) proposed that depression emerges out of a learning history characterized by: (1) not receiving positive reinforcement from the environment for certain behaviors and (2) an increase in the aversive consequences following other behaviors. Over time, the behaviors of depressed individuals become increasingly driven by *negative reinforcement* (i.e., reducing distress and avoiding negative consequences) and behavior that is typically reinforcing (e.g., going for a walk on a sunny day) stops producing positive consequences. This in turn leads to the extinction of potentially reinforcing behaviors. For instance, if a person's efforts to develop friendships are consistently met with rejection or lack of interest from others (i.e., not reinforced), she might stop attempting to make connections (i.e., the behavior is extinguished).

According to Ferster, a decrease in response-contingent positive reinforcement results in several behavioral consequences that propagate depression. First, he proposed that people *turn inward* and focus on their internal hardship at the expense of observing and responding to potential sources of positive reinforcement in their environments. Second, because a limited set of behaviors are being positively reinforced, depressed individuals' range of adaptive behaviors narrow, and they develop increasingly passive behavioral repertoires. Last, as attempts to actively engage the environment are not often positively reinforced, the behavioral range of depressed individuals becomes focused on avoiding and/or escaping anticipated aversive consequences of interactions within their environments. In sum, Ferster's behavioral model proposes that depression arises primarily from a chronic lack of positive reinforcement from the environment, which ultimately contributes to an increased focus on internal negative experiences, reduced engagement in adaptive behaviors, and increased avoidance behaviors.

Although Ferster (1973) argued that avoidance behaviors play a central role in depression, this construct has only recently become the focus of systematic study. Dr. Keith Dobson and his colleagues at the University of Calgary (Calgary, Alberta, Canada) created a measure to capture distinct types of avoidance: behavioral social (I avoid attending social activities), behavioral non-social (Rather than try new activities, I tend to stick with things I know), cognitive social (I try not to think about problems in my personal relationships), and cognitive non-social (I avoid making decisions about my future) (Ottenbreit & Dobson, 2004). This has given researchers a common metric with which to study different types of avoidance and their implications for depression. To date, studies have shown that all forms of avoidance are associated with depressive symptoms in non-clinical college samples (Moulds, Kandris, Starr, & Wong, 2007) and differentiate adults suffering from MDD from control participants (Ottenbreit, Dobson, & Quigley, 2014). This line of research is still in its infancy, and crucially, future study is required to investigate the role avoidance plays in adolescent depression.

Similar to Ferster's (1973) behavioral model of depression, Lewinsohn (1974) also emphasized the importance of response-contingent reinforcement. Specifically, he proposed that the rate that individuals receive response-contingent reinforcement is influenced by: (1) the number of events that would be reinforcing for the individual; (2) the availability of those events in the environment; and (3) the behavior of the individual required to generate the positive reinforcement. For example, someone at risk for depression might at once have a small number of events that he would find reinforcing, *and* those events are scarce in his present environment. Furthermore, people at risk for depression may lack some basic social (e.g., making appropriate eye contact; nodding and smiling to indicate engagement) and non-social (e.g., persevering at challenging activities; trying new things) behaviors that might impede their receipt of positive reinforcement in their environments. For instance, if an adolescent has poor social skills and struggles with making conversation, his attempts at forming friendships with classmates might be rejected (lack of positive reinforcement).

Importantly, Lewinsohn emphasized the subjective experience of environmental rewards in understanding their impact on mood and functioning. This concept has strongly influenced more recent behavioral models of depression (e.g., Martell, Dimidjian, & Herman-Dunn, 2013) that focus on the *functional analysis* of behaviors to understand the development of depression and guide treatment. Functional analysis assumes that all behaviors can be understood in light of what immediately precedes (antecedents) and proceeds from (consequences) them. Consider, for an example, an adolescent who joins a pick-up basketball game after school. Without exploring the antecedents and consequences of this behavior, it is tempting to view this as a positively reinforcing activity likely to be associated with a boost in mood. However, if the adolescent only joined the game because he was pressured by his parents to "get more involved" (antecedent), was picked last on a daily basis, and was teased for not playing well (consequences), our view of this behavior necessarily changes. Modern behavioral models of depression focus on the interplay between the antecedents, consequences, and overall contexts in which behaviors occur to understand the role these behaviors have in the development and maintenance of depression.

Social Cognitive Learning Models of Depression

Collectively, social cognitive learning models focus on individuals' beliefs about their ability to act on and influence their environments. Bandura's (1986) Social Cognitive Theory (SCT) is a broad description of how human beings construct knowledge and regulate action. Within SCT, Bandura describes processes that moderate how individuals exercise agency within their environments. *Perceived self-efficacy*, defined as an individual's beliefs regarding their capacity to produce change in her environment, is proposed to be the foundation of human agency (Bandura, 1999). From an SCT perspective, believing that one's actions will lead to desired outcomes provides the central motivation to act or persevere in difficult circumstances.

According to SCT, depression arises at least partly due to low perceived self-efficacy. Bandura (1999) described three pathways through which self-inefficacy may ultimately contribute to depression. First, people with low self-efficacy may possess standards of self-worth that they view as unattainable. Repeated failures to obtain achievements perceived as central to one's self-worth results in diminished motivation and depressed mood. Increases in depressed mood further lower self-efficacy beliefs (e.g., Kavanagh & Bower, 1985), creating a vicious cycle that worsens depressive symptoms. Second, perceived social inefficacy reduces individuals' ability to generate supportive social environments for themselves (Holahan & Holahan, 1987). Within SCT, supportive relationships are thought to enhance personal efficacy because close others can model effective coping strategies and perseverance, and also provide coping resources. Thus, perceived social inefficacy increases risk for depression by limiting the availability of stress-buffering social support and reducing an individual's personal coping resources. Finally, low self-efficacy impacts individuals' ability to exert control over depressotypic cognitions. For instance, low efficacy to control ruminative (i.e., passive, repetitive cognitions about depressed mood; see Nolen-Hoeksema's Response Styles Theory section below) thinking in response to negative events is implicated in the onset and chronicity of depression (Kavanagh & Wilson, 1989).

Research has supported the association between low self-efficacy and depression in adolescents. In one study, Bandura, Pastorelli, Barbaranelli, and Caprara (1999) examined the prospective associations among several facets of perceived self-efficacy and depressive symptoms in a large sample of children and adolescents. Low social and academic self-efficacy was directly associated with increased depressive symptoms. Further, both forms of self-inefficacy had indirect effects on future depression, such that they reduced academic achievement, increased problem behavior, and decreased prosocial behaviors, which, in turn, contributed to increased depression. In another sample of adolescents, Muris (2002) found that, in addition to social and academic self-efficacy, emotional self-efficacy (i.e., belief in one's ability to cope with negative emotions) was associated with depressive symptoms. Finally, Jenkins, Goodness, and Buhrmester (2002) found that two facets of adolescent social self-efficacy (beliefs regarding abilities to provide emotional support and navigate interpersonal conflicts) predicted depression among early adolescents, although the effect of interpersonal conflict management was stronger.

Closely related to Bandura's SCT is Rotter's (1966) construct of locus of control (LOC), which refers to the extent to which people believe that they can control events or outcomes in their environments. People who believe that outcomes are a product of their own behaviors and characteristics have an internal LOC, whereas individuals who ascribe outcomes to factors outside their control (e.g., chance, fate) have an external LOC. Consistent with research on self-inefficacy and depression, people possessing a more external LOC are at highest risk for depression. For example, in an early meta-analysis, higher externality was moderately associated with depressive symptoms across several adult populations (e.g., psychiatric patients, college students) (Benassi, Sweeney, & Dufour, 1988). Furthermore, externality is prospectively associated with future depressive symptoms and fewer periods of wellness among psychiatric patients (Harrow, Hansford, & Astrachan-Fletcher, 2009). Although the body of studies is smaller, research has replicated the relation of a more external LOC to depression in adolescents (e.g., Dunn, Austin, & Huster, 1999; McCauley, Mitchell, Burke, & Moss, 1988).

Taken together, both SCT (Bandura, 1986) and Rotter's (1966) theory of LOC propose that individuals suffering from depression view themselves as being at the mercy of their environments. We will see this general theme of perceived helplessness again in some of the cognitive theories of depression described below.

Cognitive Theories of Depression

Cognitive theories focus on the thought patterns, attitudes, and beliefs that are implicated in the development of adolescent depression. For the most part, cognitive theories employ a *diathesis-stress* approach to understanding depressive symptoms, wherein a pre-existing cognitive vulnerability (diathesis) interacts with SLEs in the individual's environment to increase risk for depression. Importantly, cognitive vulnerability factors share the following characteristics: (1) they are *traits*, meaning they represent enduring, stable features of the individual that precede depression; (2) they are endogenous, meaning they emerge from within the individual; (3) they are latent, meaning they are considered to be dormant until triggered by negative life events and are causally linked to the appearance of symptoms; (4) they *specifically* predict depression, and not other psychiatric symptoms or disorders (see Ingram, Miranda, & Segal, 1998).

In the ensuing section, we will focus on three cognitive theories of depression that have received substantial empirical support in adult and adolescent populations: Beck's Cognitive Theory (Beck, 1976), the Hopelessness Theory (HT: Abramson, Metalsky, & Alloy, 1989), and the Response Styles Theory (RST: Nolen-Hoeksema, 1991; Nolen-Hoeksema, Wisco, & Lyubomirsky, 2008). All three theories propose a diathesis-stress model of depression, but differ in their descriptions of the exact nature of the cognitive factors that confer vulnerability to depression.

Beck's Cognitive Theory

Beck's Cognitive Theory of depression (Beck, 1976) proposes that depression vulnerability arises from *dysfunctional attitudes* developed in the face of adverse childhood experiences. Specifically, dysfunctional attitudes crystallize through the process of deriving meaning from these early stressful experiences over time (Beck, 2008). Sets of related dysfunctional attitudes become organized into maladaptive *schemas*, defined as stored knowledge about oneself and one's prior experiences surrounding a broad theme. Schemas are the foundation of cognitive vulnerability in Beck's model; a given negative schema may lie dormant until it is triggered by an event thematically related to the schema content, and once active, the negative schema fuels the systematic negative biases that characterize depression (see the Information-Processing Models of Depression section of this chapter, below).

For instance, an adolescent who grew up being persistently berated by over-critical caregivers might develop dysfunctional attitudes like, "No matter what I do, it's never enough," "If I can't complete a task, there is something wrong with me," and "If something isn't just right, then I've failed." These attitudes might organize into the maladaptive schema, "I'm a failure." According to Beck, the activation of such depressogenic cognitions by schema-congruent life events increases the chances of developing the *negative cognitive triad*, which is a sufficient proximal cause of depression. The negative cognitive triad involves negative patterns of thinking about oneself (e.g., self-denigrating beliefs), the world (e.g., belief that life is unfair and others are hostile), and the future (e.g., belief that nothing will ever change).

Much of the research testing Beck's Cognitive Model in adolescent samples has operationalized cognitive vulnerability using participant reports of dysfunctional attitude content. The existing prospective research has generally confirmed the association between dysfunctional attitudes and future depression in children and adolescents. For instance, two studies on large samples of adolescents recruited from school settings found that higher scores on the Dysfunctional Attitudes Scale (DAS: Weissman & Beck, 1978) predicted higher depressive symptoms (Marcotte, Lévesque, & Fortin, 2006) and major depressive episodes (Lewinsohn et al., 1994) up to 2 years later. Other studies have explicitly examined the role of cognitive vulnerability in a diathesis-stress framework by prospectively assessing both dysfunctional attitudes and stress. Results have generally been consistent with hypotheses derived from Beck's model – greater dysfunctional attitudes predict increases in depressive symptoms (Abela & Sullivan, 2003; Hankin, Wetter, Cheely, & Oppenheimer, 2008) and the onset of depressive episodes (Lewinsohn et al., 2001), among adolescents reporting high, but not low, levels of life stress.

Although far less studied, an equally important element to defining cognitive vulnerability to depression is the structural characteristics and organization of negative schemas (i.e., the relative interconnectedness of information contained within them). Given that self-relevant information is processed more efficiently than non-self-relevant information, it is more interconnected in the self-schema. When schema content is highly interrelated, the activation of one element readily triggers a network of other related beliefs and attitudes, and thus, there is greater subsequent influence on emotions and information processing (see Dozois & Dobson, 2003). Dr. David Dozois at Western University (London, Ontario, Canada) developed the Psychological Distancing and Scaling Task (PDST: Dozois & Dobson, 2001a), which measures the relative interconnectedness of negative and positive self-schemas. Studies using the PDST have confirmed that depressed adults exhibit more tightly organized negative self-schemas and more loosely organized positive self-schemas compared to healthy controls (Dozois, 2002) and adults with anxiety disorders (Dozois & Dobson, 2001a; Dozois & Frewen, 2006). Importantly, schema interconnectedness possesses the core characteristics of a marker of cognitive vulnerability, in that it remains stable after depression remission (Dozois & Dobson, 2001b) and predicts recurrence (Dozois & Dobson, 2003). Despite compelling evidence for the importance of schema organization for understanding adult depression, no studies to our knowledge have been conducted in youth.

Hopelessness Theory

In its initial conceptualization, the HT of depression (Abramson, Seligman, & Teasdale, 1978) posited that depressed individuals have a particular *attributional style* (i.e., a manner in which they understand why they have certain experiences) when it comes to understanding why negative life events occur. In HT, depression is characterized by internal (e.g., It's my fault), global (e.g., I can't do anything right), and stable (e.g., Things will always be this way) views of negative events, and this *negative* attributional style is a proximal predictor of MDD. The original HT was further refined by Abramson and colleagues (1989) to specify three particular cognitive styles implicated in depression: (1) viewing oneself as defective and insufficient following negative events; (2) forecasting catastrophic consequences for negative events; and (3) viewing negative events as global and stable. Over time, these particular attributional styles are hypothesized to evolve into a state of hopelessness, and ultimately, MDD.

In addition to specifying particular patterns of thinking that lead to depression, HT posits that hopelessness arising from negative attributional styles contributes to a specific subtype of MDD: hopelessness depression. Hopelessness depression is characterized by the following cluster of symptoms: hopelessness (criterion symptom), sadness, retarded initiation of voluntary responses, suicidal ideation, initial insomnia, low energy, self-criticism, concentration difficulties, psychomotor retardation, brooding or worry, lowered self-esteem, and dependency. To meet criteria for hopelessness depression, an individual must present with hopelessness for at least 1 week and endorse at least four of the other associated symptoms (Alloy et al., 2006). In support of a distinct hopelessness subtype of depression, studies have shown that symptoms hypothesized to be part of the hopelessness depression cluster are more strongly associated with the negative attributional styles described above than symptoms not belonging to the cluster (e.g., Alloy & Clements, 1998; Joiner et al., 2001).

Recent comprehensive reviews of cross-sectional and prospective tests of HT in child and adolescent samples (Abela & Hankin, 2009; Garber, Korelitz, & Samanez-Larkin, 2012; Jacobs, Reinecke, Gollan, & Kane, 2008) have found general support for HT. Most prospective studies have examined negative attributional styles as an underlying cognitive vulnerability that interacts with life stress to predict increased depressive symptoms and the onset of MDD. Importantly, there is evidence that each type of cognitive style implicated in HT (i.e., attributions about causes, consequences, and the self) interacts with life stress to predict depression in children and adolescents, although evidence is strongest for negative attributions about *causes* (see Abela & Hankin, 2009).

Despite convincing evidence for HT in adolescent samples, the majority of the diathesis-stress literature takes the standard approach of treating each of the three attributional styles separately, and thus ignores the interrelationships among these attributional styles. This approach may thus not capture important aspects of adolescents' cognitive vulnerability. To address this short-coming, the late Dr. John Abela developed the *weakest link* approach to operationalizing cognitive vulnerability (Abela & Sarin, 2002). This approach uses an individual's highest score on the three negative attributional style scales (i.e., causes, consequences, or self) to assess his or her cognitive vulnerability to depression. In a number of studies, Abela and his colleagues showed that the interaction between an individual's weakest link and stress was a better predictor of future depression compared to models taking the traditional approach of examining attributional styles separately (Abela, Aydin, & Auerbach, 2006; Abela, Parkinson, Stolow, & Starrs, 2009; Abela & Sarin, 2002).

Nolen-Hoeksema's Response Styles Theory

RST (Nolen-Hoeksema, 1991, 2004) provides a basis for understanding how an individual's typical pattern of responses to depressed mood influences the duration and intensity of their ensuing mood disturbance. Two distinct response styles were initially proposed: rumination and distraction.[1] According to RST, rumination is defined as "repetitive and passive thinking about one's symptoms of depression and the possible causes and consequences of these symptoms" (Nolen-Hoeksema, 2004, p. 107). "Passive thinking" involves fixating on problems and the associated emotions without taking action. In contrast, a distracting response style involves focusing one's attention on external aspects unrelated to mood state. In its initial form, RST proposed that individuals who engage in ruminative responses to depressed mood were likely to increase the severity and duration of their depressive symptoms, while distraction would be more associated with reductions in their symptoms.

Research conducted with samples of dypshoric and non-dysphoric college students has demonstrated that a ruminative state can be experimentally induced by instructing individuals to focus on the causes, consequences, and meanings of their current feelings. These studies have consistently demonstrated that experimentally induced rumination increases negative affect among dysphoric, but not non-dysphoric, participants (see Nolen-Hoeksema et al., 2008, for a review). This increase in negative affect is hypothesized to trigger a search for explanatory causes, attempts to repair moods, and efforts to engage existing coping strategies, which ultimately leads to a downward spiral of worsening depressed mood

---

1 Studies of children and adolescents that assess response styles using the Child Response Styles Questionnaire (CRSQ: Abela, Rochon, & Vanderbilt, 2000) have identified problem-solving as a third response style in addition to rumination and distraction. However, in these studies, the problem-solving subscale possessed relatively few items and was highly correlated with distraction. Therefore problem-solving was combined with distraction as a single response style separate from rumination (Abela, Aydin, & Auerbach, 2007). For the purposes of this chapter, we simply refer to the "distraction and problem-solving" subscale of the CRSQ as "distraction" in the adolescent studies we review in this section.

over time (Moberly & Watkins, 2008). Longitudinal research on adult samples has borne out this hypothesis – a tendency to ruminate when dysphoric is associated with prolonged depressive symptoms in both nonclinical (Nolen-Hoeksema & Davis, 1999; Roberts, Gilboa, & Gotlib, 1998) and clinical (Ciesla & Roberts, 2007; Robinson & Alloy, 2003) samples.

In adolescent samples, prospective studies have consistently shown that a trait ruminative response style increases vulnerability to worsening depressive symptoms (Abela, Aydin, & Auerbach, 2007; Burwell & Shirk, 2007; Hilt, McLaughlin, & Nolen-Hoeksema, 2010) and major depressive episodes (Abela & Hankin, 2011; Alloy et al., 2012; Nolen-Hoeksema, Stice, Wade, & Bohon, 2007). Importantly, in response to early criticism regarding the overlap between self-reported rumination and depressive symptoms, researchers have identified two response styles that are independent of depressive symptoms: brooding ("a passive comparison of one's current situation with some unachieved standard") and reflection ("a purposeful turning inward to engage in cognitive problem-solving") (Treynor, Gonzalez, & Nolen-Hoeksema, 2003, p. 256). Recent prospective research has confirmed that ruminative brooding, but not reflection, is prospectively associated with increased depressive symptoms among adolescents (Bastin, Mezulis, Ahles, Raes, & Bijttebier, 2014; Mezulis, Simonson, McCauley, & Vander Stoep, 2011; Paredes & Zumalde, 2014).

Despite the strong support for rumination as a vulnerability factor for depression, the complementary hypothesis that the distraction/reflection response style is associated with *decreases* in depression over time has received mixed support. Some prospective studies have confirmed the hypothesized effect of distraction (e.g., Abela et al., 2007), but others have found no prospective association between distraction and depressive symptoms (Abela, Brozina, & Haigh, 2002), or have found that distraction/reflection actually predicts worsening depression (Mezulis et al., 2011; Paredes & Zumalde, 2014). Clearly, an important avenue for future study is to clarify the characteristics of a distracting/reflective response style in order to determine its precise relationship to the development of adolescent depression.

Information-Processing Models of Depression

An essential component of Beck's Cognitive Theory (see above) is that, when activated, cognitive vulnerability factors (e.g., schemas, dysfunctional attitudes) systematically influence how information from the environment is processed. These negative information-processing biases are thought to be the proximal causes of the changes in affect, behavior, and motivation that constitute depression (Beck, 2008).

Below, we review some of the literature on the information-processing biases that are present in adolescent depression. This review is not exhaustive, and there are many additional elements of information-processing theories not covered (see reviews by Foland-Ross & Gotlib, 2012; Gotlib & Joormann, 2010; Phillips, Hine, & Thorsteinsson, 2010). Below, we focus on negative biases in attention, memory, and emotion-processing, as well as deficits in cognitive control.

Attentional Biases

Some of the earliest research on information-processing in depression tested whether depressed individuals preferentially attend to mood-congruent (i.e., negative) stimuli. A commonly used method to examine this question is the *dot-probe task* (Joormann & Gotlib, 2007), in which a pair of stimuli (words or faces) of different valences (one neutral, one emotional) is presented. Participants are then asked to make a response to a probe that replaces either the neutral or emotional stimuli. Biases in attention are measured by computing the difference between response times to probes that replace emotional stimuli, compared to probes that replace neutral stimuli. More rapid responses to probes that replace emotional stimuli suggest that attention is biased towards the emotional stimulus.

Whether or not depressed individuals show negative attentional biases depends on the duration of the stimuli. In general, when emotional stimuli are presented subliminally (e.g., for 14 ms), depressed individuals do not differ from healthy controls in terms of how rapidly they respond to probes replacing negative stimuli. However, when emotional stimuli are presented supraliminally (i.e., presented for longer durations, up to 1000 ms), clinically depressed adults exhibit attentional biases towards sad, but not happy, fearful, or angry, emotional stimuli (Gotlib, Krasnoperova, Yue, & Joormann, 2004). Although far fewer in number, studies suggest that clinically depressed adolescents (Hankin, Gibb, Abela, & Flory, 2010) as well as youth at high risk for developing depression (Joormann, Talbot, & Gotlib, 2007; Kujawa et al., 2011) exhibit a similar attentional bias to negative emotional stimuli. The discrepancies in the attentional bias literature between subliminal and supraliminal stimulus presentations have led to the conclusion that, unlike anxiety, depression is not characterized by automatic orientation to negative stimuli, but instead involves impairment in disengagement from negative stimuli once attention is captured (Joormann & Gotlib, 2010).

Depressed individuals also may exhibit an attentional bias *away* from positive emotional stimuli compared to healthy individuals. In the dot-probe task, this means that participants respond more rapidly to probes replacing neutral stimuli compared to those replacing positive (e.g., happy) stimuli. A meta-analysis of adult studies suggests that the magnitude of this bias away from positive stimuli is small but statistically significant (Peckham, McHugh, & Otto, 2010). Armstrong and Olatunji (2012) conducted a meta-analysis of adult eye-tracking studies of attentional biases and found that depression is characterized by both blunted orienting of attention, and less sustained attention, to positive stimuli. Given the small number of studies, it is unclear whether an "anhedonic bias" (Armstrong & Olatunji, 2012, p. 714) in attention exists among adolescents. However, one study reported attentional bias away from positive stimuli among depressed adolescents with comorbid anxiety disorders (Hankin et al., 2010). Clearly, future research is needed to clarify the nature of attentional biases among depressed adolescents.

Memory Biases

Cognitive models of depression propose that, when depressive self-relevant schemas are activated, mood-congruent (i.e., negative) information becomes more readily accessible from memory. One commonly used method to assess negative memory biases is the Self-Referential Encoding Task (SRET), in which participants view negative and positive interpersonally oriented words and are asked: "Does this word describe you?" After completing the task, participants are asked to recall as many adjectives as they can in any order. Depressed adults (Dozois & Dobson, 2001a) and adolescents (Auerbach, Stanton, Proudfit, & Pizzagalli, 2015) endorse more negative and fewer positive words as self-descriptive, and recall more negative and fewer positive adjectives. Further, Auerbach et al. (2015) also found that there may be specific neural activity that underlies these self-referential processing biases in depressed adolescents. This negative bias in the recall of explicitly encoded (i.e., encoded in conscious awareness) material is one of the most reliable and robust cognitive biases found in MDD (Gotlib & Joormann, 2010; Kircanski, Joormann, & Gotlib, 2012).

There is less consistent evidence regarding negative memory biases for information that is encoded outside of conscious awareness (i.e., implicitly) (Gotlib & Joormann, 2010). Recognition biases in implicit memory are most commonly measured in studies involving priming, wherein investigators quantify the extent to which later responses are shaped or affected by previously encoded information. For instance, word completion tasks ask participants to first encode a list of positive and negative words, and later complete a series of word fragments (e.g., hop _____). Word fragments are counterbalanced such that half can be completed to form previously encoded words, and half form words from a new, unprimed list. Participants who complete more primed versus unprimed negative words show a negative implicit memory bias. Although mean effect sizes were small, a recent meta-analysis of word completion and other implicit memory tasks found evidence for negative biases in depression (Gaddy & Ingram, 2014). Further, implicit memory biases were stronger in studies employing self-relevant stimuli, consistent with the findings regarding explicit memory biases.

In addition to biases in what information depressed individuals recall over short periods, research also has focused on the content of long-term *autobiographical* memories recalled in response to cue words. An extensive body of research has shown that depressed individuals tend to report *overgeneral* autobiographical memories (OGMs) (Williams et al., 2007); that is, they tend to recall personal events that belong to a category of experiences (e.g., When I go to the mall) and/or events that occurred over an extended timeframe (e.g., My summer vacation), rather specific, time-limited events (e.g., I visited my mother last Thursday afternoon). This is conceptually important because recalling OGMs may allow individuals to avoid potentially distressing content, which, in the long run, may impair problem-solving and, ultimately, maintain or exacerbate depressive symptoms (Williams et al., 2007).

The degree of overgeneralization of autobiographical memories is most commonly assessed using the Autobiographical Memory Task (AMT: Williams & Broadbent, 1986), wherein participants recall the first memory that comes to mind following a series of cue words. Recalled memories can then be categorized as specific or overgeneral. A series of recent studies have provided compelling evidence that OGM, indexed using the AMT, acts as an underlying vulnerability for adolescent MDD, particularly in the face of stress. Consistent with the adult literature, clinically depressed adolescents report greater OGMs (Kuyken, Howell, & Dalgleish, 2006; Park, Goodyer, & Teasdale, 2004), as do participants at elevated risk for developing depression (Kuyken & Dalgleish, 2011) and adolescents who have remitted from a previous episode of MDD (Kuyken & Dalgleish, 2011; Park, Goodyer, & Teasdale, 2002). To our knowledge, there are two studies that have provided evidence for OGM as a vulnerability factor in a diathesis-stress framework. First, Sumner et al. (2011) reported that, among adolescents with a history of MDD, OGM prospectively predicted depression recurrence, but only among those who also reported high levels of chronic interpersonal stress. Similarly, another study found that OGM was prospectively associated with increases in depressive symptoms, but only for those who reported high scores on a measure of emotional abuse during the follow-up period (Stange, Hamlat, Hamilton, Abramson, & Alloy, 2013).

Emotion-Processing Biases

There is an emerging literature that suggests that, along with preferentially orienting attention towards negative emotional stimuli (i.e., negative attentional biases), depressed individuals also show negative biases in identifying emotional facial expressions. Compared to non-depressed participants, adults with MDD are both slower and less accurate at identifying neutral facial expressions, and more often misinterpret neutral stimuli as sad (Leppanen, Milders, Bell, Terriere, & Hietanen, 2004). Furthermore, clinical depression is associated with both less accuracy in identifying happy facial expressions (Mandal & Palchoudhury, 1985a) and enhanced accuracy for sad expressions (Mandal & Palchoudhury, 1985b). More recently, researchers have used a facial morphing paradigm (i.e., the facial expression intensity changes continuously from neutral to the target emotion) to develop a more fine-grained understanding of depressive biases in the processing of subtle differences in emotion-processing. Using this methodology, Joormann and Gotlib (2006) found that depressed adults required both greater intensity to identify happy expressions and lower intensity to identify sad expressions compared to healthy controls. This pattern was replicated in a sample of adults with remitted depression who underwent a negative mood induction (LeMoult, Joormann, Sherdell, Wright, & Gotlib, 2009), providing preliminary evidence that these processing biases may act as underlying vulnerability factors to MDD.

The literature on emotion-processing biases in depressed adolescents is limited. Using the same facial morphing paradigm described above, Joormann, Gilbert, and Gotlib (2010) found that, contrary to the adult literature, youth at high risk for MDD required greater intensity to identify *sad*, but not happy, facial expressions. We (Auerbach, Stewart, Stanton, Mueller, & Pizzagalli, 2015) recently examined emotional-processing biases in adolescents by recording their accuracy at identifying facial expressions (sad, happy, neutral, fearful) at various intensities (e.g., 10%; 60%). Consistent with adult studies, we found that depressed adolescents were less accurate for low-intensity happy faces, but *more* accurate for low-intensity sad faces, compared to non-depressed adolescents. Further, we found that deficits in processing happy faces were associated with neural abnormalities in the left dorsolateral prefrontal cortex, an area of the brain implicated in regulating and processing emotions. In sum, there is some intriguing evidence to suggest that depressed adolescents show negative emotion-processing biases, but this literature is in its early stages. Future studies are required to fully delineate the nature and extent of these biases in adolescent depression, to reconcile inconsistencies across studies, and to determine whether these biases are prospectively associated with the development of MDD and/or the exacerbation of depressive symptoms.

Deficits in Inhibition and Cognitive Control

As we alluded to in the section on attentional biases above, there is emerging evidence to suggest that depression is associated with difficulties in disengaging from negative information (Kircanski et al., 2012). The ability to inhibit irrelevant information, regardless of valence, is crucial to humans' ability to adaptively respond to environmental demands. The amount of information that can be temporarily stored for cognitive manipulation is limited; therefore, to effectively focus our attention, we must suppress information irrelevant to what we are doing from occupying precious space in our temporary information stores. Compared to non-depressed adolescents, depressed adolescents show pronounced deficits in their general inhibition abilities (Wagner, Muller, Helmreich, Huss, & Tadic, 2015).

Dr. Jutta Joormann and Dr. Ian Gotlib have conducted a series of experiments to assess the inhibition of emotional information, specifically. This research has employed the negative affective priming task (Joormann, 2004), which measures how quickly participants respond to emotional targets (positive or negative) after trials containing emotional distractors that they are instructed to ignore. Adults with MDD (Goeleven, De Raedt, Baert, & Koster, 2006; Joormann & Gotlib, 2010), elevated depressive symptoms (Joormann, 2004), and euthymic, previously depressed participants (Joormann, 2004) show deficits in inhibition of negative emotional information compared to never-depressed subjects. Relatedly, compared to controls, depressed individuals show deficits in forgetting previously memorized negative information (Joormann & Gotlib, 2008). Importantly, across the studies reviewed above, the inhibition deficit is *specific* to negative information; depressed individuals do not differ from non-depressed controls in their proficiency at inhibiting positive information. To our knowledge, these promising findings on disinhibition in depression await replication in adolescent samples.

Summary

In this chapter, we reviewed research on etiological models that have improved our understanding of how adolescents develop depression. Adolescents' environments play a prominent role in triggering episodes of depression, and many of the diathesis-stress models we described identify characteristics that place youth at risk for depression in the face of negative life events. From a clinical perspective, developing a deeper understanding of etiological models of depression may enhance confidence with delivery of early-session psychoeducation, and, further, it may facilitate richer and more accurate case conceptualizations. Perhaps most importantly, understanding the processes that likely cause and maintain our patients' illness may help build a more profound capacity for empathy and a better language with which to work on presenting problems, potentially informing targets for treatment and ultimately, contributing to more effective clinical outcomes.

3 Assessment

In graduate school, one of us (RPA) had a clinical supervisor who often said, "You don't know until you ask, and what you don't ask, you'll never know." The statement is as obvious as it is intuitive; however, it also underscores the importance of conducting a thorough assessment. Such an assessment allows clinicians to better understand how symptoms of depression cohere, and ultimately, it enables clinicians to work collaboratively with patients to develop a comprehensive case conceptualization. There is a wide range of assessment tools available. Nevertheless, as we are focused on integrating assessment into CBT, the present chapter focuses on tools that may be utilized both at the outset and throughout treatment. Specifically, the chapter will provide a rationale for conducting a thorough assessment during the initial sessions as well as providing session-to-session assessments. To that end, it will provide an overview of gold-standard diagnostic interviews and narrow-band severity indicators (e.g., self-report measures, observational methods, and third-party report of patient symptoms). Additionally, given the high prevalence of self-harm and suicidality in the context of depression, relevant assessment tools targeting these features will be discussed.

Assessment Goals

Prior to choosing which approach and instruments to utilize, it is important to identify the central aim for a given assessment. Assessment goals include, but are not limited to, diagnosis, treatment planning, treatment monitoring, and evaluation (Essau & Ollendick, 2010). During treatment, assessment often spans the initial two to three sessions; however, it also should be integrated more fluidly throughout subsequent sessions. In fact, treatment success often is contingent on the quality and depth of the initial assessment as well as the ongoing assessment throughout the course of treatment – which will necessarily facilitate a more comprehensive case conceptualization. It is important that chosen instruments are reliable and valid and adequately address the clinical issues in question.

CBT for depressed adolescents is thought to be time-limited in that a given treatment course may range from approximately 12 to 18 sessions. A thorough assessment at the onset of treatment helps clarify problem areas or treatment goals for both the clinician and patient, and it provides important clinical information regarding antecedents, triggers, rationale for potential symptom fluctuations, and resources (i.e., interpersonal, coping). Many clinicians use the more formal diagnostic tools outlined below while others pursue an ad hoc approach to develop an understanding of the presenting symptoms. These initial assessments are very commonplace relative to subsequent session-to-session assessments. By contrast, fewer clinicians provide formal week-to-week assessments to track symptom change over time.

There are a number of advantages to more systematic assessment as this information may be seamlessly integrated into the treatment framework. First, there are a number of freely available self-report measures of depressive symptoms (e.g., Center for Epidemiologic Studies Depression Scale, Mood and Feelings Questionnaire), and consequently, we encourage clinicians to have patients complete these measures before each session. This allows clinicians to track symptom changes, and additionally, it provides a window of understanding as to what types of symptoms may be changing from session to session (i.e., affective versus somatic versus cognitive). In doing so, this may serve to help the clinician identify symptom changes facilitated by different CBT skills and may reveal chronic issues that persist throughout treatment and require renewed focus. Second, we encourage clinicians to use the information that is collected by creating session-by-session symptom trajectories (Figure 3.1). This allows the therapist and patient to identify trends and productively explore what transpired in a given week that contributed to symptoms improving (e.g., successfully completed weekly CBT assignments, positive interactions with parents) or worsening (e.g., conflicts with friends or parents, difficulty in school). This granular week-to-week analysis provides a road map for clinicians to follow, and ideally, it helps shape the behavioral and cognitive strategies employed. Moreover, studies have shown that tracking patient progress over the course of treatment, and then feeding this information back to the patient, may significantly improve patient outcomes (Lambert et al., 2003; Lambert, Harmon, Slade, Whipple, & Hawkins, 2005). *Last*, weekly assessments provide objective versus subjective assessments of symptom change. Clinicians encourage patients to *act like scientists* by exploring the *what, why,* and *how* with respect to ongoing changes which occur in the context of treatment, and thus, it is important for clinicians to *practice what they preach*. Whether symptom information is obtained with pen and paper, through the use of a tablet, and/or through mobile phone apps is unimportant. Rather, collecting the hard, empirical data will provide a more objective account of the overall treatment, which, in our estimation, provides a stronger framework for the treatment itself. In light of the importance of assessments, in the proceeding sections, we have outlined different tools and strategies in which assessment may be integrated into a clinician's everyday practice. Understandably, it may not be realistic for clinicians to utilize all the tools described in the proceeding passages. Nevertheless, our aim is to provide the range of options available, and, critically, to underscore how these tools may be utilized to facilitate treatment efficacy.

Diagnostic Interviews

In general, unstructured interviews are helpful for building rapport with patients and may be tailored to address an individual's presenting issues. These interviews allow clinicians to observe a patient's behavior, especially in response to different types of questioning that may be more or less taxing. At the same time, from a psychometric perspective, such

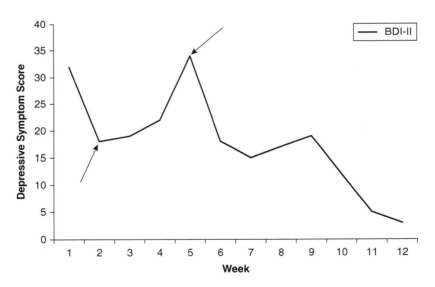

Figure 3.1 Tracking Depressive Symptoms from Session to Session

Note: CBT underscores the importance of patients collecting data on their experience as opposed to relying on subjective recall. In the example in Figure 3.1, a patient's weekly Beck Depression Inventory-II (BDI-II) symptoms were assessed prior to each weekly session. Using Figure 3.1, it is then easy for a clinician to explore in a collaborative way what changes occurred from week to week, which may have influenced the rise and fall of depressive symptoms. Despite its relative simplicity, this may be a valuable tool to motivate participants to adhere to mutually agreed-upon therapeutic goals as well as outline what is and is not working in the therapy.

an approach does not possess sufficient reliability as the interviews may vary substantially from patient to patient. Structured and semi-structured diagnostic interviews are more labor-intensive and time-consuming as compared to unstructured interviews and paper and pencil questionnaires, and in some instances, these interviews may require formal training. However, there is a substantial upside. The clinician is provided with a wealth of information as well as a context for the symptoms. Further, these interviews provide an opportunity for the clinician to better evaluate each symptom, and, based on the aggregate of information, determine if a given individual meets diagnostic criteria for depression and other comorbid disorders. As mentioned earlier, clinicians have myriad options when choosing diagnostic instruments. The exemplars described below are by no means exhaustive. Rather, they were selected given their reputation in the field, accessibility, psychometric properties (i.e., reliability and validity), and diversity of scope (i.e., psychosocial contexts versus diagnoses).

HEADS-ED

Given the importance of building trust and beginning to forge a therapeutic alliance with adolescent patients in the initial sessions, a formalized assessment can, at times, seem like an unnatural introduction to treatment. A potential happy medium may be to utilize the HEADS-ED tool as a starting place (Capelli, 2011; see heads-ed.com). This brief semi-structured interview (10–15 minutes) is a validated tool that, when administered effectively, provides a wealth of psychosocial information related to the following important domains: (1) **H**ome (e.g., How do you get along with your parents/family?); (2) **E**ducation (e.g., How are your grades?); (3) **A**ctivities and peers (e.g., What are your relationships like with friends and what types of activities do you do?); (4) **D**rugs and alcohol (e.g., How often do you use drugs or alcohol?); (5) **S**uicidality (e.g., Do you ever have thoughts of wanting to end your life?); (6) **E**motions, behaviors, thought disturbance (e.g., How has your mood been lately?); and (7) **D**ischarge resources (e.g., Are you currently seeing or have you ever seen a therapist?). In the context of patients in your office, it may be sufficient to begin with the *HEADS* component before proceeding with a more formalized assessment of symptoms and thus omitting the *ED*. While it is likely that most clinicians would address each of these issues during initial sessions, the tool provides a handy checklist, and critically, it structures the interview in a natural way by allowing the adolescent to better describe the context in which symptoms may have emerged. In many ways, the interview provides a loose structure for guided exploration that would be consistent across patients, and further, beginning with these questions, as opposed to probing symptoms from the onset, may allow adolescents to develop a comfort level before beginning a dialogue about symptoms that, for some, may be challenging and difficult to articulate. Therefore, the HEADS-ED interview may provide a safe means to develop therapeutic rapport before conducting a formalized assessment of symptoms.

In addition to being a wonderful clinical tool, the developers of HEADS-ED have made resources about the interview publicly available online – complete with training videos. This is an invaluable resource to learn different ways to probe adolescents using open-ended questions. Further, the HEADS-ED interview may provide an informative starting point to better understand the symptoms discussed during the structured and semi-structured diagnostic interview below. By referring back to this contextual information, clinicians may find that it results in greater fluidity throughout the session, and potentially, expedites the formal (and potentially longer) assessments.

Stress and Adversity Inventory

Major models of mental and physical health underscore the importance of understanding the impact of both current and lifetime stress, as this may have profound implications for the course and treatment of a given disorder. Interpersonal stress, in particular, is a robust predictor for both the onset and course of adolescent depression (e.g., Auerbach et al., 2014), and therefore, we believe that it is essential to quantify the impact of stress, especially as this may inform a clinician's case conceptualization and treatment approach. The Stress and Adversity Inventory (STRAIN: Slavich & Epel, 2010) provides an online approach to systematically assess a broad array of acute (e.g., deaths of loved ones, romantic break-ups) and chronic (e.g., persistent health issues, school difficulties) stressors. The STRAIN (http://www.uclastresslab.org/products/strain-stress-and-adversity-inventory) can be completed online prior to the initial appointment or while an adolescent waits for the initial appointment as it necessitates about 25–35 minutes (approximately 220 questions). Upon completion, the system immediately generates a clinician-friendly report describing an individual's cumulative life stress – including data on severity, frequency, timing, and duration. Such background information can be woven into the assessment process, and ultimately, may inform the therapist's understanding of key factors contributing to the initial onset and maintenance of an adolescent's depressive symptoms, as well as potential treatment targets.

Kiddie Schedule for Affective Disorders and Schizophrenia

The Schedule for Affective Disorders and Schizophrenia for School Age Children Present and Lifetime Version (K-SADS-PL: Ambrosini, 2000;

Kaufman, Birmaher, Brent, Rao, & Ryan, 1996) is a semi-structured interview that is administered by clinicians to the parent and adolescent (ages 6–18 years). While the K-SADS-PL is extremely thorough, one of the primary challenges is that the interview requires between 90 and 120 minutes, and it needs to be administered by well-trained mental health professionals. The instrument was designed to assess current and past psychopathology based on DSM-IV-TR diagnostic criteria (American Psychiatric Association, 2000), and by interviewing both the parent and child, the assessment may obtain summary ratings, which may increase the reliability of diagnoses. Moreover, depending on the age of the patient, it may be helpful to corroborate the presence (e.g., hallucinations, delusions) or absence (e.g., externalizing behaviors) of reported symptoms with parent report of a child's symptoms. In addition to systematic questioning about depressive disorders, the interview may provide important information about comorbid disorders, and given the high rates of comorbidity between depression and anxiety, this may be helpful in unpacking the temporal course and development of related mental illnesses. Presently, the K-SADS-PL is freely available (http://www.psychiatry.pitt.edu/node/8233) through the University of Pittsburgh, Department of Psychiatry.

Mini International Neuropsychiatric Interview for Children and Adolescents

The Mini International Neuropsychiatric Interview for Children and Adolescents (MINI-KID: Sheehan et al., 2010) is a structured diagnostic interview used to assess current and past psychopathology (i.e., internalizing and externalizing disorders) in youth based on criteria from the DSM-IV-TR. In general, the interview necessitates 20–30 minutes, and it provides a strong overview of the presence or absence of symptoms using easy-to-follow skip-out procedures. Despite its relative brevity, as compared to more extensive diagnostic interviews (e.g., K-SADS), it has demonstrated relatively high reliability and validity (Sheehan et al., 2010). Given the length and sound psychometric properties, this diagnostic interview may be more easily integrated, relative to the K-SADS-PL, in the context of treatment.

Self-Report Questionnaires

While structured and semi-structured diagnostic interviews provide a comprehensive assessment for symptoms of mental disorders, these interviews often require extensive training and considerable time to administer. As a result, a series of self-report questionnaires has been developed to assess clients' subjective experience of depressive symptoms. Such questionnaires are relatively easy to administer, and typically, require little time to complete. In contrast to interviews that have the capacity to diagnose depressive disorders, self-report questionnaires are typically limited to assessing the frequency and severity of depressive symptoms. Self-report instruments have been utilized for both clinical and research purposes, and despite the potential for response bias, many possess strong reliability and validity.

There are several advantages to self-report measures. First, many teens have difficulty sharing their symptoms of depression. Thus, self-report measures provide a more private space to express what symptoms are affecting them without having to verbalize them to a clinician (particularly in the initial sessions). Second, the administration of self-report questionnaires does not require extensive clinical training (e.g., an administrative assistant can oversee administration in the waiting room). Last, self-report measures can be readministered throughout clinical practice, and thus, it allows the clinician and patient alike to amass objective data regarding symptom change over time. Further, depressive symptom inventories also may provide clinicians with a road map regarding how to better target treatment by identifying relatively more severe symptom clusters.

Beck Depression Inventory – Second Revision

The Beck Depression Inventory-II (BDI-II: Beck, Steer, & Brown, 1996) is a commonly used self-report measure of DSM-IV depressive symptoms. In general, the BDI-II is not an instrument that yields diagnoses. The measure contains 21 items that assess the presence of cognitive-affective and somatic symptoms during the previous 2 weeks. Item scores range from 0 to 3, with higher total scores reflecting greater depressive symptom severity. Standard cut-offs for the BDI-II include: (1) 0 – 13 = minimal depression; (2) 14 – 19 = mild depression; (3) 20 – 28 = moderate depression; and (4) 29 – 63 = severe depression. In general, the BDI-II possesses strong reliability and validity (Beck et al., 1996).

Center for Epidemiological Studies Depression Scale

The Center for Epidemiologic Studies Depression Scale (CES-D: Radloff, 1977) is among the most widely used self-report depressive symptom scales, and it is publicly available. The CES-D is comprised of 20 items, and the questionnaire is based on existing measures including the original BDI (Beck & Steer, 1991), the Zung Self-Rating Depression Scale (Zung, 1965), the Minnesota Multiphasic Personality Inventory for Depression Scale (McKinley & Hathaway, 1944), and an unpublished depression checklist developed by Gardner (1968). The CES-D assesses depressive symptoms from the general population, and to date, the application has been broad-based, ranging from epidemiological and treatment studies to ongoing clinical assessment in the context of treatment. Results from a principal component analysis divide the items into four primary subscales: depressed affect, positive affect, somatic and retarded activity, and interpersonal. CES-D scores range from 0 to 60, and higher scores indicate greater severity of depressive symptoms, with a score of 16 indicating moderate depression. Research examining the psychometric properties of the CES-D across diverse samples has found that the measure is reliable and valid. Irwin, Artin, and Oxman (1999) revised and abbreviated the original version (CESD-R), and the revision is more in line with the depressive symptoms included in the DSM-IV.

Mood and Feelings Questionnaire

The Mood and Feelings Questionnaire (Angold et al., 1995; Messer et al., 1995) is a self-report measure that provides a balanced report of affective, cognitive, and somatic symptoms in depressed adolescents. There are two versions of the questionnaire: the short version (13 items) and the long version (33 items). Both instruments have demonstrated excellent test–test reliability and validity, and they have been used extensively with child and adolescent samples. Another exciting feature of this questionnaire is that it also contains short and long parent versions, which assess their children's symptoms. All of these measures are publicly available (devepi.duhs.duke.edu/mfq.html), and therefore, can be easily integrated into everyday practice.

Observational Methods

There are inherent strengths to interviews and self-report measures, but the power of observation should not be understated. Depression is a disorder that compromises our mood, thoughts, and behaviors. Some patients may lack the insight or the capacity to accurately report their symptoms. At the same time, for a trained clinician there are key characteristics or features of the depressed individual to observe.

One of the more noticeable symptoms is psychomotor retardation and agitation. Again, returning to graduate school, a supervisor once expertly explained the symptoms as follows. Psychomotor retardation and agitation are similar to what happens when we slow down and fast-forward DVDs, respectively. More specifically, an individual struggling with psychomotor retardation will typically speak and move more slowly as if he/she were moving in slow motion. Conversely, individuals who are experiencing psychomotor agitation will speak quickly, often not finishing sentences or thoughts, and have difficulty sitting still. In a vacuum, these symptoms may be more easily noticed. However, if a person has never been in your office before, it will be difficult to ascertain what a given individual's baseline behavior may be as there is no reference point. Thus, a helpful question to pose is whether or not anyone has commented on how fast or slow the patient's speech and movements have been lately (or elicit a third-party report from a parent or teacher). While the patient may not have insight into these recent changes, it is likely that someone (e.g., parent, teacher, peer) in the patient's life has taken stock.

Depression is often characterized by weight gain or loss (change of 5% of body weight in 1 month). Understandably, this is not a phenomenon one can easily ascertain during an initial session. However, for longstanding patients, unintended weight gain and/or loss is observable. Alternatively, for new patients, clinicians should ask whether they have experienced recent weight gain or loss, and if so, how much and in what period of time. When asking such questions, it is important to state clearly whether weight loss or gain was intended or could be accounted for by any recent changes (e.g., new medication)? Additionally, when working with children and adolescents, weight gain and loss should be viewed in the larger context of "typical growth" and pubertal change.

Fatigue is another symptom that may be observed in the context of an assessment or throughout the session. Many patients struggling with depression report significant fatigue despite sleeping more. Coupled with this overwhelming fatigue, many patients have a diminished capacity to concentrate. Such patients may not realize that their concentration is limited or may simply note that they feel tired. However, throughout the interview, it is important to note how often a patient needs questions repeated, provides non-sequiturs to question prompts, loses the thread when responding to specific questions, and has difficulty engaging in the conversation. It also is important to ascertain whether the patient acknowledges diminished concentration and if concentration varies as a function of environmental contexts (school versus friends).

Third-Party Reports

Multi-informant assessments provide clinicians with an array of perspectives as they gather information through different lenses and from diverse environments. Generally, there is greater reliance on third-party reports for children and adolescents, as clinicians often seek information from peers, teachers, and parents. To that end, the child and adolescent field has a variety of reliable, valid, and systematic options. With regard to standardized third-party reports of a patient's symptoms, Achenbach (1991) has created a series of instruments that may be completed by a patient's parents and teachers. These tools are reliable and valid gold-standard measures in the field, and thus, they provide important information in both understanding and treating a patient's symptoms.

Child Behavior Checklist

The Child Behavior Checklist (CBCL: Achenbach, 1991; Achenbach & Rescorla, 2001) is an instrument that is typically completed by the parent of a given child, and it is often used in conjunction with the Youth Self-Report (YSR), which assesses overlapping constructs (Achenbach, 1991). The instrument contains two sections. In the first section, the respondent is asked general information about his/her child (e.g., Please list any organizations, clubs, teams, or groups your child belongs to) and then a parent is asked to compare his/her child's present activity to that of other children of the same age. In the second section, there are 120 statements describing potential behavioral and emotional problems, and respondents are asked to indicate that these statements are "not true," "somewhat or sometimes true," or "very true or often true." The CBCL can be used with children and adolescents ages 6–18, and there is also a version for children 1.5–5 years of age (Child Behavior Checklist – Language Development Survey: CBCL – LDS). Historically, scoring the CBCL was time-consuming; however, there is now a computer scoring system that computes the various subtests and scores (i.e., internalizing versus externalizing). The CBCL has strong reliability and validity, and it has been broadly utilized across cultures. As the CBCL provides normative scores, it is helpful in understanding whether the presence of symptoms is typical or normal as opposed to clinically significant.

Teacher's Report Form

Similar to the CBCL, the Teacher's Report Form (TRF: Achenbach, 1991) is often paired with the YSR, and it assesses a child's behavioral functioning as well as internalizing and externalizing symptoms. Teachers may provide invaluable information about a child's emotional intelligence and social functioning within an academic environment. The full version of the TRF also includes options for adaptive functioning and academic performance sections, and while these sections are certainly helpful, they are not obligatory. In general, the TRF possesses strong test–retest reliability, internal consistency, and interrater reliability, as well as acceptable criterion validity. The instrument can be scored manually, and there is also computerized scoring available. Normative scores and cutoffs are provided.

Suicide and Self-Harm Risk Assessment

The careful assessment of suicide and self-harm is essential when working with patients struggling with depressive symptoms and disorders. While only a small percentage of depressed patients attempt suicide and engage in self-harm, these are issues that need to be explored with caution and care. In general, assessment of risk should include an examination of: (1) predisposing vulnerabilities; (2) triggers or precipitating events; (3) affective, cognitive, and behavioral status; and (4) contradictions (e.g., perceived coping resources). Additionally, clinicians should broadly assess suicidal intent, motivations for suicide and lethality of potential attempts, and whether these issues arise in the face of chronic or acute suicidality (Berman, Jobes, & Silverman, 2006). The issues of suicidality and self-harm are further complicated as there are many individuals who deliberately harm themselves without lethal intent (i.e., non-suicidal self-injury: NSSI) (for example, see Nock, 2009). In an effort to better understand risk for suicide, Goldston (2003) reviewed approximately 60 instruments assessing constructs such as the presence of, risk/propensity for, and the intentionality/lethality of suicidal behaviors. Goldston (2003) cautions that few measures are predictive of attempted suicide, and all measures possess strengths and weaknesses. At the same time, two recommended scales include the Beck Scale for Suicide Ideation (BSI) and Linehan's Reasons for Living (LRFL), which we have detailed below. Additionally, we also provide background information on the Columbia Suicide Severity Rating Scale, a brief interview that can be seamlessly integrated into sessions, especially when dealing with high-risk youth. Finally, the Self-Injurious Thoughts and Behaviors Interview (Nock, Holmberg, Photos, & Michel, 2007) is discussed. The interview extensively probes NSSI and suicidality, which provides a means of differentiating these important, distinct behaviors. Regardless of the clinician's assessment strategy, ultimately one must ascertain whether the patient has a specific plan in place, and if so, what is the potential timeline of these events in order to develop an effective plan of action to ensure safety.

Beck Scale for Suicide Ideation

The BSI (Beck & Steer, 1991) is a 21-item self-report measure that examines the presence and severity of suicidal ideation, and it was adapted from the Scale for Suicide Ideation (SSI: Beck, Kovacs, & Weissman, 1979), an interview-administered rating scale to assess suicidality. Specifically, the measure assesses: (1) an individual's suicidal plans; (2) suicide deterrents; and (3) passive and active suicidal ideation. The BSI contains five screening items regarding active versus passive intent to commit suicide, and positive endorsement of such items prompts specific follow-up questions. The BSI has been validated in both adolescent (Steer, Kumar, & Beck, 1993) as well as adult inpatients and outpatients (Beck & Steer, 1991). Principal factor analysis indicates that there are three factors: desire for death, preparation for suicide, and actual suicide desire. Higher scores on the BSI indicate greater intensity of suicidality (scores range from 0 to 38).

Linehan's Reasons for Living Inventory

The LRFL Inventory LRFL (Linehan, Goodstein, Nielsen, & Chiles, 1983) is a 48-item self-report measure that assesses an individual's beliefs and expectation for not committing suicide. An underlying assumption of the measure is that adaptive beliefs and sufficient reasons for living serve as a buffer against suicidality, and consequently, the instrument examines between-person differences with respect to the "reasons of living" in individuals who engage in suicidal behaviors from those who do not. The LRFL contains six factors: survival and coping beliefs, responsibility to family, child-related concerns, fear of suicide, fear of social disapproval, and moral objections. The instrument possesses strong internal consistency (Linehan et al., 1983) as well as test–retest reliability (Osman, Jones, & Osman, 1991). It also contains moderate concurrent validity with measures of suicide ideation (e.g., Bonner & Rich, 1991; Cole, 1989).

Columbia-Suicide Severity Rating Scale

The Columbia-Suicide Severity Rating Scale (Posner et al., 2008) provides a suite of tools, including a screener, lifetime history module, and suicidality since last visit. The modules are accessible and freely available (www.cssrs.columbia.edu/), and importantly, they are easy to follow, with interactive training materials online. By and large, information is obtained relatively quickly (~5–10 minutes), and the modules can be very helpful in conducting risk assessments.

Self-Injurious Thoughts and Behaviors Interview

The Self-Injurious Thoughts and Behaviors Interview (Nock et al., 2007) is a publicly available, structured clinical interview that assesses the presence, frequency, severity, age of onset, and other characteristics of suicidal thoughts and behaviors as well as non-suicidal thoughts (i.e., thoughts pertaining to the intentional destruction of one's bodily tissue without the intent to die) and behaviors (i.e., the intentional destruction of one's bodily tissue without the intent to die). The interview has been used widely in research. However, for self-injurious and suicidal patients in a clinical setting, it also may be appropriate, especially, if it is important to assess a lifetime history of suicidality and NSSI. For patients reporting suicidality and/or NSSI, the interview requires approximately 20–30 minutes, and it is strongly recommended that clinicians receive training prior to administration.

Summary: An Ounce of Prevention is Worth a Pound of Cure

Despite a number of effective psychotherapeutic and pharmacological treatments for depression, only a minority of individuals receive treatment (e.g., Garber, Webb, & Horowitz, 2009). In part, there remain significant barriers to mental health services, which leave the vast number of depressed individuals untreated. As a response to this glaring need, programs such as the National Depression Screening Day (NDSD) provide individuals with ready access to screens for depression and related mood disorders. These screens are held across hospital, university, and community settings, and further, individuals with internet access also may complete a brief survey online. NDSD is intended to provide a brief survey of depressive symptoms, and ideally, if an individual has a positive screen, he/she is referred for mental health services. Coupled with the NDSD, many states also provide mandatory yearly wellness visits during which children and adolescents are prophylactically screened for a wide range of physical and mental health problems. These visits are critical, as there are more optimal outcomes when symptoms are treated earlier in the disease course. Overall, the NDSD and wellness visit campaigns target an unmet gap in services by identifying risk and channeling patients to needed services.

Future Directions

Nezu, Nezu, Friedman, and Lee (2009) indicated that, in the last 100 years, nearly 300 measures of depression have been developed. The astonishing volume of instruments is indicative of: (1) the significance and impact of depression; (2) an evolving understanding of the phenomenon; and (3) an ingenuity of how to more accurately and succinctly assess it. At the same time, it also underscores a more ominous matter. Specifically, our instruments, whether interview, self-report, observation, or informant-based, do not always *tell the whole story*. In a way, the tools that we utilize are often limited by what an individual says, reports, and does. Moving forward, it will be invaluable to identify behavioral indicators and biomarkers that predispose individuals to depression. Such markers will enable clinicians to institute prevention strategies that may, ultimately, buffer individuals from the deleterious impact of depression. Until that time, clinicians and researchers are encouraged to use the gold-standard interviews and indicators in the field.

4 Setting the Stage

For those of you who have worked with adolescents, it may not be surprising to hear that there is enormous heterogeneity in how and why a teenager may end up in your office. In most instances, it begins with a phone call from a concerned parent. This phone call is an invitation into the family's life, and the conversation is an opportunity to learn about the teenager – to identify how current symptoms may be impacting an adolescent's development, relationships, academic performance, and behaviors. During this conversation it is important for you, as the therapist, to convey your approach to psychotherapy, describing your therapeutic modality, in broad strokes, as well as your tactical approach and experience with treating depression in adolescence. In many ways, this initial contact is a *mini-interview* for both parties, and importantly, it is crucial to provide families with enough information to make an informed decision about their child's treatment. Albeit brief, these initial phone conversations should cover basic details about your practice, including, but not limited to: (1) therapeutic approach (i.e., modality, frequency of sessions); (2) session length; and (3) fee structure (including insurance coverage). This basic information will ensure a high degree of transparency about your practice, which, ultimately, may avoid any confusion throughout the treatment.

Before initiating treatment, it is important for the parent and child to consent and assent, respectively, to the policies in your practice.[2] This process is an ideal opportunity to outline the limits of confidentiality (i.e., following guidelines about the duty to report) and review important boundaries and expectations in the context of clinical care. This can, at

---

2 A psychotherapist–patient services agreement should detail thorough descriptions of psychological services, professional fees, insurance reimbursement, limits of confidentiality, information pertaining to patient professional records, patient rights, and contact information. Ideally, this document should be written in a style that is accessible and clear. The patient should receive a copy of the form that is signed by the legal guardian, adolescent, and therapist.

times, be a challenging conversation. On the one hand, legal guardians of minors may have access to all clinical information; however, from a treatment perspective, this could jeopardize an adolescent's willingness to disclose key clinical information. Thus, we often ask parents to "waive" this right, but underscore that any issues concerning patient safety will be disclosed in a manner that is consistent with legal statutes and ethical guidelines. In a conversation with a parent and adolescent about confidentiality, it is important to draw clear therapeutic boundaries while emphasizing that safety is paramount:

THERAPIST: The limits of confidentiality are very clear in the eyes of the law. Whenever issues around safety arise – whether it be maltreatment, self-injury, or suicidal thoughts or behaviors – we'll work cooperatively to ensure that no harm comes to your daughter or others.
PARENT: So, when would there be limits to confidentiality?
THERAPIST: It's been my experience that it's important to maintain a trusting therapeutic environment, and in this way, it's important for your daughter to feel that she can tell me things without the fear that I'll disclose this information to her parents.
PARENT: That makes sense. I want her to have a space to feel like she can work out her problems.
THERAPIST: Exactly. We want to cultivate this space, which I think will lead to more optimal outcomes. And, if there are times when your daughter wants to share important information with you about her treatment, we can arrange to do so in the context of our sessions.
PARENT: That would be great. Thanks for making this clear to me.

In most instances, parents are on board with this approach, as there is an implicit understanding that this is the best practice to obtain better clinical outcomes. Once there is agreement about the approach moving forward, it is time to begin the therapeutic work.

Psychoeducation

"Knowledge is power" (Bacon, 1597). The power of knowing offers a sense of control, and in the context of psychotherapy, it is essential for youth to regain a locus of control over their symptoms (see Chapter 2). Most often, psychoeducation is woven throughout the course of treatment; however, it is helpful to use psychoeducation as a tool during the initial sessions to paint a clear picture about: (1) what constitutes depression (i.e., symptoms); (2) how CBT works and/or may differ from other forms of talk therapy; and (3) what are realistic expectations about treatment. In this day and age, it is typical for patients to search online for answers about depression and treatment, and although this type of initiative should be lauded, the reliability of the information derived may be *hit or miss*. Thus, using a spirit of guided discovery (described in detail below), psychoeducation may help fill in the gaps in a more organic way, which also may help patients receive more complete answers.

Talking with a Patient about Major Depressive Disorder

Almost without exception, adolescents recognize that depression encompasses feeling persistently sad. Yet, it may be surprising that many youth are unaware that MDD includes other symptoms that cohere to form a syndrome:

THERAPIST: It sounds like the sadness has been overwhelming for the past 6 weeks. What other symptoms have you been experiencing during this time?
PATIENT: Um, I've been pretty irritable, especially around my parents.
THERAPIST: That's good to know. Irritability plays a big part in depression for a lot of people. It's definitely something we should keep an eye on and try to learn ways to better manage it. Would it surprise you to learn that depression could include other symptoms as well?
PATIENT: Like what?
THERAPIST: Good question. So, depression can include as many as nine symptoms, and to meet criteria for the disorder, a person would need to experience at least five of the nine symptoms for a minimum of 2 weeks.
PATIENT: I didn't realize this.
THERAPIST: I wanted to raise this issue because depression can look quite different across people. Some may have sleep problems and are really tired; others may have a change in their appetite and low self-esteem. It'll be important for us to understand how you experience depression.
PATIENT: Sure . . . makes sense. I guess I never thought of it in this way.
THERAPIST: By identifying the main symptoms of your depression, we can better track if specific symptoms change during our work together.

There are many approaches to psychoeducation. It may be more expedient to simply tell an adolescent about the symptoms or even provide a handout that may be reviewed together. However, it has been our experience that engaging adolescents in a conversation about their own symptoms provides a more instructive platform and, ultimately, has more personal salience. During these conversations, it is helpful to discuss the heterogeneity of depressive symptoms and experience (e.g., onset, course, recurrence) as well as to delineate differences among cognitive, affective, and somatic symptoms, especially as this may help a patient obtain a more fine-grained understanding of whether specific environmental contexts trigger different types of symptoms. Again, in this way, depressed adolescents obtain a deeper understanding of their symptoms, which may provide a greater sense of control.

Initiating a Conversation about Cognitive Behavior Therapy

In addition to providing an understanding of depression symptoms (and other comorbid disorders), it is essential to provide a road map about what to expect in CBT. For many adolescents, this will be their initial foray into psychotherapy, and while they may have developed certain assumptions through friends, pop culture (e.g., television, movies), and parents, their expectations for treatment may not be entirely accurate. Thus, it is incumbent upon the therapist to clarify what a patient can reasonably expect from treatment, and critically, what a therapist expects from a patient (e.g., between-session assignments). Similar to psychoeducation regarding depressive symptoms, information about CBT will be integrated throughout the course of treatment. In the initial sessions, it is key to address the following issues: (1) past experience in therapy; (2) knowledge about CBT; and (3) expectations about therapy.

THERAPIST: I know you mentioned that you've been in therapy before. What was your experience like?
PATIENT: Umm. I went and saw this guy once a week. We talked about stuff.
THERAPIST: So, it sounds like you were going weekly. Do you know what type of therapy you did with him?
PATIENT: It was for my depression. Not sure what it was called.
THERAPIST: No problem. What kind of things did you work on?
PATIENT: We just kind of talked, but it didn't really go anywhere.
THERAPIST: I see. It sounds like you would have preferred for things to be clearer. Would you mind if I tell you a little about CBT?
PATIENT: I guess.
THERAPIST: Great.

By obtaining a sense of a patient's past therapeutic experience, it will help a therapist become more nimble with respect to approaching or avoiding different styles of interaction. Also, it provides a clean transition into describing the CBT framework. By and large, CBT requires more active participation from a patient. It is critical for a therapist to delineate how the flow will progress, including: (1) developing a clear structure for the session (see Chapter 5); (2) working through CBT skills in session; and (3) assigning weekly exercises. For many patients, it is essential to foster greater intrinsic motivation to complete in-session and weekly assignments; however, we emphasize that simply attending one session each week will not suffice to overcome depression. Rather, it will require challenging oneself, and critically, applying the skills in the *real world* to determine what works, what does not work, and then, exploring how to utilize the skills more effectively from situation to situation. For many patients, this challenge may seem daunting, particularly given the negative cognitions (e.g., pessimistic thoughts about the benefits of engaging in weekly assignments) and symptoms (e.g., lack of interest, indecisiveness) that so often define depression. Yet, it also is important to emphasize that this process will happen in a step-by-step and gradual manner.

Providing an overview of the CBT format is instructive for adolescents (and parents), as it helps clarify expectations for therapy. In a similar way, it may be helpful to discuss *how* symptoms can change in the course of treatment. For the majority of CBT responders, symptom reduction is a gradual, and, at times, frustrating process. From session to session there may be minor improvements and at times spikes in their symptom scores; however, the general trajectory is in the direction of reduced depressive symptoms and enhanced well-being. These minor spikes may be associated with negative life events, struggling with new skill acquisition, or other setbacks, but by tracking the symptoms over time (see Chapter 3), the therapist and patient can examine symptom change in a broader temporal perspective. This may provide key fodder to defuse negative automatic thoughts that arise during challenging periods (e.g., I'm never going to get better; CBT isn't working). Other patients experience symptom change in a jigsaw-like fashion. For example, improvements in somatic symptoms (e.g., improved sleep and less fatigue) may precipitate renewed energy to challenge negative automatic thoughts that contribute to low self-worth. Alternatively, effective use of cognitive strategies may mollify negative automatic thoughts in social situations (e.g., negative automatic thought: Nobody wants me around; challenge: There is no evidence that no one wants me here), which may provide the opportunity for an adolescent to experience pleasure. For some, there may be *sudden gains* (Tang & DeRubeis, 1999; Tang, DeRubeis, Beberman, & Pham, 2005). *Sudden gains* are defined as a significant symptom reduction (i.e., >11 points on the Beck Depression Inventory; Beck & Steer, 1987) during a single between-session interval, and critically, these sudden gains are associated with better long-term outcomes. As a whole, there is no *right way* for symptoms to improve, and incorporating this information into treatment may reduce patient anxieties and foster more realistic expectations about symptom change.

Collaborative Empiricism and Guided Discovery

Collaborative empiricism and guided discovery form the foundation of CBT. Effective CBT, by its very nature, requires therapists to work in concert with adolescents to identify problem areas, formulate goals, and develop a cohesive plan of action. Not surprisingly, few adolescents respond well to an overly didactic approach, and thus, forging a partnership wherein teens are actively involved in the therapeutic process is critical. There are a number of different ways to frame the therapeutic relationship; however, underscoring the adolescents' inherent expertise regarding their own life is empowering:

THERAPIST: Before we discuss specific treatment goals, I wanted to talk to you about an important aspect of CBT.
PATIENT: OK.
THERAPIST: In brief, although I'm the expert on CBT, you're the expert on your life. I only see you once a week. You live in your skin 24/7. You know the ins and outs of your negative emotions, innermost thoughts, and problems in your life. To effectively target your goals, it's more effective to work together – similar to the way a coach guides a player.
PATIENT: What do you mean?
THERAPIST: Good question. From session to session, we'll use your experiences to guide our approach to therapy. In doing so, we'll work together to determine what are effective strategies to target the goals you've outlined.

This example highlights the importance of clarifying the therapeutic dynamic – one in which the therapist learns from and works with the patient. As we discuss in Chapter 6, collaborative empiricism refers to the process of working jointly with an adolescent to better understand the presentation of symptoms and problems, and critically, designing approaches to test potentially problematic or dysfunctional interpretations (i.e., negative automatic thoughts, core beliefs, depressogenic schema) arising from these experiences.

Guided discovery is an essential component of collaborative empiricism in which a therapist asks strategic questions to guide patients through their own thoughts and experiences (Beck & Dozois, 2011). When successful, this approach helps patients to shift their perspectives:

PATIENT: I tried to do the thought records, but they really don't do anything.
THERAPIST: That sounds frustrating. Walk me through why they're not helpful.
PATIENT: So, they take too much time. And, I don't want to carry a piece of paper around with me.

THERAPIST: I'm with you. A lot of patients don't like carrying a notebook or worksheet with them. I wonder if there are other ways to complete the thought records.
PATIENT: Not sure. But, this isn't working.
THERAPIST: Got it. Rather than doing the assignment in the moment at school, are there other times that might feel less intrusive?
PATIENT: I guess at home.
THERAPIST: If you did them at home, when would you do it and how might they help you manage your mood?
PATIENT: Probably at night – so that I could think about the different thoughts and feelings that popped up throughout the day.
THERAPIST: I guess if you did this at home, we can determine if this was helpful or not.

When working with adolescents, there will be many opportunities to *clash ideas*. Needless to say, depressed teenagers who are struggling with low mood and energy may not jump at the opportunity to engage with CBT assignments. One approach, which we have not found terribly effective, is to consistently reiterate the importance of doing weekly assignments. Conversely, we have had more success in working collaboratively with a patient to learn why a given assignment is challenging, and then adapting the exercise to meet the demands and restrictions of their schedule. This example illustrates *where* the patient struggled with the assignment – completing the thought record in school. However, by listening to what is being said, it was clear that the patient was not fundamentally opposed to the exercise. Thus, through guided discovery, the therapist was able to reconstruct a plan of action, and in doing so, empower the patient to choose where and when the assignment could be completed.

Collaborative empiricism and guided discovery help to engage patients in and foster a curiosity about the process of CBT, which will likely improve intrinsic motivation to actively pursue therapeutic goals and facilitate ongoing case conceptualizations (Friedberg & McClure, 2002). Although it may be tempting, at times, to try to actively persuade adolescents to share your perspective, this may prove to be a Sisyphean task. Rather, take a step back. Be curious. And, ask adolescents to help you understand their perspective and feelings. By trying *to meet them where they're at*, there may be an opportunity to learn from them, and critically, help them consider alternatives through carefully laid questions.

Therapeutic Alliance

One of the knocks on CBT is that it may be overly focused on techniques, interventions, and on targeting surface-level symptoms, and ultimately underemphasizes the alliance between therapists and patients. It is incumbent on each therapist to bring CBT to life, and similar to other modalities, it begins with developing a strong therapeutic alliance. Bordin (1979) posited that the alliance consists of three primary components: (1) the *bond* between therapist and patient; (2) therapist–patient agreement on the *goals* of treatment; and (3) therapist–patient agreement on the *tasks* of treatment. Each component offers a means of strengthening the overall alliance, and at different times in the treatment course, the focus will necessarily shift among them. When working with youth, therapists must channel their inner *Swiss Army knife*. Meaning, there are commonalities across the skill sets one needs to develop and to maintain a strong therapeutic relationship, and a therapist must be dexterous in the use of these techniques to nurture a trusting and secure alliance with adolescent patients. In our view, there a number of key strategies that will enable therapists to foster strong therapeutic alliances: (1) express authentic empathy, understanding, and validation; (2) reduce distress; (3) elicit and incorporate client feedback; and (4) self-disclose (in an appropriate fashion). No one strategy will work for every patient, but using these approaches in targeted ways may facilitate the therapist–patient alliance.

Empathy, Understanding, and Validation

A broad range of therapies emphasize the importance of empathy, understanding, and validation (see Beck, 2005). Nevertheless, when it comes to treating depressed adolescents, this may be easier said than done. Adolescents are wildly interesting individuals – they dream big, think bigger, and act in unimaginable ways. For our part, this is what is so exciting about working with this population. Adolescents also are prone to mood swings and a disarming bluntness. Consider the following exchange from a teenager one of us (RPA) was treating:

PATIENT: I'm here because my parents are making me.
THERAPIST: I'm sorry that you're being forced to be here. This hardly seems fair to you.
PATIENT: Don't try to get inside my head. I'm not talking.
THERAPIST: I understand. Listen, perhaps we can find a middle ground here. We can sit in silence for 40 minutes. Or, we can talk about something that is of interest to both of us.
PATIENT: I doubt we have anything in common.
THERAPIST: I think you might be surprised. Why don't we give it a chance? Pick anything of interest to you – music, sports, movies.
PATIENT: Whatever. I guess I can talk about movies. It's better than staring at you for 40 minutes.

In this example, which unfortunately is not uncommon, the patient has been coerced into coming to therapy – never an ideal setup for a therapist.

This may engender a variety of negative automatic thoughts, "This guy can't help me" or "If I'm rude, he'll back off." As therapists, it is important not to let our agenda get in the way of doing our job. Meaning, during initial sessions, it is ideal to educate patients about the structure of sessions and create a list of goals (see Chapter 5). For challenging patients, however, a successful initial session may simply allow for the possibility of a second session. The example above emphasizes the importance of validating the patient's experience – it is unfair to be forced to attend therapy. At the same time, by shifting the focus away from *doing therapy*, it may allow the patient to perceive the therapist differently. By defusing the anger a patient might feel about the process and conceding control about what to discuss, it may empower a patient to better connect with the therapist.

Certainly, not all patients will present with such hostility and frustration. Nevertheless, different challenges will arise across treatment. For example, it is not uncommon for patients to resist and/or struggle with completing weekly assignments. It is important to explore why these assignments were incomplete or challenging. While there may be instances when youth merely forget to do the assignments, there may be more to it. It could be that the assignments themselves elicit distress, or they do not understand how to complete the assignments. In general, it is very challenging to track one's thoughts and mood, and rather than jumping to conclusions that patients are not working hard enough, this could instead be used as an opportunity to validate their experience and work collaboratively to find strategies to better facilitate the process. In the end, patients need to feel supported. Evincing empathy, understanding, and validation does not guarantee positive outcomes. Nevertheless, we firmly believe that it will increase the odds that patients feel understood, which, over time, may lead to increased engagement in treatment and in turn, more optimal therapeutic results.

Reduce Distress

A theme that is underscored throughout this book is the importance of mood tracking and assessment. Indeed, obtaining *quick-and-dirty* mood ratings at the beginning and end of each session (e.g., On a scale from 1 to 10, with 10 being the worst you have ever felt, how do you feel now?) allows a therapist to explore whether any distress was alleviated during the session. This attenuation of negative affect is important when working with adolescents. Adolescents are in a critical period of transition – simultaneously becoming autonomous from parents and more reliant on same-aged peers. This push-and-pull process is normal; however, as they learn to navigate new types of peer and romantic relationships, stress, tension, and conflict are not uncommon. A seasoned CBT therapist affords time within the session to address the week-to-week stressors, and the co-problem-solving is another platform to convey empathy and understanding. When patients' stress and negative affect are alleviated, it serves to strengthen the therapeutic alliance (see DeRubeis and Feeley, 1990; Webb, Auerbach, & DeRubeis, 2012), as it: (1) provides more confidence in the therapist/treatment; (2) reduces negative cognitions about treatment; and (3) enhances patients' competency in skill utilization and emotion regulation.

There are several other related benefits to actively helping patients reduce distress in session. First, distress reduction provides therapists with a degree of credibility; having demonstrated the efficacy of a given skill, patients may be more apt to *buy into* the therapeutic process. Second, in short-term therapy, each session is a testing stage for a given skill. If skills are successful in session, it may provide the necessary traction and momentum for patients to utilize and generalize the skills in different environmental contexts. Last, many CBT skills seem relatively straightforward, but patients often attest that they are unwieldy and challenging to use in *real life*. Both are true, and it can be challenging to integrate new strategies to manage ongoing distress in one's life. At a minimum, it requires a departure from reflexive bad habits that may exacerbate negative emotions. Practicing the skills may foster greater patient confidence in utilizing the CBT skills outside of the session.

THERAPIST: We're reaching the end of the session. At the start of the session you noted that your mood rating was 7/10. How would you rate your mood now?
PATIENT: I would say that it's about 4/10. I'm definitely feeling a bit better.
THERAPIST: That's really encouraging. Going from 7/10 to 4/10 in about 50 minutes is very impressive. How do you think you could use what we discussed in our session today to more actively monitor and manage your mood outside of our sessions?
PATIENT: I guess that I could track my mood.
THERAPIST: Great. Tracking your mood can definitely be helpful. What else?
PATIENT: I guess also identifying and challenging my thoughts using those thought records. That seemed to be helpful.
THERAPIST: Yes, the real test will be seeing what happens when you apply these skills over the next week.
PATIENT: I can give it a shot.

By reducing distress in the session, a therapist may improve the alliance and foster greater trust in the therapeutic process. Taken together, this may provide a key building block to address the therapeutic goals outlined by the patient.

Elicit and Incorporate Feedback

In principle, eliciting feedback should be a routine component of therapy; however, many therapists, irrespective of experience level, fail to do so. There are a number of well-intentioned reasons why therapists elect to ignore this helpful practice. To optimize the time in session, particularly as it relates to skill building and role-playing, therapists may not want to be derailed for fear of taking time away from imparting key therapeutic skills. Alternatively, therapists might fear that eliciting feedback may shift the focus from the patient to the therapist. In their mind, maintaining a patient-focused approach may be the best means of addressing identified therapeutic goals. Yet another reason is that feedback from patients may feel uncomfortable. Despite our intentions to help patients, these efforts may, at times, be perceived as dismissive and invalidating. Although this is unlikely to be the therapist's intention, eliciting feedback may help us identify problem areas that interfere with the therapeutic process.

THERAPIST: How did you feel about today's session?
PATIENT: It was fine.
THERAPIST: It's really helpful for me to learn about things you liked in the session. And, critically, I want to hear about things that you didn't like, too.
PATIENT: What do you mean?
THERAPIST: Although it's not my intention, there may be times when things I say rub people the wrong way. If you're ever bothered by something I say or don't say, would you be comfortable letting me know?
PATIENT: OK. I'll let you know.

There are different approaches to eliciting feedback. Whereas some therapists prefer to do this in the beginning of a session, others feel that it is most helpful at the end. There is no *best way* per se, and frankly, there are advantages to both approaches. Receiving feedback at the beginning of a session may allow therapists to revisit a challenging session from the previous week, and additionally, it may afford the necessary time and therapeutic space to adequately explore in the session (i.e., by prioritizing this on the agenda). Alternatively, some therapists prefer to integrate this at the end of the session so as not to disrupt the flow of a given session. Regardless of when the feedback is elicited, integrating it into each session is crucial.

Eliciting feedback should be done in a routine way, and if the practice is established within the first or second session, therapists will find that it is fairly straightforward. Exemplar feedback questions are presented in Box 4.1.

> **Box 4.1**
>
> **Beginning of a Session**
>
> - What thoughts do you have about last week's session before we get going today?
> - We're at the halfway point in therapy. What have you liked or not liked about our work together?
> - Last week we didn't really agree about everything. How did that make you feel?
>
> **End of a Session**
>
> - What did you think of today's session?
> - What did you find challenging about the session this week?
> - What did you find helpful or unhelpful about today?

Feedback can be obtained through direct questions, and yet, for others it may be easier to provide this in written form (i.e., a worksheet provided to a patient at the end of a session). The use of open-ended questions increases the likelihood that an adolescent provides a more in-depth response. When framed as a yes–no option, adolescents may choose to deflect the question, which would be a missed opportunity to probe burgeoning or ongoing problems in therapy.

Understandably, an adolescent may not feel confident in voicing discomfort and frustration to a therapist, and therefore, it is important for a therapist to be transparent about this potential power dynamic.

THERAPIST: As part of our ongoing work together, I'm going to ask you for feedback. This will allow me to help you better address your goals.
PATIENT: Sounds good.
THERAPIST: How likely are you to tell me if something is bothering you about the therapy?
PATIENT: I'm not sure. Honestly, I probably wouldn't say anything.
THERAPIST: That is pretty common. Just to be clear, giving me constructive feedback is not rude, and you won't hurt my feelings. In fact, quite the opposite. By telling me what is and is not working, it may help you better achieve your goals.
PATIENT: OK, I'll think about it.
THERAPIST: Great, thank you for considering this. It's something we'll revisit each session.

Despite the challenge for the therapist and the patient, eliciting feedback is a critical part of effective CBT (Spielmans, Pasek, & McFall, 2007). The feedback is instructive for a therapist to necessarily adapt to patients' needs, and moreover, it teaches adolescents that they have the power, through effective communication, to shape their interpersonal relationships in spite of challenging power dynamics. The adolescent patient learns a valuable lesson about optimal ways to convey feedback, especially as this may relate to providing challenging information to authority figures. At a minimum, adjustments made in the context of the therapy will provide additional ammunition to dispel depressogenic cognitions (e.g., No one listens to me; Nothing will ever change), and ultimately, it also will serve to strengthen therapeutic relationships.

Self-Disclose

"Good fences make good neighbors" (Frost, 1915). The same is true in therapy, as it is important to have clear boundaries with patients. The issue of self-disclosure has been sharply debated among clinicians, and there are valid arguments to be had on whether or not to self-disclose. To be clear, self-disclosure is not an all-or-nothing enterprise. Self-disclosure should be conveyed in an authentic manner, one in which a therapist feels comfortable with the depth and breadth of information that is divulged.

PATIENT: I'm not a good student. I'll never be a good student. I'm just not that smart.
THERAPIST: There's no denying it, your grades are on the lower end. But, in my mind, grades don't always reflect intelligence.
PATIENT: Tell that to my parents.
THERAPIST: It may surprise you, but when I was your age, I really struggled in school. We had moved to a new city, and I had a tough time adjusting.
PATIENT: Really?
THERAPIST: Really. It took me a long time to pull out of it. But, it started with changing how I approached the work, and importantly, getting extra help at school. I didn't want to do it at first, but in the end, it really helped me.

For an adolescent patient, exhibiting a degree of imperfection may make the therapeutic experience feel more approachable. Moreover, for some patients, judicious self-disclosure may foster a greater connectedness and identification with the therapist.

Alliance-Interfering Behaviors

Although the chapter has already outlined a number of different strategies to improve therapeutic outcomes, it also may be important to highlight several *alliance-interfering behaviors*. All of us, at some point in our career, have

56 *Setting the Stage*

exhibited these, and almost without fail, it results in taking a step backward, or worse, a patient dropping out of treatment. With this in mind, we view this as a critical area of therapeutic self-monitoring and growth.

Invalidating Environments

Invalidating environments arrive in a number of shapes and sizes; however, perhaps the most common miscue is being perceived as judgmental. As all therapists will readily attest, therapy is not about being right or wrong. Rather, it is creating a non-judgmental space for adolescents to explore their experiences. Being judgmental will stop therapy in its tracks, as most adolescents will simply shut down.

Box 4.2

Judgmental Exchange

PATIENT: I know that I shouldn't be doing this, but I've been cutting myself at night.
THERAPIST: You have?
PATIENT: It's the only thing that makes me feel better in the moment.
THERAPIST: That can't be true. There has to be a better way. We've talked about this.
PATIENT
(hesitantly): I guess.

Non-Judgmental Exchange

PATIENT: I know that I shouldn't be doing this, but I've been cutting myself at night.
THERAPIST: Seems like things have really been challenging over the past week.
PATIENT: Yes. I know I shouldn't be doing this . . . it just kind of happened.
THERAPIST: What happened over the last week that was different than other weeks?
PATIENT: I'm fighting more with my mom. She just doesn't get me. School is a disaster. And, my girlfriend and I are on the outs.

Self-injurious behaviors definitely warrant careful clinical attention and may signal a worsening of symptoms. However, casting judgment will push a therapist farther away from being able to connect and to help a patient. Cultivating a non-judgmental environment will encourage patients to bring challenging material to a given session, and ideally, through guided discovery, it will help the therapist and patient uncover the causes of those behaviors (e.g., cutting as an attempt to down-regulate negative affect) and help teach patients different strategies to address similar issues in the future.

Another issue that many therapists have encountered is not being completely present in the context of a session. Whatever the reason (e.g., long day; feeling tired; distracted by a previous patient; personal problems), our patients deserve our very best. Thus, it is ideal for each therapist to create a schedule that affords the necessary time to prepare for each session and decompress between sessions. At a minimum, a therapist should review patients' files before the session begins. In this way, the therapist will be ready to contribute to the agenda setting at the beginning of each session. For example, therapists may wish to refresh their memory about the weekly assignment, and further, map out the skills and issues to address in the forthcoming session (as well as prepare any needed handouts). While it may seem more efficient to schedule back-to-back patients throughout the day, it is important for therapists to take stock of what is needed to decompress and re-energize between patients.

Perfectly Imperfect Therapists

"To err is human" (Pope, 1711: see Pope & West, 2014). Therapists make mistakes. Despite our best efforts and dedication to patient care, there are a number of ways that we err. These include, but are certainly not limited to, formulating incorrect case conceptualizations, under- or overestimating a patient's ability, forgetting key information provided by a patient, and many, many other things. At a bare minimum, apologize. When done so in a timely and authentic manner, an apology may foster a better connection between therapist and patient.

PATIENT: The conversation with my mom went terribly.
THERAPIST: I'm sorry to hear this. Can you help me understand what happened?
PATIENT: I told her about my cutting, and she totally freaked out. She grounded me. She took away my phone. And, she's not letting me see my friends.
THERAPIST: I didn't anticipate that your mom would react like this. I'm very sorry – I really misread the situation.
PATIENT: I never should have said anything to her. I knew she couldn't handle it.
THERAPIST: I think you had a better read on the situation than I did.

Therapists are only human and not omniscient, a point that should be acknowledged with patients. While these situations can be challenging, if plans are constructed in a collaborative way – as opposed to therapists pushing their own agenda – it may reduce the likelihood that therapists shoulder all the blame. Thus, therapists and patients can step back and reflect, as co-investigators, where a treatment approach may have gone astray.

Another important avenue to cultivate therapeutic success is to seek feedback and supervision from colleagues (Pretorius, 2006). After post-doctoral training and licensure, it is important to keep pushing ourselves as therapists. Although we may become more confident in our clinical judgment and therapeutic abilities as years pass, greater confidence does not necessarily reflect greater competence. Eliciting feedback from colleagues is a very effective way to continue maturing. This practice ensures that therapists are being CBT-adherent, and critically, using best practices to facilitate optimal outcomes with patients.

Triangulating the Guardian

Adolescents do not always agree with their parents' decisions. However, it is a poor practice to align oneself with the adolescent at the expense of the parent. This may seem obvious; however, when a therapist is desperate to forge a bond with a challenging patient, stranger things have happened. At all costs, resist this temptation.

Box 4.3

Triangulating

PATIENT: My dad is such an idiot. First he yells at me for putting a tiny dent in the car. Then, he yells at me for forgetting to take out the trash. He just completely overreacts to everything.

THERAPIST: Yeah, he seems to be really laying into you of late – which isn't really what you need.

Non-Triangulating

PATIENT: My dad is such an idiot. First he yells at me for putting a tiny dent in the car. Then, he yells at me for forgetting to take out the trash. He just completely overreacts to everything.

THERAPIST: You sound pretty upset with your dad. Help me understand what's happening at home.

Although finding this common ground in the short term may improve the relationship, it is not going to help an adolescent patient in the long term. It is important to help a patient find different ways of discussing and managing challenging home environments with parents. Critically, therapists should never knowingly drive a wedge between a child and parent; rather, it is essential for effective therapists to observe adolescents' frustration and anger and work cooperatively to help them manage emotions in more effective ways.

Motivational Interviewing

As intimated throughout this chapter, building rapport with adolescents can be quite the challenge. Initially, adolescents may be unwilling to change, and resistance may manifest itself as taciturn responses, late arrivals to appointments, incomplete weekly assignments, and general aloofness. No doubt, this process is frustrating, and perhaps not surprisingly, Trepper (1991) describes clinical work with adolescents as an *adversarial sport* – one in which the therapist rarely wins (Naar-King & Suarez, 2011). The overarching aim of motivational interviewing (MI) is to use a collaborative, person-centered approach that helps youth identify *their* reasons for change (Naar-King & Suarez, 2011). When MI is integrated with CBT for internalizing disorders, research has demonstrated improved treatment engagement and outcomes (see Burke, Arkowitz, & Menchola, 2003; Flynn, 2011; Hettema, Steele, & Miller, 2005).

Originally, MI was developed as a brief intervention for problem drinking behaviors in adults (Miller, 1983). However, given its widespread success in fostering increased motivation for change (for review in adolescents, see Naar-King & Suarez, 2011), there has been a natural extension to broader mental health problems (e.g., anxiety, obsessive-compulsive disorder, depression) and health behaviors (e.g., sexual risk, cigarettes, eating behaviors) as well as a downward extension to youth populations. A common misconception of MI is that the approach is based on a specific theory, but Miller and Rose (2009) contend that MI is a grounded theory that emerged after careful analysis of recorded sessions. Nevertheless, it does bear close relation to the transtheoretical model of change (TTM: Prochaska & DiClemente, 1984). The TTM provides an organizing framework to understand the different stages of change (precontemplation, contemplation, preparation, action, maintenance), and it is believed that individuals move back and forth (and not necessarily in a linear fashion) though these different stages when challenges and obstacles present themselves. MI also is consistent with, but not derived from, Deci and Ryan's (1985) self-determination theory, which examines the effect of intrinsic (i.e., internal) versus extrinsic (i.e., external) motivation on mental health and health behaviors. As a whole, MI was developed to capitalize on client-centered counseling skills while providing a goal-oriented platform to promote behavioral change (Naar-King & Suarez, 2011).

Autonomy, Collaboration, and Evocation

MI is not a compendium of discrete techniques, but rather, it is a general style of interacting (Miller, 2008). From a thematic perspective, MI underscores the importance of: autonomy, collaboration, and evocation (ACE: Naar-King & Suarez, 2011). This framework provides the basis for responding to resistance and leveraging person-centered skills.

Autonomy

A recurring theme throughout this book is that adolescence is a key developmental period in which youth become increasingly autonomous (Rudolph, 2008), and accordingly, effective therapy allows teens to assert their autonomy by shaping the therapeutic content (e.g., goals, weekly assignments). By genuinely fostering and respecting a teen's autonomy, therapists will more successfully elicit *change talk* – a discussion of what behavioral changes are needed and how these changes will be achieved. Conversely, when adolescents sense that their autonomy is devalued, it often elicits resistance:

PATIENT: These weekly assignments are a total waste of my time.
THERAPIST: I understand what you're saying. But, it's been my experience that these assignments will help you get better.
PATIENT: I don't want to do them.
THERAPIST: I think you'll find that if you do them, you'll feel somewhat better. You should give it a try before you reject it.
PATIENT: Whatever.

It can be challenging for depressed teens to engage with weekly assignments. On the one hand, patients may not have sufficient motivation to complete exercises, which are time-consuming and require great effort. Yet, there is a rich empirical literature detailing the short- and long-term benefits of incorporating between-session exercises. In the exchange above, the therapist is well intentioned but fails to respect the adolescent's autonomy. Consequently, rather than fostering motivation, the adolescent's position became more entrenched. Using an MI approach that is sensitive to the patient's autonomy may help reduce resistance and increase engagement:

PATIENT: These weekly assignments are a total waste of my time.
THERAPIST: It must be frustrating to be asked to complete these assignments. What would be helpful?
PATIENT: What do you mean?
THERAPIST: It may not surprise you, but there have been many patients who've hated these weekly assignments. In these cases, it's been really

helpful for me to learn from patients about what might work between sessions.
PATIENT: I don't know. I've never really thought about it.
THERAPIST: One place to start is to think about your treatment goals. What do you think we can do to best address these goals?
PATIENT: I'm not sure. I don't have a lot of time.
THERAPIST: I totally understand that. Let's start with one of your goals, perhaps the one you think is the highest priority. I'd love to hear some of your thoughts on how to best address this goal.
PATIENT: Yeah. OK.

When using an MI approach, the therapist is not trying to coerce the patient, but rather, guides the patient and elicits ideas about what change looks like and how it might be achieved. This is best accomplished by providing authentic validation of the adolescent's experience (i.e., many patients dislike weekly exercises) and creating space to explore the patient's ideas. Being supportive of an adolescent's desire for autonomy may help a teen feel less constrained and increase willingness to engage in treatment.

Collaboration

Similar to CBT, MI underscores the importance of forging a partnership between the therapist and patient. This collaborative process creates a road map for the therapist and patient to follow. A critical part of the challenge is to guide, but not steer, where the adolescent travels. Again, when using an MI-consistent approach, the adolescent is responsible for directing when and how behavioral change occurs.

PATIENT: Honestly, I think the best solution is for me to not talk to my mom or dad.
THERAPIST: Right now communicating with your parents is challenging.
PATIENT: You got that right. They're so stupid. They just don't get it.
THERAPIST: It certainly seems that you're an ocean apart on this issue. I guess I wonder what not talking to them will look like. How will this decision impact you?
PATIENT: I don't really care.
THERAPIST: OK, let's think this through together. My goal is to help you create an environment that feels less stressful and more supportive.
PATIENT: Well, that's not home.
THERAPIST: I get that. How will not speaking to your parents impact you?
PATIENT: I'll be stressed out all the time when I'm home. But, I just won't be there.
THERAPIST: I see, so not talking to your parents will add to your stress.

PATIENT: In a way. But, it seems better than where I'm at now.
THERAPIST: One of the goals you outlined at the onset of treatment is "getting along better with my parents."
PATIENT: Yes, but only if they're being reasonable.
THERAPIST: On the one hand, your relationship with your parents is really rocky and you feel unheard. On the other hand, you've also expressed to me that these relationships are important. I wonder if the communication has to be all-or-nothing.
PATIENT: I guess I would need to talk with them about some things – rides, school, money.
THERAPIST: Perhaps this is an area to build from – starting small?

Generally speaking, adolescents do not respond well to directives (e.g., It's really better for you to learn to speak with your parents). An MI approach elicits adolescents' reasons for learning to re-approach a given obstacle (e.g., I will need to eventually speak to parents for rides, money). Moreover, collaboration allows the adolescent to build self-efficacy as well as develop trust in the therapeutic process.

Evocation

Part of the challenge of working with resistant and (initially) unmotivated teens is the clipped and glib responses (e.g., no, yup, don't know) that often follow different lines of questioning. MI provides an arena to evoke reasons for and against behavioral change. It is essential to *get teens talking*. Two approaches that are antithetical to this tenet are: (1) providing unsolicited advice and (2) asserting the *righting reflex*. Despite sound intentions, unsolicited advice tends to shut down patients. It decreases a patient's perceived autonomy, and particularly in the early sessions, it may make assumptions about what is and is not possible within a teen's life. Similarly, the righting reflex – a tendency for therapists to be overly didactic about the "right way" to do things – prevents a teen from thinking through the pros and cons of a given situation (Miller & Rollnick, 2002). This effortful contemplation is a key component to building intrinsic motivation. While Naar-King and Suarez (2011) aptly note that it is not realistic for adolescents to view all change as pleasurable (or desirable), by evoking change talk, adolescents may internalize the motivation to change, especially when it adheres to their own personal values.

Learning to Roll with Resistance

There are a number of clever mnemonic devices in MI to help keep therapists on track. Perhaps the most well known is OARS: open-ended questions, affirmations, reflections, and summaries. When these techniques are used together and integrated into CBT, it helps nurture a supportive environment for change talk.

Open-Ended Questions

As mentioned earlier in this chapter, open-ended questions are essential to learn about an adolescent's experience, and while there is certainly a time and place for yes–no questions, whenever possible, these should be minimized. In the early going of a therapeutic relationship with a depressed teen, it can be challenging to sustain a conversational flow, and open-ended questions convey the explicit message that a therapist is interested in how a teen thinks, feels, and behaves.

Affirmations

Affirmations allow a therapist to positively reinforce and validate adolescents' efforts, decisions, and behaviors. Well-planted, and genuine, affirmations may sustain change talk. For example, when therapists affirm patients' efforts and choices (It was brave of you to talk with your boyfriend about setting certain limits), it often prompts teens to continue discussing their own reasons why it was important to choose a given course of action. Despite the many benefits of affirmations, therapist should be cautious about how and when they are used. Adolescents may be unaccustomed to hearing this type of positive reinforcement, and there are times when affirmations may make some teens feel uncomfortable, particularly if they elicit negative automatic thoughts (e.g., It's only a matter of time until I disappoint my therapist). Thus, although affirmations are important to use, the associated impact should be carefully gauged.

Reflections

Naar-King and Suarez (2011) assert that active listeners use reflections to express empathy as well as to test clinical hypotheses about how teens experience their environment. Reflections are often divided into simple and complex. A simple reflection is a careful restating of an adolescent's words without adding meaning or emphasis to the content. A simple reflection conveys to the patient that the therapist *gets it*:

PATIENT: Being depressed just sucks. Every day is a struggle.
THERAPIST: Every day is a struggle for you.

By contrast, complex reflections are used to *push* the conversation between a therapist and patient in a specific direction. A *double-sided reflection* highlights a teen's ambivalence or mixed feelings. Miller and Rollnick (2002) suggest using "and" versus "but" in these reflections, and importantly, ending the statement on the positive side of change. For example, "On the one hand you find thought records to be annoying, and on the other hand, doing thought records has helped you 'get out of your head'." The overarching goal is to have adolescents explore the ambivalence, and potentially, identify the pros and cons of different behavioral choices. Reflections also may be used to express a patient's implied emotions (You're feeling totally hopeless). These types of reflections, especially when they are a slight over-reach, may elicit vibrant change talk:

PATIENT: I'm just stuck. I'm not getting better.
THERAPIST: You're feeling totally hopeless.
PATIENT: Well, not totally hopeless. Things are not as bad as they were a month ago.
THERAPIST: What do you mean?
PATIENT: I'm actually going to school every day. And, I've started to hang out with a friend or two on the weekends.

Carefully embedded over-reaches (i.e., feeling totally hopeless) may evoke discussion that counters a therapist's reflection, and by consequence, adolescents may find themselves explaining why symptoms are improving, treatment is working, and/or life is becoming less stressful (as opposed to delineating the converse). With all reflections, timing and intensity are important.

Summaries

An underutilized tool in therapy is to periodically summarize content throughout the session. This is of particular import when working with a depressed patient. Depression compromises attention and energy, which are essential for maximal comprehension. Intermittent summaries ensure that a therapist and patient are *on the same page*. For example,

> I just want to see if I understand. The depression started after your family moved. At that point, you started a new school and had a difficult time making new friends. Then, because you registered late for soccer, you couldn't join the team, which is something you love. Now, you're feeling stuck, and you don't have a sense of how to "turn this around."

If something was omitted from a summary, it provides an opportunity for a patient to assert key content. After summaries, a therapist can then transition to different topics as outlined on the agenda.

Taken together, MI is consistent with the collaborative spirit of CBT and is a valuable approach to building and maintaining relationships with adolescents; however, delivering MI techniques requires careful training, practice, and supervision. The information above provides the broad strokes of a technically sophisticated approach, and to obtain proficiency, it is recommended that clinicians consult the many accessible resources that are available (see Miller, 1983; Miller & Rollnick, 2002; Naar-King & Suarez, 2011).

Summary

In sum, good therapy is not dissimilar to spinning plates. As therapists, we need to be mindful of the many plates in concurrent motion – tracking of our approach (e.g., collaborative empiricism, guided discovery), disseminating skills (e.g., CBT tools), and building sound therapeutic relationships (e.g., alliance). If our attention drifts to only one of these plates and is neglectful of the others, something will fall out of place and jeopardize the integrity of the therapy. Being an effective CBT therapist is more than just knowing the skills; it is learning to impart these skills in a collaborative and engaging manner while helping adolescents to manage their emotions and thoughts in non-judgmental and nurturing environments.

5 Starting

There's no denying it, the early sessions of CBT are busy. Within these sessions, therapists are charged with forging warm and trusting relationships while, at the same time, conceptualizing presenting issues, planning treatment, introducing the cognitive model, and working on initial interventions. Fortunately, the right structure and approach will maximize the likelihood for success in these early sessions, and critically, set the table for the remainder of therapy. Below we describe the major tasks accomplished within the early sessions of CBT, provide an outline for Session 1 as well as a general structure for Session 2 and beyond, and delineate some early-session behavioral interventions.

Major Elements of Early Sessions

Identifying Presenting Issues

Almost invariably, depressed adolescents (and their families) come to therapy feeling overwhelmed by the multitude of problems and stressors they face. Collaboratively organizing and prioritizing patients' presenting issues has both short- and long-term benefits. First, this process can make problems seem less overwhelming and may reduce distress and bolster motivation (short-term). Second, identifying key issues allows therapy to target areas that give patients the greatest *bang for their buck*; that is, areas that are most likely to contribute to substantial reductions in symptoms (long-term).

To identify patient problems, we adapt an approach described by Kuyken, Padesky, and Dudley (2009). First, we ask open-ended questions focused on problems in the *here and now* (e.g., What issues have bothered you the most in the last week or so?). Patients are encouraged to actively participate in the process by writing brief descriptors of their issues (e.g., missing school; not feeling motivated) using their own words. Many adolescents will be able to come up with a short list of three to five general problems. However, it is also helpful to probe for chronic problems that may not be identified as a current issue by the adolescent and/or problems that reflect avoidance (and therefore, may not be coupled with distress).

THERAPIST: In addition to what you've already told me, what are the things that you want to be doing but aren't?
PATIENT (Alana): Umm, I dunno. I haven't been jogging lately.
THERAPIST: What's been holding you back?
ALANA: I don't feel like I have the energy for it anymore.
THERAPIST: How important is it for you to get out of the house?
ALANA: Pretty important. It used to really help my mood.
THERAPIST: How would you feel about adding something about this to your problem list?
ALANA: Yeah, it makes sense. It should probably be on there, anyway.

After a short list of problems is created, it is helpful to explore the unique meaning of each problem in the patient's life. Here, the therapist can express genuine curiosity about how the problem impacts functioning across various domains of day-to-day life (e.g., school, home, relationships).

THERAPIST: Maybe let's start with feeling sad all the time. How does this impact you?
ALANA: Well, I definitely do a lot less when I'm sad. Like, I don't paint anymore.
THERAPIST: OK, so feeling sad seems to affect your interests and activities. Anything else?
ALANA: I'm not really sure.
THERAPIST: Well, what might your closest friends say about how sadness has affected you?
ALANA: Umm, well some of my friends would probably say that I never call them to make plans; they usually have to call me if they want to get together.
THERAPIST: So sadness is having an effect on your friendships. What other relationships are affected?

Specifying examples of the objective, measurable impacts that problems have on patients' lives will facilitate prioritizing those causing the most damage. Asking patients to rate the subjective severity of each problem may further augment the assessment by quantifying the impact. Further, subjective ratings carry the added benefit of providing a means to assess progress towards alleviating the problem later in therapy.

When collaboratively prioritizing problems, factors to consider include: the functional impact, the patient's subjective distress, the likelihood of the patient changing, and the length of time the issue has persisted. We find that starting with problems that have a high impact *and* are likely to change substantially over the first half of therapy sets the patient up for success. It also is important to consider contingencies among presenting issues. For example, a patient may need to address the problem, "I don't like opening up about my personal life" before "I don't have any close friends." Critically, problems related to patient safety (e.g., risk for self-harm) (see Chapter 8) and problems that threaten therapeutic effectiveness (e.g., homework non-compliance) should be identified and addressed before other issues are targeted.

Cognitive Case Conceptualization

Case conceptualization refers to "a process whereby therapist and patient work collaboratively to first describe and then to explain issues a patient presents in therapy" (Kuyken et al., 2009, p. 3). A good case conceptualization parsimoniously guides treatment and contributes to its effectiveness (Persons & Tompkins, 2011). Generic approaches to cognitive case conceptualization (e.g., Beck, 2005; Persons, Davidson, & Tompkins, 2001; Persons & Tompkins, 2011), such as the one we present here, draw on elements from disorder-specific models (e.g., Beck, Rush, Shaw, & Emery, 1979) and higher-level cognitive theory to flexibly describe and generate hypotheses about a given patient. Although the *heavy lifting* related to case conceptualization occurs in the pretreatment assessment (see Chapter 3) and initial sessions, case conceptualization is an ongoing empirical process. Hypotheses derived from the initial formulation are continuously tested, revised, and, where appropriate, removed in later sessions.

Below, we list and describe the major components of cognitive case conceptualizations for depressed adolescents. A sample written case formulation (Alana) is provided.

Problem List

The patient's presenting issues are listed in order in the formulation. For each item, we find it helpful to include the central and/or typical moods, behaviors and negative automatic thoughts (NATs). NATs, which we describe in more detail in Chapter 6, are rapid, evaluative, non-purposeful thoughts that seem to *pop into* one's mind in response to situations. Along with moods, thoughts, and behaviors, recent situations that illustrate the problem can be listed as well. Together, these elements give a cross-sectional, *here-and-now* view of the adolescent's current struggles and functioning.

Schemas, Intermediate Beliefs, and Compensatory Strategies

According to the cognitive model (Beck, 1976), schemas are essentially summaries of early experiences surrounding particular themes that act as lenses through which later, similarly themed experiences are interpreted. Intermediate beliefs occupy the intermediary level of thought between schemas and surface-level automatic thoughts. Typically, these represent assumptions (if–then statements) or rules that apply across situations (e.g., If something isn't just right, I've failed; I must always be polite). Schemas and intermediate beliefs are the *mechanisms* that explain why the current problems arose from precipitants and why they are maintained by activating situations. Interventions that directly elicit and work to change maladaptive schemas and intermediate beliefs often occur in later sessions, but hypotheses about their content can be generated from early-session data. One possible option is to use common threads in activating situations or NATs to shed light on the likely content of deeper-level cognitions. For example, an adolescent who reports NATs like, "She doesn't really care about me," "He thinks I'm crazy," and "She only hangs out with me when she's bored" in interpersonal activating situations (e.g., a friend breaks plans; an argument with a romantic partner) might possess the core schema, "I'm unlovable."

Compensatory strategies describe what adolescents generally do when their schemas and/or intermediate beliefs are activated by triggers. At one time, these strategies may have been adaptive, such as learning to stay quiet and not speak your opinion in a household with an alcoholic parent. However, in the adolescent's current context, these strategies are unhelpful, and may serve to trigger or maintain depressive symptoms and problems.

Predisposing Factors

According to Beck's Cognitive Theory, maladaptive schemas and intermediate beliefs develop in response to adverse childhood experiences that color individuals' early learning history (Beck, 1976; see Chapter 2). We recommend working with patients in a Socratic and less didactic fashion (e.g., How do you think your early childhood problems with your father have impacted how you view yourself?) to generate one to three particularly powerful experiences that could account for the schemas and/or intermediate beliefs listed in the conceptualization. For instance, abuse and neglect in childhood are strongly and robustly associated with future

MDD, as well as other psychopathology (see Harkness & Lumley, 2007), and depressogenic schemas, specifically (Lumley & Harkness, 2007).

Precipitating Factors

Precipitants are large-scale events that cause or trigger the index episode of depression. In short, they are the *stress* component of diathesis-stress models of MDD (see Chapter 2). Typically, depressive episodes are precipitated by multiple events and so the conceptualization should focus on the main ones. For adolescent patients with chronic depressive symptoms, reporting on precipitants of their episode may be difficult. In these circumstances, it may be useful to focus on what life events or circumstances: (1) caused the adolescent and family to seek treatment (or more intensive treatment) and/or (2) worsened symptoms to the point that the patient could no longer cope alone.

Activating Situations

Activating situations can be distinguished from precipitating factors by their smaller scale and more isolated impact on moods, thoughts, and behaviors. Like precipitating events, though, activating situations are hypothesized to trigger dormant, depressogenic schemas, resulting in negatively biased information processing (see Chapter 2), negative moods, and maladaptive behaviors. For example, both having a parent move out of the home (precipitating factor) and a friend not returning a text message (activating situation) might trigger an underlying, maladaptive self-schema (e.g., I'm unlovable).

Summary

The summary presents a brief description of the therapist's working hypotheses based on the formulation. It can be thought of as the 2-minute blurb that could be presented to colleagues at group supervision. It paints a picture of how the patient developed their schemas and dysfunctional attitudes and describes the main ways in which they are currently being activated to contribute to the adolescent's symptoms and presenting issues.

Strengths and Assets

Incorporating strengths into the conceptualization allows the patient and therapist to bring abilities and skills from areas of strength to bear on problems and difficulties. This may open up a broader list of intervention options for the treatment plan and maximize patient resilience

(Kuyken et al., 2009). Furthermore, a side effect of assessing and/or working with strengths is that this may elicit *positive* emotions. Positive emotions have salutary effects on cognition; they *broaden* the scope of attention and thoughts that come to mind, thus allowing people to think and act more flexibly and creatively (Fredrickson, 2001, 2013). In the context of CBT, this could help depressed adolescents more effectively navigate the shifts in perspective required for interventions like challenging NATs (see Chapter 6). Indeed, individualizing CBT for depression to capitalize on patient strengths may contribute to more rapid improvement of depressive symptoms (Cheavens, Strunk, Lazarus, & Goldstein, 2012).

Setting Goals

If a time-limited course of CBT were a nautical voyage, therapy goals would be the ship's compass. Taking the time to set appropriate goals at the outset of therapy will ensure that the ship is safely guided to land; failing to do so may leave therapist and patient stranded at sea. One of the most commonly used and (in our opinion) most useful tools for goal-setting is to create SMART goals (Doran, 1981). Below we briefly describe the relevance of each component of SMART goal-setting to CBT with depressed adolescents.

Specific

Presenting goals are concrete and are linked to specific anticipated behavioral changes. Asking patients questions like, "How exactly would you know you are making progress on this goal?" often helps in developing more specific aims.

Measurable

Where possible, patients should be encouraged to quantify goals in terms of observable phenomena (e.g., behaviors) in their day-to-day lives. Given the negative cognitive biases in MDD (see Chapter 2), depressed adolescents may not notice, or may downplay, progress towards goals when these are assessed subjectively.

THERAPIST: So what would you most like to see change as a result of treatment?
ALANA: Well, I want to not feel depressed and angry all the time.
THERAPIST: That makes a lot of sense to me. If you weren't feeling depressed and angry all the time, how would you be feeling instead? [Framing goals as meaningful growth.]

ALANA: I guess I would be happy. And more carefree – like when I was a kid.
THERAPIST: Great. How does a goal of feeling more happy and carefree sound to you?
ALANA: Pretty good, I guess.
THERAPIST: What would we notice in your daily life if you were more happy and carefree? [Eliciting specific examples.]
ALANA: Probably I would spend more time with Kristy and Amber. I might do more fun things with mom and dad too, like we used to.
THERAPIST: Anything else?
ALANA: Well, maybe I would start back at my art.
THERAPIST: How often would you like to see your friends? [Eliciting measurable frequency data.]
ALANA: Well, I would want to see them at least twice on the weekends, and a weeknight.

In this example, the therapist operationalized the goal of "feeling more happy and carefree" using specific behaviors (e.g., spending time with friends) that could be objectively tracked (weekly frequency). For goals involving symptom change, therapist and patient may create a scale that they track throughout sessions (e.g., below 5/10 sadness 5 days a week). Behavioral goals may be measured in terms of their frequency (e.g., jog two times per week), duration (e.g., cook with mom for 30 minutes), and/or intensity (e.g., get 20 math problems done).

Attainable

The majority of patient goals should be realistically achievable during the course of therapy. It is important to meet patients *where they are at*, and, where necessary, help them appraise the suitability of their goals given their current functioning and/or previous experience. We recommend starting smaller to maximize the likelihood of success, particularly with depressed patients who may be prone to personalizing setbacks (e.g., I'm a complete failure). Further, there are always opportunities to make a goal more ambitious later in therapy.

ALANA: Well, I would want to see them at least twice on the weekends, and a weeknight.
THERAPIST: Wow, that's pretty frequently. How often do you see Kristy and Amber right now?
ALANA: We actually haven't hung out since school started. I just feel too tired.

THERAPIST: Hmm. When you were feeling better, how often did you used to spend time with them?
ALANA: In the school year, we'd go to someone's house most weekends. We'd sometimes do homework together after school, maybe a couple of times a month.
THERAPIST: So you'd like to spend more time with Kristy and Amber, but, since you've been feeling depressed, you haven't seen them since September. When you were feeling better, it sounds like you hung out twice a week at most. How does this affect your goal for therapy?
ALANA: Three times a week might be too much. Maybe I should try for once a week.
THERAPIST: Sounds great. We'll check in on this goal later, and we can increase it if we need to.

Adolescents frequently have goals regarding changes they would like to see in others (e.g., I'd like my boyfriend to listen to me more). These types of goals are not under the patient's direct control and so there is no way of maximizing their attainability. Therapist and patient can collaboratively reframe *goals for others* to be more under the patient's control (e.g., I'd like to more effectively communicate my needs to my boyfriend).

Relevant

Generating goals that extend directly from the patient's presenting issues ensures that the therapeutic focus is on symptom reduction and functional improvement. Additionally, adolescent patients are likely to be more invested in goals stemming from high-priority presenting issues. Alana's treatment plan (Box 5.1) presents an example of how goals can map directly on to presenting issues.

Time-Limited

A hallmark of CBT is its structured, time-limited course, and therapy goals follow suit. We find it helpful to set a mix of short-, medium-, and long-term goals (Kuyken et al., 2009), to label them as such, and to check on them throughout treatment. Short-term goals can be accomplished in four to six sessions, medium-term goals by the end of treatment, and long-term goals in a year or more (i.e., post-treatment). For Alana's presenting issue, "Feeling sad all the time," short-term goals include, "hang [with Kristy and Amber] once per week" and "Paint for fun two times per week for 20 minutes," a medium-term goal would be "Feel 4/10 or less sadness most days," and a long-term goal might be "Stay depression-free when I have setbacks."

Box 5.1 Cognitive Behavioral Case Conceptualization and Treatment Plan for Alana

Identifying Information

A 16-year-old white female high school sophomore, not working, living with biological mother, father, and 12-year-old brother.

Problem List

1 *Feeling sad all the time*

Thoughts:	"She doesn't really care about me"; "People don't know the real me"; "I'm the last person that they call"
Emotions:	sad, depressed, despair
Behaviors:	seek reassurance from closest friends; stay quiet/withdrawn in groups
Recent Situations:	at home with no plans on weekend night; waiting for text from Kristy

2 *Anxiety and avoidance of activities*

Thoughts:	"Something bad is going to happen"; "My neighborhood is not safe"
Emotions:	fear, anxiety
Behaviors:	staying indoors on weekend; no longer jogging as before
Recent Situations:	mom asked to walk to the store; friend asked to meet at park

3 *Problems with school work*

Thoughts:	"What's the point?"; "I'm going to fail anyway"; "I'll never understand this"
Emotions:	frustration, hopelessness
Behaviors:	give up on difficult problems; avoid homework; argue with parents
Recent Situations:	working through difficult chemistry problem

4 *Relationship with parents*

Thoughts:	"They don't understand me at all"; "They are liars"
Emotions:	anger, resentful
Behaviors:	yell at parents; walk out of conversations; isolate in room
Recent Situations:	compliment from mom on appearance; dad saying, "I love you"

Schemas, Dysfunctional Attitudes, and Compensatory Strategies

- "I'm unlovable" (self)
    - Strategies: keep most people at "arms length"; with closest friends, don't express needs
- "I'm broken and cannot be fixed" (self; future)
    - Strategies: give up (on relationships, when things are hard); refuse offers of help
- "People have bad intentions" (others)
    - Strategies: do not disclose personal details to people; avoid meeting new people
- "The world is not safe" (world)
    - Strategies: limit time alone outside of the house; hypervigilance

Predisposing Factors

Sexual assault by a stranger in her neighborhood when she was 14. A group of kids from her school posted mean comments about her on Facebook for several months afterward. Grandfather died suddenly of a heart attack when she was 12 years old. Mother suffers from depression and verbalizes self-critical thoughts.

Precipitating Factors

Boyfriend of 6 months ended relationship suddenly because she "wouldn't go far enough" (sexually). Began taking practice SATs in school. Close friend started spending time with a new group of friends.

Activating Situations

Friends cancelling plans/not responding; studying for exams, doing difficult homework; parents giving compliments, people trying to help; being alone in public places.

Summary

Alana has a history of awful things happening in her environment suddenly and unexpectedly (i.e., grandfather's death; sexual assault). Further, some of her early learning experiences indicated that responsibility for these things should be directed inward (i.e., mother modeling self-criticalness) and have led her to believe that she is broken and unworthy of love (i.e., being bullied). She has had two recent interpersonal stressors that have activated her beliefs that she is unlovable, unfixable, and that people generally have bad intentions. Her symptoms of depression are maintained by ongoing problems in friendships that are perpetuated at least partly by a combination of Alana's avoidance of group activities and seeking reassurance that the relationship is "OK". She has reduced or eliminated many of her previously enjoyed activities (jogging, going to the market) because of her beliefs that the world is unsafe and threatening, and this increased isolation is worsening her depressive symptoms. Her deepening sadness and isolation have colored her approach when completing school work; she no longer sees a reason to devote time to school because she doesn't see it making a difference. Similarly, offers to help and expressions of love from her parents directly conflict with her beliefs, leading to heated arguments.

Strengths and Assets

Stable home life (parents employed) and supportive family; continued school attendance in the face of life circumstances; no history of alcohol/substance abuse; athletic; talented artist (painting, sketching).

Treatment Plan

Presenting Issues	Goals
1 Feeling sad all the time	<ul><li>Feel 4/10 or less sadness most days</li><li>Better relationship with Kristy/Amber; hang out once per week</li><li>Paint for fun two times per week for 20 minutes</li></ul>
2 Anxiety and avoidance of activities	<ul><li>Be able to go to the park with family</li><li>Start jogging again; at least once per week outside</li><li>Feel 5/10 or less anxiety most days</li></ul>
3 Problems with school work	<ul><li>Schedule 1 hour after school on weekdays for homework/readings</li><li>Apply for summer internship at fine arts college</li></ul>
4 Relationship with parents	<ul><li>Accept compliments from parents; say "I love you" back to them</li><li>Do one fun thing with mom/dad every week</li></ul>

Treatment Modality, Frequency, and Duration

Individual cognitive behavioral therapy delivered in weekly sessions over the course of 16 weeks. Taper to biweekly or monthly sessions for four additional sessions. Negotiate booster sessions as needed.

Interventions

1. Activity scheduling focused on spending more time with family/close friends and doing previously enjoyed activities (painting).
2. Identifying NATs generated about interpersonal situations (friends, family), as well as situations where she feels afraid/threatened (e.g., asked to go to the store).
3. Use cognitive restructuring to challenge NATs related to friends and family not caring or not understanding, as well as hopeless thoughts about school work.
4. Use a series of behavioral experiments to gradually test out beliefs and assumptions related to safety of her immediate environment. Create coping cards containing anxiety management strategies to assist in completing these experiments.
5. Social skills practice/role-playing for challenging interpersonal situations (e.g., accepting compliments).
6. Schema change methods (continuum methods, positive data logs) to work on her beliefs that she is unlovable and unfixable.

Adjunctive Treatment

Pharmacotherapy; consecutive family therapy sessions.

Obstacles

1. Alana's core belief that "people have bad intentions" may make establishing a strong therapeutic alliance difficult. Finding ways to build her trust in early sessions will be paramount for later work.
2. Alana views herself as beyond "fixing," and has previously rejected help from concerned others. In response to setbacks, Alana may disengage from session or drop out from treatment.
3. Warmth and acceptance from others are threatening to Alana, because they challenge her ingrained belief that she is fundamentally unlovable. Positive interpersonal exchanges, either within or outside of sessions, may trigger anger and defensiveness.

Planning Treatment

A treatment plan briefly describes the therapist's course of action based on the adolescent's presenting issues and goals. Therapy is akin to building a house and the treatment plan provides the blueprint for construction. Treatment manuals are not blueprints for the house; however, they do include many of the tools necessary to get the job done. Every adolescent's blueprint is unique because they bring different materials (e.g., their presenting issues; previous experiences) to the job site. The blueprint therefore takes into account the tools that have been effective across many builds (e.g., challenging NATs with thought records) and the available materials to individualize the job and ultimately create the desired house (i.e., attain the patient's therapeutic goals).

Written treatment plans flow naturally from the case conceptualization and include the following elements: a list of patient goals, the treatment modality, duration, and frequency, an ordered list of interventions, any required adjunctive treatment, and perceived obstacles to treatment. Perceived obstacles generally include therapist predictions about difficulties that might arise based on the case conceptualization. For instance, an adolescent with the underlying assumption "If I can't be perfect, I'm no good at all" might have difficulties surrounding homework (e.g., procrastination, avoidance). The second half of Box 5.1 shows Alana's treatment plan. The listed interventions for Alana address items from her problem list, work towards her therapy goals, or both. For example, activity scheduling (fun events with parents; socializing with close friends; painting) may address her problems of "feeling sad all the time" and "relationship with parents," as well as goals related to these problems.

Answering the following questions also may be helpful when creating a treatment plan for adolescent patients: (1) *Do the interventions prioritize presenting issues most linked to functional impairment and/or risk of harm?* Unplanned speed bumps and detours are the rule, not the exception, in therapy. It is fair to assume that not all of our *best-laid plans* will be fully (or even partially) realized, and consequently, the ones that *are* completed need to be most vital for improvement. The next key issue is whether there is patient motivation and investment in the treatment course: (2) *Are the patient and their family on board with the treatment plan?* Getting adolescents to *buy in* to a treatment plan increases their likelihood of follow-through. Further, there are often several equivalently effective approaches that could be taken, and a patient's strong preference may serve as a guide for the therapist (see Brent, Poling, & Goldstein, 2011). Adolescence captures a wide developmental range: (3) *Are the treatment plan and proposed interventions developmentally appropriate?* Therapists should consider and take into account an adolescent's developmental history and timing of developmental milestones when crafting potential interventions (see Friedberg & McClure, 2002). For example, an adolescent who is reading and writing well below grade level might benefit from simplified versions of cognitive and behavioral interventions with fewer verbal demands. Although the questions above are not an exhaustive list of questions relevant to treatment planning, carefully considering the themes above may translate into more effective outcomes for depressed adolescent patients.

The Anatomy of Session 1

The most important goal of Session 1 is to maximize the probability that the patient returns for Session 2. This simple truth underscores the foremost priority of the first session: building rapport and trust. Secondary goals include exposing patients to the key elements of CBT sessions (e.g., agenda setting), providing psychoeducation about the course of therapy and the cognitive model, creating a preliminary list of problems and goals, and setting the first homework. This is *a lot*, and touching on all of the elements we describe below should not be done at the expense of setting the foundation for a strong therapeutic relationship.

With this important caveat in mind, the elements to include in a first therapy session are presented in Box 5.2, and we provide brief descriptions of the content to focus on at each step.

Box 5.2   First Session Structure

- Set the agenda
- Mood rating (e.g., rate depressed mood from 1 to 10)
- Elicit patient's experience of coming in for the first session
- Elicit patient's experience with his or her depression (symptoms, functioning, causes)
- Create a problem and goal list
- Elicit previous therapy experience. Introduce the cognitive model and the general structure of CBT
- Assign first session homework (activity log)
- Summary of first session
- Feedback (elicit both positive and constructive feedback)
- Mood check

Setting the Agenda

At the outset of Session 1, the therapist should introduce the rationale for agenda setting and then work together with the patient to create the session's written agenda. Whenever possible, we find it beneficial for patients to put an item on the agenda. This sets the tone for therapy as a collaborative partnership and underscores the active role that the adolescent will be expected to take. Further, it indicates that the adolescent's opinions, needs, and priorities will be central to therapy, which may contradict the patient's expectations and/or previous experiences. Most adolescents will be unfamiliar with setting an agenda, so the therapist may need to model appropriate items and provide feedback to patients regarding their contributions.

THERAPIST: Let's start by setting an agenda for the session, which we'll do at the start of every session. The reason we do this is so we make sure to get to the most important points and to keep us on track. Does that sound good?
PATIENT: OK.
THERAPIST: I have some specific things I think are important to cover today, but before I get to those, I want to hear your priorities. So, what is on your mind that you'd like to focus on today?
PATIENT: Well, I don't really know what we are doing in therapy. Is it just talking about your feelings?
THERAPIST: Sounds like you'd like to know more about what to expect in therapy, and maybe get an idea of what specifically you'll be asked to do. Have I got that right?
PATIENT: Yeah, that's it.
THERAPIST: What might we call that as an agenda item?
PATIENT: I dunno . . . "more about therapy"?
THERAPIST: That sounds great.

Mood Rating

In addition to week-to-week assessments of depressive symptoms using formal instruments (see Chapter 3), adolescents provide an initial, subjective rating of their in-the-moment affect. We use a unipolar rating of depressed mood from 1 (not at all depressed) to 10 (the most depressed I've ever felt). These simple rating scales serve two primary purposes. First, it demonstrates that emotions exist along a continuum versus being *all-or-nothing* (i.e., never sad versus always sad). Second, it provides an opportunity to determine whether different CBT skills (e.g., challenging NATs) reduce distress in session.

Elicit Experience of Coming to Session

Coming to therapy can be nerve wracking for anybody, and adolescents may have a less clear idea of what to expect compared to adults. Asking about this experience allows the therapist to quickly address concerns or confusion the patient might have and normalize first session anxiety. This also may serve as a smooth bridge to psychoeducation about CBT and provide opportunities to debunk common therapy myths.

THERAPIST: Before we get going with our main work for today, I wanted to ask you how you felt about coming here today.
PATIENT: Pretty nervous. I didn't want to come.
THERAPIST: First session nerves are really common. What made you not want to come in?
PATIENT: I didn't want you to psychoanalyze me. Like, I didn't want to be some freak on some doctor's couch talking about my mother.
THERAPIST: I get that; I wouldn't be interested in doing that either. It sounds like you have some expectations about what therapy is like. Would you be interested in hearing more about CBT?
PATIENT: Sure.

Discuss Patient's Depression

Psychoeducation about MDD is covered in detail in Chapter 4. Briefly, in Session 1, we recommend engaging the patient in a discussion of her current symptoms and functioning using open-ended statements like, "Tell me what your depression is like for you." Where possible, probe for information that will inform the cognitive case conceptualization such as the patient's problems, her perception of what is causing her problems/symptoms (e.g., major life events), data on her home and school life, as well as relationships (family, friends, partners). This is also an opportunity to assess the patient's knowledge about the symptoms of MDD and to normalize her experiences (e.g., When you say "nothing is fun any more," that's actually one of the most common symptoms of depression). Finally, during this discussion, the therapist can determine if anything has changed (symptoms, functioning, environmental stressors) since the last meeting (e.g., the initial assessment).

Creating a Problem and Goal List

Discussing symptoms may naturally transition into identifying a concise list of problems, which can be shaped into therapeutic targets, as we described in the sections above.

Introducing the Cognitive Model and Structure of CBT

We often begin this discussion by asking the patient about her previous therapy experience. This information may create a natural segue into describing the basic tenets of CBT; the therapist can build on

82 *Starting*

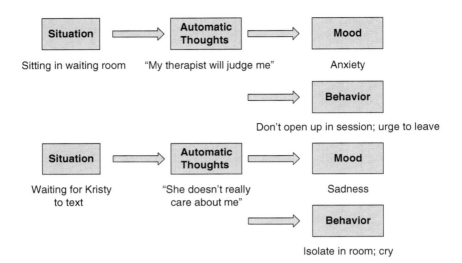

Figure 5.1 Example of Simple Diagram Illustrating Cognitive Model

the patient's existing knowledge of cognitive interventions or contrast her previous experience with CBT. Ultimately, we seek to impart the bottom line of the cognitive model – there is a dynamic relationship among thoughts, emotions, and behaviors. Ideally, this is illustrated using concrete examples of recent situations where the patient's thinking impacted her mood and/or behavior. With sufficient examples, the therapist and patient can summarize the connection between thoughts and moods across situations using a basic diagram (e.g., Figure 5.1). It is important to underscore that CBT aims to *modify* distorted cognitions by systematically evaluating their accuracy. If the patient has difficulty coming up with examples, the therapist can draw on information the patient has already provided in session.

THERAPIST: Can you think of a time in the past couple of days when you noticed a change in your mood – like feeling more sad?
PATIENT: Uhh, everything kinda blends together. I always feel the same.
THERAPIST: Depression can definitely feel that way. You mentioned you felt distressed when you came in today – can you say more about that?
PATIENT: Yeah. I felt really nervous sitting in the waiting room.
THERAPIST: OK. So you're out in the waiting room before your appointment; what was going through your mind just before you noticed feeling nervous?

PATIENT: Well, I feel so crappy right now that I was worried you would judge me.
THERAPIST: So you had the thought, "my therapist will judge me." Have I got that about right?
PATIENT: Yeah, that's it.
THERAPIST: What was the connection between that thought and how you felt in that moment?
PATIENT: It made me feel more anxious, and worse about being here. I wanted to get up and leave.
THERAPIST: OK, so you noticed that your thinking had a strong impact on how you felt, and led to urges to avoid the situation. This is something that CBT focuses on a lot – the connection between how we think and how we feel and behave. In fact, a lot of what we will do together is to learn how to change your thinking to improve your depression and anxiety. How does that sound?

Assigning Homework

In CBT, homework is the vehicle through which patients build and generalize therapy skills. Greater homework adherence predicts better outcomes in CBT for adolescent depression (Gaynor, Lawrence, & Nelson-Gray, 2006), and adherence in early CBT sessions increases the likelihood of later homework completion (Addis & Jacobson, 2000). Therefore, it's crucial to set patients up for success with their first homework assignment.

Devoting more time to assigning and reviewing homework, eliciting patient reactions to homework and troubleshooting obstacles, and providing a clear rationale are therapist behaviors that predict greater homework adherence (Jungbluth & Shirk, 2013). In addition to these strategies, it may be helpful for patients to brainstorm potential homework (e.g., plan an outing with a friend as a means to increase activity and reduce isolation), as this may increase the patient's intrinsic motivation. For some adolescent patients, the term "homework" may be loaded with negative connotations; session time may need to be devoted to differentiating between school homework (i.e., relatively arbitrary, sometimes unpleasant) and therapy homework (i.e., mutually agreed upon, designed to maximize helpfulness and feasibility). An alternative – and less loaded – term can also be substituted (e.g., weekly assignment).

Common first session homework items include activity monitoring (described below), refining the goal/problem list, brief readings about CBT, thinking of potential Session 2 agenda items, and/or tracking changes in mood and accompanying thoughts or images.

Session Summary

The end-of-session summary is a concise highlight reel of important takeaway points that emphasizes central CBT themes. These are facilitated by briefer section summaries sprinkled throughout the session (e.g., summarizing work on the third agenda item) and by having the patient write down key points as they arise. Generally, the therapist models the first session summary, but the patient can take over this responsibility in later sessions. A critical benefit of having patients summarize the key points of session is that therapists can gauge the extent to which teens understood and retained the in-session work and discussions.

Feedback

Adolescence is a developmental period characterized by an increasing need for autonomy and control. Eliciting feedback about sessions is not only crucial for resolving misunderstandings and shaping treatment, but is also central for building rapport (see Chapter 4). Eliciting feedback about what the patient may not have liked is equally important as, if not more important than, hearing what went well. It takes a lot of courage for adolescent patients to give their therapist constructive feedback. This can be acknowledged both directly (e.g., That couldn't have been easy to share; thank you so much for letting me know) and by *responding* with adjustments to future approaches.

Mood Rating

This rating again focuses on how the patient is feeling *at that moment* and uses the same scale as the pre-session rating. Patients may use the pre- and post-session ratings to observe *in vivo* changes in their mood in response to their therapeutic work. When pre- to post-session changes in mood are observed, therapists can probe to discover what session elements may have contributed to the boost in mood.

Session Content and Structure: Session 2 and Beyond

Adolescence is a period of considerably heightened stress compared to childhood (Garber et al., 2002), which may stem from the extensive biological and psychosocial changes that typify this developmental period (McClure & Pine, 2007). Maintaining a clear session structure in therapy may help adolescents organize and manage their chaotic external and internal experiences, promoting self-control and self-regulation (Friedberg & McClure, 2002). Box 5.3 outlines a structure that may be used from Session 2 to termination.

> **Box 5.3   General Early Session Structure**
>
> - Set the agenda
> - Check-in:
>   - Rate depressed mood (1–10)
>   - What happened in the week between sessions?
>   - Summary of key points from previous session
> - Review of last week's homework
> - Discuss patient-generated agenda items and/or priorities based on patient problems/goals
> - Assign new homework for next week
> - Summary of key points from current session
> - Feedback (elicit both positive and constructive)
> - Rate depressed mood

Book ending therapy sessions with habitual mood checks gives adolescents repeated practice with identifying mood states and rating their intensity and provides opportunities to compare their mood between sessions and to adjust session content based on mood if needed. Some adolescents may need to be reined in during check-ins; any complex descriptions of between-session events requiring more than a few minutes can be added to the agenda. Asking adolescents to summarize take-home points from the previous session reinforces key learning, presents opportunities for mastery, and gives the therapist a sense of how important therapy skills and concepts may or may not be sinking in.

It is critical to allow time to fully review all homework items from the previous session with adolescent patients. This increases the likelihood that the patient will continue to do homework (Jungbluth & Shirk, 2013) and emphasizes that these tasks are valued and important to therapy. After the homework review, the *meat* of the session will vary from patient to patient and is guided by the problem and goal list. Common early-session targets include maintaining and building rapport, reinforcing the cognitive model in session and with basic homework activities, and behavioral activation (BA). Teaching and practicing therapy skills with adolescents is easiest when they are embedded in the context of the patient's problems, interests, and strengths. For instance, using a patient's agenda item "my fight with Amy" to practice identifying NATs and reinforce the cognitive model allows the patient to see a therapy skill work in a context that matters to him.

Whenever possible, adolescent patients and therapists should keep written records of important points from session and skills to practice.

Additionally, frequently evaluating and updating the patient's problem/goal list is especially helpful in early therapy sessions. Referring to the problem/goal list can be worked into the feedback portion of every session (e.g., How have we done with working on your problems and goals this session?) and more major check-ins on therapeutic progress are formal agenda items to consider every three sessions or so. Relatedly, the initial sessions should involve actively testing, scrutinizing, and adjusting the preliminary cognitive case conceptualization.

Behavioral Activation Strategies

Behavioral techniques, such as activity monitoring and scheduling, are commonly employed in the early stages of CBT for depression. We recommend that therapists working with depressed adolescents *start* with BA interventions as early as possible. Research suggests that BA techniques, in isolation, are as efficacious as the full CBT package at treating adult MDD and preventing relapse (Dimidjian et al., 2006; Dobson et al., 2008). Further, BA interventions may be *more* helpful for patients with severe depressive and anhedonia symptoms (Beck, Rush, et al., 1979; Dimidjian et al., 2006). In short, there is strong evidence for the tremendous antidepressant effects of these interventions.

There are also more subtle reasons to start with behaviors. First, BA interventions are relatively simple and intuitive, making them easy to implement. This feature is especially important for adolescents who may struggle with self-reflection and personal insight, or for younger patients, who may need more practice before cognitive interventions become helpful. Second, BA techniques may provide critical initial symptom relief that will facilitate the application of later interventions. Third, the simplicity of BA techniques makes these activities more likely to engage adolescents' interest and attention, which fosters motivation and engagement in therapy. Last, BA interventions provide a wealth of data about patients (e.g., day-to-day accounts of how they spend their time), which can be invaluable for informing an initial cognitive case conceptualization. Below, we describe two BA techniques frequently employed in early sessions with adolescent patients: activity monitoring and activity scheduling.

Activity Monitoring

The goal of activity monitoring is for patients to gain insight into the link between what they are doing and how they are feeling. Most commonly, patients use some variation of a weekly activity log (Figures 5.2 and 5.3) that lists the days of the week and hours of the day and provides a space

	Ex. Day	Monday	Tuesday	Wednesday	Thursday	Friday	Saturday	Sunday
Early morning–9	Morning Routine Anxious (8)							
9–10								
10–11								
11–12								
12–1	Poetry Club Happy (5)							
1–2								
2–3								
3–4	Basketball Practice Lonely (6)							
4–5								
5–6								
6–7								
7–8	Movie with Dad Relaxed (7)							
8–9								
9–12								

Figure 5.2 Example Activity Log with Hourly Blocks of Time

Instructions: Track your activities and associated moods. When you complete an activity, grade it for mood (M) on a scale from 0 (the worst you ever felt) to 10 (the best you ever felt), and *name a one-word emotion* to describe your mood.

	Ex. Day	Monday	Tuesday	Wednesday	Thursday	Friday	Saturday	Sunday
Early morning-9								
9–12								
12–2	English Report Frustrated (5)							
2–5	30-min Jog Accomplished (7)							
5–8	Lunch with Marie Sad (2)							
8–10								
10–12								

Figure 5.3 Example Activity Log with Larger Blocks of Time

Instructions: Track your activities and associated moods. When you complete an activity, grade it for mood (M) on a scale from 0 (the worst you ever felt) to 10 (the best you ever felt), and *name a one-word emotion* to describe your mood.

to write in information pertaining to each block of time. However, we take a decidedly non-judgmental stance about the exact tool used for tracking activities, so long as they are tracked. Many of our patients have successfully made use of their personal day planners, electronic schedulers, and/or smartphones to record activities and mood. Therapist and patient can collaboratively and creatively tailor the exercise to suit the patient's needs.

How to Monitor

In activity monitoring, patients take brief notes about activities they engaged in during the day, ideally for each day of the week between therapy sessions. However, the rigor with which these data are collected varies from patient to patient. The most intensive option is to have patients record their activities and other data every hour on the hour. This approach likely provides the most accurate information by virtue of its lower memory requirement, but it also places the greatest burden on the patient and therefore may be impractical under many circumstances. Alternatively, therapist and patient can work collaboratively to establish set *check points* during each day at which time the patient reports on a block of time. For instance, an activity log could be completed at meals and right before bed. This method tends to be more feasible than the hour-by-hour option, but may yield less reliable information because it relies on retrospectively recalling events and internal experiences. A compromise between the two approaches above is to use *time sampling*, wherein patients choose portions of each day of the week (e.g., 6 p.m. to 8 p.m. on Monday) to monitor intensively (i.e., hour-by-hour). In this approach, the selected blocks of time need to be varied and representative; they should include times throughout the day, and both weekday and weekend sampling.

Factors to consider when selecting a specific approach to activity monitoring include the patient's age, symptoms (particularly memory, attention, and concentration deficits), motivation, and written language abilities.

THERAPIST: So, in this chart, there is room to write a description of what you were doing for each hour of each day and to rate your mood. What do you think about giving it a try this week?
PATIENT: Well, it seems like a lot . . .
THERAPIST: Filling it out for every hour of every day is a lot to ask. What do you think would be more doable?
PATIENT: I dunno, maybe half the days to start?

THERAPIST: That's a great plan. Maybe we could do three weekdays and one weekend day, so that we get information about both types of days. Is there anything else to adjust to make this more helpful?
PATIENT: I'm worried I'll forget to do it. And I don't want to carry the form around at school.
THERAPIST: Totally understandable. What about using your phone in some way to help you out?
PATIENT: Yeah, that could work. I could set the alarm for times I need to fill it out. Maybe I could take notes on my phone at school and use them to finish the form at home.
THERAPIST: Those are really great ideas.

What to Monitor

First and foremost, all activity monitoring assignments involve brief descriptions of what the patient is doing from hour to hour. These descriptions should strike a balance between including enough information to be distinct and useful while not being burdensome for the patient. We recommend a discussion about what to record when patients are engaged in the same general activity for an extended period of time (e.g., in class). It is unlikely for a patient's mood to remain unchanged for, for example, a 4-hour period while taking morning classes. In this case, the patient would be encouraged to note changes in contextual factors (e.g., working on biology homework versus taking an English quiz) that might be linked to variations in mood. As we will describe below, this level of detail is helpful for bridging to activity scheduling, and can be used to highlight the role of thoughts in altering mood across contexts.

In addition to the activity description, patients can be asked to record the intensity of their mood (e.g., sad, angry, anxious, stressed) in the time frame. We find that it is simplest to use a unipolar scale. For example, when rating depressed mood, patients are encouraged to use a rating from 1 (no depressed mood) to 10 (worst/most intense depressed mood). Prior to completing the activity monitor, patients may benefit from anchoring the scale with concrete examples of when they felt that intensity of depressed mood (e.g., 1 = my 13th birthday party; 5 = a hard chemistry assignment; 10 = when my dog died). Instead of, or in addition to, mood ratings, patients can rate the level of mastery and pleasure associated with activities (Beck, 1995, 2011; Beck, Rush et al., 1979). *Mastery* refers to the sense of accomplishment one feels when doing an activity, while *pleasure* is a rating of the delight and satisfaction that accompany the action. Ratings of pleasure and mastery can be especially useful for choosing the types of activities that are most intrinsically reinforcing (i.e., those high in mastery and/or pleasure) that should be *scheduled* throughout treatment. Finally, patient and therapist may choose to adjust the basic activity log to track salient behaviors, such as sleep (duration and quality ratings) or use of substances.

Rationale for Assigning Activity Monitoring

Providing a rationale for completing an activity log will increase the likelihood of the patient following through (Beck, 1995, 2011). Where possible, this should be anchored in the patient's description of his current problems.

THERAPIST: From what you've told me so far, you are feeling overwhelmed at school and less motivated to spend time with your friends and family. Do I have that right?
PATIENT: Yeah. And my friends have stopped calling too, 'cause I've been saying "no" to hanging out.
THERAPIST: Ah, I see. I wonder if it might be helpful to keep careful track of how you are spending your time nowadays using this activity log. Basically, it asks you to keep track of the activities you are doing, along with how you feel while doing so.
PATIENT: OK, I guess.
THERAPIST: Have you ever used a schedule like this before?
PATIENT: Yeah, once in 7th grade I used something like that to plan homework time.
THERAPIST: Oh yeah, how was that?
PATIENT: For a while I was more organized and I usually got more done. Then I stopped.
THERAPIST: Do you think something like that could also work in therapy?
PATIENT: Maybe. If I was more organized, I might feel better.
THERAPIST: Yeah, that sounds logical. What else might you find out if you wrote down what you were doing and how you were feeling?
PATIENT: Well, I dunno, it might show when I feel the worst during the day.
THERAPIST: Yes, it might. Also, on the flip side, it could show when you feel the best. Would you be up for learning more about how to use this activity log?

Reviewing Activity Monitoring

There are two primary goals to keep in mind while reviewing a patient's activity monitoring homework: (1) emphasize the connection between behaviors and mood and (2) identify behaviors to change (i.e., increase, decrease, or replace) that could improve the patient's mood and functioning. There are many good ways to approach an activity log review; we recommend focusing on the broad questions listed in Box 5.4.

> **Box 5.4   Questions to Consider When Reviewing a Patient's Activity Log**
>
> - Which activities are associated with the least depression and/or the most mastery/pleasure?
> - Which activities are associated with the most depression and/or the least mastery/pleasure?
> - How balanced is this schedule (i.e., which activities are over- or under-represented)?
> - Do moods shift dramatically or are they relatively stable?
> - Are there obvious interruptions to normal routines (e.g., sleep, meals, school attendance)?
> - Are there activities that the patient is avoiding?

The simplest approach is to have patients briefly describe each entry and rating. Then, an open-ended question like, "What did you notice from doing this activity?" is often enough to begin discussion of the impact of behaviors and contexts on mood. The therapist also may highlight the patient's highest and lowest mood ratings and ask for additional context. Further, highlighting times when similar or identical activities are associated with disparate mood ratings can provide a nice transition to identifying NATs (i.e., patients discover that their attributions about the situation impacted their mood at the time; see Chapter 6 for a detailed discussion).

Descriptions of important events associated with relatively high or low depressed mood are critical for informing activity scheduling. Crucially, though, not all activities associated with low mood should be decreased, and not all those associated with more positive mood should be increased. For example, a patient may endorse relatively low levels of depression while watching TV, but this may reflect the mild relief associated with avoiding a distressing task, like finishing math homework, rather than actual pleasure or enjoyment. Similarly, a patient may engage in a behavior that is typically naturally reinforcing, like light exercise, but report a lower mood because of contextual factors (e.g., walking alone versus with a friend). In sum, it's important to elicit contextual information surrounding affect-laden events to both emphasize the mood–behavior connection and inform future activity scheduling.

Activity Scheduling

Adolescents coping with depressive symptoms gradually lose sources of reinforcement in their environments. Activity scheduling aims to systematically and purposefully build back reinforcing activities into the patient's life, which interrupts the downward spiral of low mood, inactivity/isolation, and negative thinking (Beck, Rush, et al., 1979). Scheduling activities, following through, and seeing even a small change in mood can instill a sense of accomplishment, which may increase the likelihood of continued re-engagement and generally build hope. An added benefit is that patients see therapy working for them, which contributes to a stronger therapeutic alliance (Webb, Beard, Auerbach, Menninger, & Bjorgvinsson, 2014) and builds mastery.

What to Schedule

In the early stages of therapy, it is often best to focus on activating *naturally reinforcing behaviors* (Martell et al., 2013). Reinforcing consequences follow logically from these behaviors, and thus, they do not rely on arbitrary, external reinforcement (e.g., giving an adolescent money in exchange for an hour of homework time). For example, an adolescent might feel a sense of accomplishment after cleaning his room and might feel more organized and on top of things. Consequently, the room-cleaning behavior might increase in the future. A patient's naturally reinforcing activities are likely to be: (1) activities associated with the least depressed mood (or highest pleasure/mastery ratings) in his activity log and (2) behaviors he enjoyed before he became depressed.

THERAPIST: So we're looking to plan activities that you are very likely to do and that will be most likely to boost your mood. Does anything jump out at you from the monitoring you did?
PATIENT: I dunno, everything was rated around the same.
THERAPIST: Yes, that's what it looks like. Well, if you think back to the summer, before you were depressed, what activities did you most enjoy then?
PATIENT: I used to do a lot of things. Now I don't do anything.
THERAPIST: Sounds like you feel like your day-to-day activities are pretty limited. I wonder though – is there any specific activity that was part of your routine and that you found fun before you were depressed, but that you have maybe stopped since you've felt worse?
PATIENT: Well, yeah, I used to practice songs on my guitar at night most school days. It was pretty fun, but I haven't done that in months.
THERAPIST: Is that something you might be willing to see if we can schedule in?

In later sessions, activity scheduling can shift to a balance of the following categories of activities: (1) self-care (e.g., exercise, healthy eating, sleep hygiene); (2) pleasure (e.g., playing the guitar for enjoyment; watching a favorite TV program); (3) tasks that must be done (e.g., homework, chores); and (4) socializing (e.g., going to the mall with friends) (Beck, 1995, 2011). Activity scheduling also can be used to explicitly target previously avoided behaviors. For example, if an adolescent patient needed to find a summer job but had been putting it off, she could break the task down into manageable activities that could be scheduled over several therapy weeks.

How to Schedule

Typically, patients write specific activities they plan to accomplish in an activity log. However, as with monitoring, the approach can be adapted to existing tools that the adolescent finds the most helpful (e.g., a wall calendar at home; smartphone). We have found it helpful to emphasize the theme of *following a plan, not a mood* with our patients. This is much easier said than done, though. In order to overcome the powerful attraction of "doing what I feel like," activities need to be carefully planned, structured, and defined, and obstacles to completion should be thoroughly vetted. Below are factors to consider when activity scheduling.

1. *Defining activity content.* Ideally, the scheduled activity is defined in specific, behavioral terms. For example, "call a friend" could be refined to "call Jordan to make a plan to hang out at my place next Friday."
2. *Frequency, duration, and intensity.* Therapist and patient should plan the frequency (i.e., days per week), duration (i.e., time in minutes or hours), and/or intensity (e.g., completing 20 math problems) of the scheduled activity. For example, "start running" might be refined to "go for a 20-minute jog two times this week." It is shrewd to err on the side of smaller, more manageable activity goals. Therapists can harness their patients' momentum later by building layers of complexity on to activities they accomplish.
3. *Timing.* The patient also needs to determine the specific day(s) and time(s) that the activity will be accomplished. An activity log from the previous week can be invaluable for identifying days and times where patients might have the most free time, and might even indicate when an adolescent patient is most likely to have success with previously avoided or difficult activities. For instance, an adolescent who is consistently most active in late morning might use this time to clean and organize his bedroom.
4. *Measuring success.* A degree of healthy skepticism about activity scheduling is expected (and encouraged) – after all, it can sound like a relatively simple solution to the complex problem of depression. With that in mind, patients can decide how to evaluate the effectiveness of

the planned activity ahead of time. Commonly, this involves rating mood before and after the activity to measure change, or tracking specific behaviors (e.g., asking the teacher for help with difficult problems). With interpersonal events (e.g., calling a friend to make plans), in particular, it can be helpful to record the exact responses of others and compare these to responses the patient anticipated (e.g., he said he was happy to hear from me and came up with a bunch of ideas of things we could do together).

Summary

"Things are achieved when they are well begun. The perfect archer calls the deer his own while yet the shaft is whistling" (George Eliot, *The Spanish Gypsy*, 2008).

The early stage of CBT is a critical learning period for both patients and therapists, and sets the tone for the structure and process of later sessions. Effectively executing the early sessions hinges on following a premeditated structure, like the one we described above, and being able to flexibly and creatively adapt the details of session content to each individual adolescent's characteristics and needs. Taking this approach gives CBT interventions their greatest opportunity to meaningfully improve patient symptoms and functioning.

6 Working

The previous chapter introduced the structure of the initial CBT sessions. In this chapter, we review a range of strategies therapists can use to identify the negative thinking patterns that are contributing to their patient's symptoms. Next, we describe a series of techniques to help patients challenge and change their negative thoughts.

Identifying Negative Automatic Thoughts

The most fundamental skills encouraged in CBT involve learning to recognize negative thoughts as they arise, or shortly thereafter (i.e., *metacognitive awareness*). Given the speed with which negative thoughts seem to automatically *pop* into one's mind, the label NATs is typically used by CBT therapists to describe this class of cognitions. Learning to become aware of one's own thought content is a foundational skill upon which more advanced cognitive skills – in particular, challenging negative thoughts – are based. Without first noticing NATs, and their role in driving negative emotions and maladaptive behaviors, patients cannot progress to more advanced cognitive restructuring skills.

Although a "basic" skill, recognizing one's own NATs is easier said than done, especially for teens. Unlike emotions, which are viscerally felt and relatively hard to ignore, thoughts are often incredibly subtle and fleeting, and thus challenging to recognize. Indeed, patients are understandably more likely to cite distressing negative emotions (e.g., I just want to *feel* better; I *feel* so depressed), or ameliorating life stressors (I just need to be at a different school; I can't stand being around my parents) as the primary problems they want to work on in therapy, rather than complaining of negative cognitions. However, cognitive work – coupled with training in behavioral skills – is the primary means through which CBT targets the negative emotional states from which patients seek relief.

To help clarify the concept of thoughts and distinguish it from felt emotions, therapists can introduce NATs to teens as typically coming in two forms: words/sentences (e.g., *That was so embarrassing!*) or pictures/images (e.g., imagining the ways in which an upcoming social interaction could go awry). The metaphor of *tuning in to your internal radio or TV station* can be especially helpful imagery for teens. The goal, of course, is not to train teens to be constantly tuning into their internal thought stream; rather, the hope is for adolescents to *catch* their negative thoughts when their affect shifts and a negative emotion arises.

It is important to highlight that the distinction between a negative thought and a negative emotion can be subtle at times, and patients commonly confuse the two. Most often, teens will mislabel a thought as a feeling. It is important for therapists to help patients distinguish the two, and to identify the negative thought(s) therein:

PATIENT: I felt so stupid.
THERAPIST: So you had the thought "I'm stupid." But what emotion did you feel in that moment?
PATIENT: I was so upset.
THERAPIST: It sounds like you felt awful. In what way did you feel upset? What emotion were you experiencing? What did you feel in your chest?
PATIENT: I felt sad. I wanted to cry.
THERAPIST: So in that moment, you thought to yourself "I'm stupid," which led you to feel really sad.
PATIENT: Yeah.

Once the therapist and patient have clarified the "hot" (i.e., emotion-generating) cognition from the negative emotion, they can progress to challenging the validity of this thought (see Challenging Negative Automatic Thoughts, below). During this discussion, therapists can use visual aids to illustrate the link between negative thoughts and emotions (Figure 6.1.).

Suggested Strategies to Elicit Negative Automatic Thoughts

(1) questions; (2) chain analysis; (3) activity log; (4) in-session NATs; (5) abbreviated thought record; (6) role play; (7) emotional themes; and (8) downward arrow.

Questions

One of the primary means through which to elicit patients' NATs is the use of appropriate, open-ended questions. Below are some suggested questions:

- *What was going through your mind right before/when you started to feel [emotion]?*
- *What were you worried/imagining might happen?*
- *What does this say about you (or mean to you)?*
- *What does this say about your future or what's going to happen?*
- *What does this say about how [the other person] feels/thinks about you?*
- *What were you thinking about/remembering?*

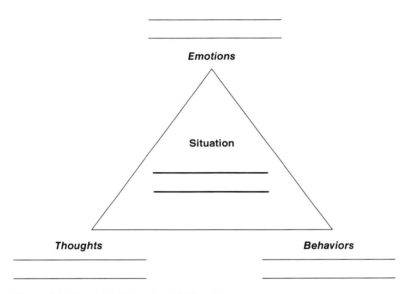

Figure 6.1 Cognitive Behavioral Triangle

Therapists also can suggest plausible NATs the patient could be having (e.g., *I may be off-base, but were you thinking _____?*), or suggest a thought that is *opposite* to the one the therapist expects the patient is having (e.g., when discussing the patient's anticipatory anxiety about an upcoming party: *So are you pumped about showing up to the party on Saturday?*). Of course, the latter strategy should be used judiciously and within the context of a good rapport between therapist and patient. The rationale for the latter strategy is that, by providing a thought that is opposite to the one the therapist expects, the patient may be more likely to identify the actual underlying NAT.

Chain Analysis

Have the patient paint you a picture of the triggering situation in detail, with as much sensory information as possible (including sights, sounds, smells). It can be easier for teens to access and recall their NATs when they're *back in the moment* and describing the event in detail. Patients may initially respond by giving an overly brief summary of the event, collapsing minutes, or perhaps hours, into a sentence or two ("She just stormed into my room and got really mad at me and then I blew up"). A therapist can ask the teen to "rewind the tape and play me the movie in real time" or "pretend you're reading me the movie script for the event. What would it say, line by line?" The more detail the patient can provide, the more likely he is to be immersed in the situation and recall his NATs.

Activity Log

As described in Chapter 5, an activity log is typically assigned as homework at the end of the first session to track the patient's daily activities and their relationships with mood. Therapists should review these activity logs in the following session. Shifts in affect on the activity log can be used as entry points to search for NATs that may have been contributing to a negative emotion:

THERAPIST: So how did the activity log go?
PATIENT: OK. Here you go [hands therapist activity log].
THERAPIST: This looks great. So let me hand this back to you [hands patient back the worksheet]. What did you notice while doing this?
PATIENT: Not much . . . I guess my mood goes up and down a lot.
THERAPIST: Interesting. Yeah, you're right. Let's zoom in on an example here. It looks like your mood was pretty low last night between 9 and 11 p.m. You wrote here that you were in your room?
PATIENT: Yeah. I was just listening to music and lying in bed.
THERAPIST: What was going through your mind right before you started to feel that low mood?

In addition to being used to track the relationship between activities and mood, the activity log can be a useful tool to anchor discussions about negative thoughts, thereby facilitating the therapist's and patient's work together to identify the NATs that popped up over the last week. Depressed teens experience numerous NATs throughout their day. However, they often do not recognize them and may need prompting by the therapist. Reviewing activity logs can be one helpful strategy to get teens to recognize NATs in their daily lives and their relationship to negative emotions. Even a partially completed activity log can be helpful for this purpose. In the case where a teen did not complete any portion of the activity log, the therapist and patient can work together to recreate one column/day of the activity log (or a few hours), or ask the patient to recall an (even slight) increase in negative affect over the last 24 hours and probe for the negative cognition(s). Alternatively, the therapist can ask the patient to describe the (emotional) *high point* versus *low point* in the day and to try to identify the NATs for each.

Homework Assignment

It is important for therapists to be vigilant for possible NATs that arise in session and to elicit them when appropriate (e.g., they are impeding the progress of the session or may reflect a rupture in the alliance). For example, this could be done if a therapist notices a shift in affect in the session and then inquires about the NAT that the patient is having at that moment (Just curious, what's going through your mind right now?), or the therapist notices apprehension from the patient about the usefulness of the current therapy activity, homework assigned, or expectations of improvement. In addition to being a useful opportunity to catch NATs *in vivo*, eliciting cognitions in session – when done in a natural and empathic way – expresses the therapist's regard for the patient's ongoing impressions and experience with therapy and the therapist's willingness to adjust the course based on the patient's needs.

Abbreviated Thought Record

Below we introduce the commonly used thought record as a means to facilitate the process of challenging NATs. However, it can also be a useful tool to help patients catch their NATs by simply completing the first three columns (*Situation, NATs, Negative Feelings*). The therapist can use an abbreviated thought record in session with the patient or assign one for homework (Table 6.1). In fact, we recommend that patients learn the thought record in this gradual manner, by becoming comfortable filling out the first three columns (to identify their NATs) and then moving on to the additional columns (to evaluate and reframe their NATs; Greenberger & Padesky, 1995).

Role Play

If the negative emotions were triggered in an interpersonal situation, then it may be helpful to engage in a role play (patient plays him-/herself and therapist takes on the role of the other individual) to attempt to recreate the situation and jog the teen's memory about the NAT. Similar to the chain analysis technique, described above, having the patient engage in a role play may help to immerse him back into the situation in question, and spark ideas about possible NATs he may have been having in the moment. Patients are, understandably, often uncomfortable about having to *act* in front of the therapist and may fear embarrassment. Therapists should judge the pros and cons of engaging in a role play, and balance the possible benefits of the exercise with the patient's comfort level.

Table 6.1 Abbreviated Thought Record

Instructions: When you notice your mood getting worse, ask yourself, "What's going through my mind right now?" and, as soon as possible, jot down the thought or mental image in the Negative Automatic Thoughts column.

Date	Situation	Negative Emotions	Negative Automatic Thoughts/Images
	Where were you – and what was going on – when you got upset?	*What negative emotions did you feel at the time?* *Also rate their intensity (0–100%)*	*What thoughts and/or images went through your mind?* *Rate how much you believe in each thought/image (0–100%)*

© J. Beck (2011). Adapted from *Cognitive behavior therapy: Basics and beyond* (2nd ed.). New York: Guilford Press, and used with permission.

Emotional Themes

If teens tend to experience certain negative emotions more than others (e.g., sadness, irritability, anxiety), it may help to narrow down the kinds of NATs they are experiencing more frequently. That is, there are differences in the *cognitive themes* that tend to underlie different emotions (Table 6.2).

For example, if a teen complains of daily surges in anxiety, it is likely that he or she is experiencing frequent NATs with a common threat-related theme (e.g., frequently worrying that something bad or embarrassing is going to happen in an upcoming social situation or at school). In contrast, if a teen has a tendency to experience much irritability or frequent bouts of anger, she is likely seeing the world through a lens of injustice. From her perspective, she is constantly being treated unfairly, not receiving what she deserves from others/the world or being disrespected by peers and/or parents. Being aware of the kinds of emotions that teens tend to experience can give therapists important clues about

102 *Working*

Table 6.2 Emotions and Associated Cognitive Themes

Emotion	Cognitive Theme	Example	Behavior
Anxiety	Perception of threat in one's environment	Worrying that something bad is going to happen in a domain that the teen cares about (e.g., friendship, dating, school, sports)	Escape; avoid
Sadness	Thoughts related to loss or failure	Loss of a relationship, perceived interpersonal rejection, perceived failure	Withdrawal; isolating; crying
Anger/ irritability	Perceived injustice or unfair treatment	Perception that one "shouldn't" be treated this way, thoughts of being disrespected	Attack, fight back (verbally or physically); passive-aggressive behavior
Guilt/ shame	Perceived wrongdoing, self-condemnation	Thoughts that you have mistreated others, let others down, or failed to fulfill your obligations; Often "should" statements directed at self (I *should* have been a better friend)	Withdrawal; apologizing

the kinds of cognitions that may be driving these emotions. This can also be an opportunity for therapists to discuss with their patients that emotions, including negative ones, generally serve adaptive functions (e.g., fear can mobilize us to avoid a real threat in our immediate environment, anger can encourage us to stand up for ourselves and others in the face of injustice). The goal is not to eliminate negative emotions, but to distinguish between healthy or natural emotions and those that are unhelpful and getting in the way of our wellbeing. The latter are the ones that are the target of therapy.

Downward Arrow

When therapists suspect that patients may be inferring a deeper meaning than revealed by their initially reported NATs, the *downward-arrow technique* (Burns, 1980; Beck, 1995, 2011) can be used to probe for these underlying cognitions. Although this is quite challenging to do effectively, the gains can be substantial – leading many patients to experience an *ah-ha moment*. For example, a teen may display strong negative affect that seems disproportional to the NAT she just reported. As a result, the therapist might suspect that there is a deeper and more negative cognition that is really driving the affect. In the example below, a 14-year-old female becomes very tearful in the session when she recounts a recent situation in which she greeted a male classmate in the hallway at school and he "ignored" her:

THERAPIST: What emotion were you feeling when he didn't respond to you?
PATIENT: Really sad. Just awful [tearful].
THERAPIST: So what was going through your mind at that moment?
PATIENT: He doesn't want to talk to me [surface-level NAT].

At this point, the therapist may think of a variety of different reasons why this classmate failed to respond to her and may move immediately to challenging the surface-level NAT, for example by asking questions such as: *What's the evidence that he doesn't want to talk to you? Are there other reasons why he may have walked right by you?* However, the intensity of the negative affect the teen reports (relative to the NAT) may be a clue that there is another, deeper cognition operating that is really driving this affect:

THERAPIST: So you had the thought, "He doesn't want to talk to me." Assuming for a moment that this is true, and he doesn't want to talk to you, what would that mean about you? [Downward-arrow question #1.]
PATIENT: That he doesn't like me.
THERAPIST: OK. So assuming for a moment he doesn't like you. What's the worst part about that? [Downward arrow question #2.]
PATIENT: That I'm going to be alone.
THERAPIST: And what does that mean about you? [Downward arrow question #3.]
PATIENT: That I'm just weird . . . no one's ever gonna wanna be with me [core beliefs: defectiveness and unlovability].

In this exchange, the therapist used a series of three downward-arrow questions to unpeel the layers of the initial NAT (He doesn't want to talk to me) and uncover a core belief, or perhaps two related ones (I'm weird; No one's ever gonna wanna be with me). This helps the therapist understand the intensity of the affect the patient initially expressed when recounting the situation. Of course she would feel this intensity of emotion if she – at a deeper level – believed that she was fundamentally flawed and, as a result, unlovable. These will be critical cognitive targets for the therapist and patient to pay attention to going forward. We will discuss challenging deeper cognitions, including core beliefs, in a subsequent section.

The downward-arrow technique often involves assuming that the initial negative thought is true, to dig deeper and ultimately uncover a core belief. Thus, it is important for therapists to use this technique judiciously and empathically, and not let patients infer that you as the therapist believe that their NAT is indeed true. Moreover, before embarking on the downward-arrow approach, therapists should ideally have developed a healthy therapeutic alliance with their patients. It also is important to note that CBT therapists often have working hypotheses about the underlying deeper thought prior to starting the downward arrow, which can help guide the therapist in his/her line of questioning.

The Bottom Line

All of the above are tools and techniques that therapists can use to help teens identify their NATs. Ultimately, the goal is for teens to develop the skills to catch their negative patterns of thinking in *real time*, and ideally, to be able to anticipate situations in which they are prone to experience strong negative emotions triggered by NATs. It is important to highlight how challenging this can be, hence the need for regular practice. We recommend that therapists encourage their patients to begin by spending approximately 10 minutes each evening reviewing their day and writing down NATs that arose (along with the accompanying negative emotions and situational triggers). Like anything else (e.g., sports; learning a musical instrument), identifying NATs is a skill that requires regular practice. To the extent that therapists can help their patients cultivate an attitude of curiosity about their mental life, teens will be more motivated to embark on the daily work of identifying their negative thinking patterns as they arise.

More broadly, the goal in this initial phase of treatment is to develop *cognitive distancing*, or an observer perspective of our thoughts[3] – in other words, for a teen to begin to transition from "I'm stupid" to "I'm having the thought 'I'm stupid'." Thoughts are, simply put, just thoughts – fleeting *events in the mind* that do not necessarily reflect reality. They may be true or untrue, or often somewhere in between. For youth and adults alike, our default mode is to go through our daily lives with little or no metacognitive awareness of the thoughts that are streaming through our mind. So to begin to reprogram our default mode and learn to observe our thought stream runs counter to decades of habit. Novice therapists

---

3 There is a proliferation of mindfulness-based therapies, including Mindfulness-Based Cognitive Therapy (MBCT: Segal, Williams & Teasdale, 2012), which focus on teaching patients an elaborated form of distancing (i.e., mindfulness). There is no formal cognitive restructuring in these therapies. They focus on changing one's *relationship* to one's thoughts rather than changing the negative *content* of these thoughts. In fact, it is interesting to note that Acceptance and Commitment Therapy (ACT), another mindfulness-based approach, was labeled "Comprehensive Distancing" in its early days (Zettle, Rains, & Hayes, 2011).

often rush too quickly from this stage out of a sense that they must start the cognitive restructuring work in a well-intentioned effort to help their patients. However, it is critical that therapists spend sufficient time guiding patients in this work of identifying their NATs as they arise, as it sets the table for the next stage: challenging NATs.

Challenging Negative Automatic Thoughts

Once teens have begun noticing their NATs, and reporting them in session, the work of challenging may begin. CBT is rooted in the cognitive model, which argues that depressed individuals are characterized not only by negative patterns of thinking, but that these thoughts are negatively biased relative to reality. Indeed, as reviewed in Chapter 2, a large and expanding body of research indicates that depressed individuals are characterized by a range of negative biases in their thinking, including memory biases (i.e., enhanced recall of negative information), interpretive biases (i.e., tendency to interpret ambiguous information in a negative way), self-referential biases (Auerbach et al., 2015; i.e., the tendency to appraise depressogenic content as being related to their own person), and forecasting biases (i.e., tendency to overpredict negative outcomes and underpredict positive ones, relative to reality; e.g., Strunk & Adler, 2009; Strunk, Lopez, & DeRubeis, 2006; Webb & Pizzagalli, in press). According to the cognitive behavioral model, these biases in thinking are, at least in part, driven by attentional biases in depression (i.e., preferentially attending to negative, rather than positive, information in one's environment; Armstrong & Olatunji, 2012). There are a variety of techniques that therapists can use to help patients identify their biases and change their negative thoughts to be more aligned with reality, and ultimately improve mood and depressive symptoms.

Suggested Strategies for Challenging Negative Automatic Thoughts

Collaborative Empiricism

At the heart of cognitive restructuring work – indeed, at the core of CBT itself – is the emphasis on therapist–patient collaboration and empiricism (Tee & Kazantzis, 2011). Collaboration refers to the fact that CBT therapists foster an atmosphere in which patients are actively involved in the process of therapy, rather than presenting themselves as all-knowing teachers who impart wisdom – in a unilateral fashion – to the passive patient. In other words, CBT is more collaborative teamwork than didactic teaching. The therapist may be the expert on psychopathology and psychotherapy, but the patient is the expert in his/her own emotions, cognitions, behaviors, and life context. In CBT, patients are encouraged to be actively involved in every step of therapy, from selecting agenda items, discussing and revising treatment goals, brainstorming and devising homework assignments, and relevant to the current topic, evaluating the validity of negative thoughts. The collaborative approach espoused by CBT can be especially important for teens given their increasing desire for autonomy and independence. The "empirical" term in collaborative empiricism refers to the fact that CBT, as we will see below, encourages a data-driven, scientific approach to working with negative thoughts and maladaptive behaviors.

The Socratic Method

Closely related to collaborative empiricism is the Socratic method (also known as Socratic dialogue or Socratic questioning), which refers to a collaborative communication style commonly employed by CBT therapists to help patients evaluate their negative patterns of thinking and to consider alternative perspectives (DeRubeis, Webb, Tang, & Beck, 2010; Overholser, 2011). At the core of the Socratic method is the judicious use of open-ended questions to gradually guide patients to consider alternative, less pessimistic perspectives on a problem. This is in contrast to trying to persuade patients – in an overly didactic fashion – of the ways in which their thinking is distorted and how they should be thinking. In addition to being one of the most distinctive stylistic features of CBT, the Socratic method is among the most challenging aspects of CBT for novice therapists to learn. When noticing a cognitive distortion in their patient's thinking, it can be very tempting for therapists to jump in and point out the flaws in their patient's thought process, and to then suggest more adaptive ways of approaching a problem. Although therapists may have the best intentions when doing so, it may not be the most effective means of getting a patient to shift her perspective. As Socrates was well aware, the point of the Socratic method is for the patient – through therapist guidance and collaborative exploration – to reach her own conclusions, which is a more solid footing for cognitive change than lecture or didactic persuasion (DeRubeis et al., 2010).[4] As well, the Socratic method may help promote autonomy and an internal locus of control in patients (Ryan, Lynch, Vansteenkiste, & Deci, 2011). It can be very helpful for new therapists to videotape or audiotape their sessions and review them, listening for exchanges in which they could have used an open-ended question, rather than a didactic statement.

---

4 In fact, from a CBT standpoint, Socrates was often rather leading, and less open-ended, in his brand of Socratic questioning, offering little room for his students to maneuver (Cooper, 1997; see especially *Euthypro* and *Crito*). As others have noted, Peter Falk in *Columbo* nicely exemplified the spirit of the Socratic method when questioning his suspects (e.g., Freeman, Simon, Beutler, & Arkowitz, 1989).

Example of Didactic Approach

Returning to the abovementioned example of the 14-year-old female who recounts a recent situation in which she greeted a male classmate (John) in the hallway at school and he "ignored" her:

Didactic approach:

PATIENT: He walked right by me! I know he thinks I'm weird.
THERAPIST: Well. That's one possibility. But I think you might be mind reading again. John may have passed right by without noticing you, or was in a rush, or even if he did notice you and didn't respond, that doesn't mean he thinks you're weird.

Socratic approach:

PATIENT: He walked right by me! I know he thinks I'm weird.
THERAPIST: Oh. I'm sorry to hear that. Did he say that?
PATIENT: Say what?
THERAPIST: Say that you're weird when he walked by you?
PATIENT: No. But he literally walked right by me! He must think I'm weird.
THERAPIST: OK. So beyond him walking by you in the hallway, what's the evidence that John thinks you're weird? [Open-ended question to explore evidence in support of NAT.]
PATIENT: Well, he doesn't talk to me much.
THERAPIST: How often does he approach you and talk to you?
PATIENT: Maybe once or twice a week he says something, maybe at our lunch table . . . or we'll chat for a second about something random in between classes.
THERAPIST: OK. And how often do you approach him?
PATIENT: Um. I don't. [The therapist can explore the reasons for this later.]
THERAPIST: Any other evidence that he thinks you're weird?
PATIENT: I guess that's the main one.
THERAPIST: OK. To be fair, let's look at the other side of it for a second. What's the evidence that he doesn't think you're weird? [Open-ended question to examine evidence against NAT.]
PATIENT: I don't know.
THERAPIST: Has he ever told you you're weird?
PATIENT: No.
THERAPIST: Has anyone else told you, "Hey, by the way, John thinks you're weird!"
PATIENT: No [laughs]. That would be weird. But it was so awkward when he walked right by me.

THERAPIST: OK, so any other possibilities why he walked by you? [Open-ended question to generate alternative explanation for situation.]
PATIENT: I guess it's possible he didn't see me. Not sure though . . .
THERAPIST: Did you guys make eye contact with each other?
PATIENT: I don't remember. He might not have seen me, I guess.

Although the Socratic approach may be more time consuming, CBT argues that, in most cases, reaching one's own conclusions – through careful therapist guidance – leads to more stable cognitive change and *buy-in* than receiving those conclusions directly from the therapist. In the above case, the therapist was able to insert some doubt in the patient's certitude, "I know he thinks I'm weird." She may not be convinced of more benign interpretations of this situation, but she is now more willing to consider alternative explanations. The therapist can follow up by asking the patient how confident she is of different explanations for why John walked by her, and importantly, what effect this exchange had on her mood.

Below we suggest additional techniques for challenging NATs. It is important to note that these are not alternatives to collaborative empiricism and the Socratic method. Rather, collaborative empiricism should pervade CBT and be used in concert with these techniques. Indeed, as we'll see below, cognitive change strategies *Examining evidence for and against NAT* and *Generating alternative thoughts/explanations* were used in a Socratic/collaborative style in the dialogue above.

Examining Evidence For and Against Negative Automatic Thoughts

One of the most commonly used strategies to evaluate the validity of NATs involves examining the evidence for and against a given NAT. In the example above, the therapist helped the patient explore the evidence for and against the NAT, "He thinks I'm weird." The purpose of this technique is to gather and clarify the evidence supporting and refuting the NAT that is driving the patient's negative affect. When doing so, it can be helpful for the therapist and patient to record (on paper or, if available, on a whiteboard) the evidence for versus against the NAT. The therapist should, of course, vary the questions, and not repeat, "What's the evidence for [NAT]?" and "What's the evidence against [NAT]?"

Depressed teens can typically easily list evidence supporting their NATs, but often struggle to gather evidence against it. As discussed earlier, given the tendency of depressed individuals to notice, focus on, and remember negative information, and to interpret ambiguous or neutral information in a negative light, this bias towards reporting evidence supporting their NAT is not surprising. As a result, it is the therapist's job to help the patient counteract this bias and to actively search for evidence that contradicts the patient's NAT. However, consistent with the spirit of CBT, it is important for the therapist to be balanced and to allow sufficient time for the patient to express his/her evidence supporting why s/he believes the NAT is accurate.

Generating Alternative Thoughts/Explanations

Often used alongside examining the evidence for and against NATs is the generation of alternative, more balanced explanations. In an effort to counteract depressed individuals' bias toward negative interpretations of events, therapists and patients can collaboratively explore other possible explanations or alternative ways of viewing a distressing situation. We previously introduced an abbreviated thought record. The full version has an additional column (Table 6.3) that guides patients in generating alternative, less negative thoughts/explanations (as well as a final column asking patients to re-rate their mood following the reframe).

Another technique to help patients consider alternative explanations is to have them imagine what they would tell a friend who is in the *identical* situation and reports the same negative thought. The strategy can help teens get enough distance from themselves to consider objectively plausible alternative explanations.

It is important to highlight that helpful behavioral change strategies or "action plans" can spring naturally from such cognitive work. For example, after a teen has identified and challenged the NAT, "I know he hates me," he may be in a better position to take appropriate steps to check in with this friend and to problem solve any tension. This also provides an opportunity for the therapist to communicate to the patient that the therapist is not exclusively focused on identifying and changing negative thinking patterns *within* the patient, but that CBT also targets actual problems and stressors in the teen's environment.

Common Cognitive Distortions (Also Known as Thinking Traps)

Depressed teens often exhibit systemic biases or distortions in their cognitive processing. Common cognitive distortions seen in depressed adolescents include: *all-or-nothing thinking* (i.e., seeing things in extreme, black-or-white terms), *catastrophizing* (i.e., fixating on the worst possible outcomes), and *mind reading* (i.e., automatically assuming what others are thinking).[5] The therapist can review these common cognitive distortions with patients. Indeed, some teens enjoy the challenge of tracking their cognitive distortions, and therapists can incorporate this activity into their patient's thought record homework (e.g., have teens not only identify

---

5 For a more extensive discussion of common cognitive distortions, see J. S. Beck (2011) and Burns (1999).

Table 6.3 Thought Record

Instructions: When you notice your mood getting worse, ask yourself, "What's going through my mind right now?" and, as soon as possible, jot down the thought or mental image in the Automatic Thoughts column. Then consider how accurate or realistic those thoughts are.

Date	Situation	Negative Emotions	Automatic Thoughts/ Images	Alternative or Balanced Thoughts	Re-Rate Emotions
	Where were you – and what was going on – when you got upset?	*What negative emotions did you feel at the time? Also rate their intensity. (0–100%)*	*What thoughts and/or images went through your mind? Rate how much you believe in each thought/image (0–100%)*	*Use the questions at the bottom to compose alternative or balanced thoughts. Rate how much you believe in each thought (0–100%)*	*Re-rate the intensity of your emotions (0–100%)*

(1) What's the *evidence* that the automatic thought is true? What is the evidence that it is not true?
(2) Are there *alternative explanations* for that event, or *alternative ways* to view the situation?
(3) What are the *implications* if the thought is true? What's the most upsetting thing about it? What's the most realistic view? What can I do about it?
(4) What would I tell a good friend in the same situation?

© J. Beck (2011). Adapted from *Cognitive behavior therapy: Basics and beyond* (2nd ed.). New York: Guilford Press, and used with permission.

their NATs, but label the common cognitive distortion). Therapists should keep track of common cognitive distortions they see their patients making, as it may inform both the cognitive case conceptualization, as well as the cognitive change strategies going forward. For example, if a patient has a tendency towards *all-or-nothing thinking* (I always screw up my friendships), she may benefit from practicing thinking in "shades of gray" (I've made mistakes with friends, but I'm usually a pretty good friend). Similarly, if a teen has a tendency to spiral into *catastrophizing* and fixating on the worst possible outcomes, he can practice more adaptive or balanced thinking by listing the following three scenarios: (1) What's the *worst* that could happen? (2) What's the *best* that could happen? followed by (3) What's the most *realistic* outcome? Having teens who frequently catastrophize first consider the worst and best extreme outcomes can help anchor their thinking when considering the most realistic or plausible outcome.

Pros and Cons

In addition to examining the *validity* or accuracy of a NAT, there may be therapeutic benefit to examining its *utility*. For example, take the case of a teen who spends a great deal of time ruminating on the fact that her boyfriend broke up with her and that she is now alone. It may not be helpful for the therapist to go about trying to challenge the validity of this or related negative thoughts. At least some of her distressing thoughts, although negative, may very well be accurate. In addition, the patient may feel invalidated and misunderstood by the therapist if he/she takes a cognitive restructuring approach. On the other hand, the patient may benefit from exploring how *helpful* it is for her to ruminate this frequently on this fact. In particular, the therapist and patient can explore the pros and cons of ruminating about the fact the patient's boyfriend broke up with her. What is the positive versus negative impact on the patient's emotions and ability to function and be productive? Such a discussion focused on the utility – rather than validity – of thoughts may increase motivation to implement strategies to reduce such repetitive negative thinking. The therapist and patient can then brainstorm different strategies for the patient to distract herself and reduce the rumination (e.g., by immersing herself in a mentally or physically engaging activity or hobby that is easily available). The latter approach can be helpful for cases in which a situation is objectively negative, yet the patient is spending an unhelpful amount of time ruminating on the event.

Behavioral Experiment

Perhaps the most powerful cognitive change strategies are behavioral experiments, as they can provide patients with direct experiential evidence against their negative cognitions. These experiments are devised collaboratively between the therapist and the patient, while brainstorming roadblocks that might get in the way of the patient completing the experiment. In addition to being potentially highly impactful, behavioral experiments can introduce some variety and excitement into therapy, as well as provide teens with the opportunity to use their creativity in designing experiments. For example, a teen who fears making a "fool" of himself in social situations and being judged negatively may test these cognitions by gradually increasing his social interactions and monitoring the outcomes. The therapist and patient can gradually work up to these behavioral experiments by developing a hierarchy of smaller experiments and beginning with some role plays in session. In such a case, it would of course be necessary for the therapist to determine that the teen has the interpersonal/conversational skill set to carry out these interactions successfully, otherwise initially building up the patient's interpersonal repertoire might be indicated.

Between-Session Homework

The therapy hour represents a tiny fraction of a patient's overall week. If the only therapeutic work occurred in session, it would be a losing battle against the other 167 hours of a patient's week, during which his negative patterns of thinking and behavior have relatively free rein. Like changing any other well-rehearsed and longstanding habits, or learning a new skill, regular practice is required to change habits of thinking and behavior. Therapists can use various metaphors to clarify the rationale for assigning homework (or, if preferred, weekly assignments) and the need for regular practice. If a patient plays a musical instrument or is involved in sports, the therapist can draw parallels between the regular, diligent practice required in learning a new instrument, song, or swing/maneuver in sport (e.g., developing well-engrained muscle memory) and the purpose of homework in CBT.

A few important issues are worth highlighting regarding the assignment of homework to teens. First, and consistent with the spirit of CBT, homework assignments should be devised collaboratively, with the therapist actively involving the patient – as much as is feasible – in custom tailoring the weekly assignment to suit the teen's needs. Paper-and-pencil assignments are not necessarily required. For example, teens may prefer adapting a thought record and completing it through the notes function on their smartphone, or setting alarms on their phone to remind them to complete a particular assignment.[6] Second, therapists should be as concrete and specific as possible about the nature of the assignment and when it will be completed (e.g., recording on a calendar the days and

---

6 For a listing of available CBT smartphone apps, see http://www.adaa.org/finding-help/mobile-apps.

times the patient has decided to complete the assignment). Third, the therapist should provide a clear rationale for the assignment and elicit feedback from the patient about the suggested activity and possible obstacles that might get in the way of completing it. Finally, and importantly, therapists should review assignments from the previous session and get patients' feedback on their usefulness.

Core Beliefs and Intermediate Beliefs

Over the course of treatment, therapists may notice certain themes recurring in the NATs reported by patients (e.g., patterns emerging from repeated thought records). These themes may point to an underlying *core belief*, which lies at the source of the patient's "surface-level" NATs. Above, we reviewed the *downward-arrow technique*, which can be used to unpeel the layers of NATs and uncover core beliefs. The Cognitive Conceptualization Diagram worksheet (Figure 6.2) can be used to help decipher core beliefs from recurring themes cutting across NATs reported in session.

As introduced in Chapter 5, core beliefs are the most deeply rooted and central beliefs individuals hold about themselves. Traditionally, the cognitive model of depression has argued that core beliefs fall into two broad categories: *helplessness/worthlessness* (e.g., I'm inadequate; I'm incompetent) and *unlovability* (I'm unattractive; I'm not good enough to be loved) beliefs (Beck, 1995, 2011). Core beliefs are considered to be the byproduct of early-life experiences (in particular, interactions with parents) and environmental feedback over one's life that one has internalized at a deep level. Core beliefs can be positive (e.g., I'm worthy of love; I'm competent). However, CBT argues that depressed individuals possess negative core beliefs, which predispose them to depressive episodes when they are activated by thematically related negative life events (e.g., a teen with an unlovability core belief that is triggered by a romantic break-up). These core beliefs serve as the lenses through which individuals filter their world (i.e., attentional/cognitive biases), which in turn further fuels these core beliefs. For example, a teen with the core belief, "I'm stupid," will be more likely to attend to and remember information (e.g., a perceived criticism from a teacher), which confirms this belief (i.e., *confirmation bias* or *Velcro–Teflon effect*).[7] Similarly, in the interpersonal domain, a teen with the core belief that she is fundamentally weird or different will have a bias towards attending to and remembering information that confirms this belief (e.g., a slightly awkward interaction with a classmate), and to interpret ambiguous or relatively neutral situations in such a way that it supports her negative core belief (e.g., perceive a neutral, or even positive, comment from a friend as a criticism).

---

7 Evidence consistent with core beliefs "sticks" like Velcro; the rest "slides off" like Teflon.

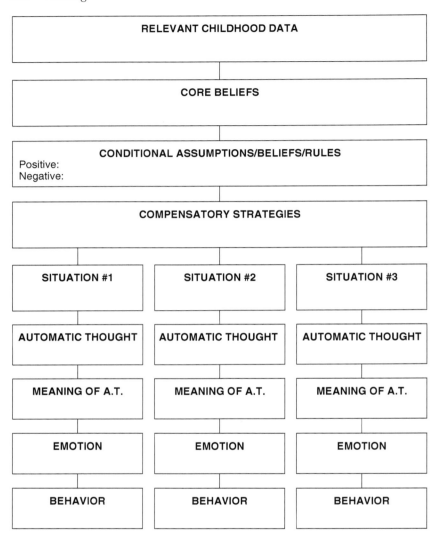

Figure 6.2 Cognitive Conceptualization Diagram.

© J. Beck (2011). Adapted from *Cognitive behavior therapy: Basics and beyond* (2nd ed.). New York: Guilford Press, and used with permission.

Intermediate beliefs, as the term implies, serve as intermediary links between core beliefs and NATs. They take the form of (typically implicit or unarticulated) *rules* (I should always put the needs of others first), *assumptions* (If I'm not loved, I'm worthless), or *attitudes* (I can't change my life, so why bother?). These intermediate beliefs are outgrowths of deeper core beliefs and, when revealed, may help the therapist and patient understand patterns of maladaptive behaviors, particularly in the interpersonal domain. For example, a teen with the core belief that she is unlovable may have the intermediate assumption, "If a guy sees the real me, he'll reject me." As a result, the teen may avoid dating for fear of ultimately being rejected.

As therapy progresses, and relevant data are gathered, the therapist can share his/her initial cognitive conceptualization and receive the patient's feedback on the extent to which it resonates with her experience. Within these discussions, therapists can explore the life experiences that initially shaped the patient's core beliefs, and importantly, how the core belief may be driving attentional and cognitive biases, and accounting for maladaptive behavioral and interpersonal patterns in the patient's present life. With sufficient exploration, patients can often report early memories when they first *felt* their core beliefs. A benefit of exploring the origins of core beliefs is that it can provide patients with a framework for understanding the roots of their current negative cognitions, maladaptive behaviors, and, ultimately, distressing emotions. More broadly, it can also help patients get a little more *distance* from their core beliefs (I'm not really "worthless," but it just feels that way because of all the experiences I had early on). It should be highlighted that a CBT therapist explores the historical origins of emotions and NATs only as a means to increase understanding of the *here and now* (i.e., always connecting the conceptualization back to current symptoms and functioning).

A cognitive conceptualization is, necessarily, a work in progress, and thus should be updated over the course of therapy as new information arises to provide a more accurate and comprehensive conceptualization. However, following an initial conceptualization, the therapist and patient can discuss what a more adaptive and realistic new core belief could be. For example, if it becomes clear that a teen holds the core belief "I'm worthless," the therapist and patient can work collaboratively to create a healthier and more accurate core belief (e.g., I'm a good person (with strengths and limitations)). Of course, the goal here is not for the patient to immediately believe this to be true at a *deep, core-belief* level, but to create a core belief that she logically considers to be more accurate and healthier, and is willing to work towards internalizing. When the patient reports feeling, at a deep level, worthless, this engrained core belief is not going to change overnight. However, the patient can be encouraged to begin recording evidence that contradicts the old core belief and supports the new, healthier one. In Figure 6.3 we present the Core Belief Worksheet that therapists and patients can use for this purpose.[8]

---

8 For a more extensive treatment of core belief work and additional core belief change strategies, see Riso, du Toit, Stein, and Young (2007) and, in particular, Young, Klosko, and Weishaar (2003).

```
Old core belief: _____

How much do you believe the old core belief right now?    (0–100) _____

    *What's the most you've believed it this week?   (0–100) _____
    *What's the least you've believed it this week?  (0–100) _____

New core belief: _____

How much do you believe the new core belief right now? (0–100) _____

| Evidence that contradicts old belief and supports new one | Evidence that support old belief with reframe (alternative explanation) |
|---|---|
|   |   |
```

Figure 6.3 Core Belief Worksheet

© J. Beck (2011). Adapted from *Cognitive behavior therapy: Basics and beyond* (2nd ed.). New York: Guilford Press, and used with permission.

In addition to gathering evidence that contradicts the old core belief and supports the new one (e.g., I helped Samantha feel better when she was upset today), a column is dedicated to recording evidence that supports the old, negative core belief, but with a positive reframe (e.g., I got in an argument with Jenny today, but that doesn't mean I'm worthless, just that we both got a little hot-headed and should have thought before we said those things. I'm going to talk to her tomorrow and apologize for my part in the argument). Through this regular work, the patient can very gradually start to reshape her core beliefs towards more adaptive ones. It is essential for the therapist to emphasize that it takes time for core beliefs to change, and underscore the importance of daily practice to challenge negative core beliefs and to bolster healthier beliefs.

Communication Styles and Cognitions

Another important factor for therapists to consider is how depressed adolescent patients interact and communicate with others. That is, what is the teen's typical communication style and how does it relate to his symptoms? Below, we describe two types of dysfunctional communication styles (passive and aggressive) that are common among depressed teens and that may generate interpersonal stress and, ultimately, increase depressive symptom severity. As described below, particular patterns of negative cognitions often underlie these communication styles, which, when uncovered, can be targeted and addressed. We also describe a healthier communication style, assertiveness, which can be introduced to teens as a more respectful (and effective) way to navigate interpersonal relationships.

Passive Communication

It is common for depressed adolescents to be overly passive in their style of communication (e.g., quiet, avoidant, submissive, overly deferential). When interacting with others in a passive way, needs and desires often remain unmet, resulting in negative emotions. For example, an adolescent may feel frustrated with himself because he did not say the things he really wanted to express in a given interaction. A teen may feel cowardly or ashamed that he was not "confident enough" to clearly express his perspective to a peer, parent, or other authority figure (including the therapist!). It is important for therapists to help their patients explore the ways in which particular negative cognitions may be contributing to their passive communication style. Examples of negative cognitions that may underlie a passive communication style include:

> *I should be quiet and respectful.*
>
> *My opinion isn't important.*
>
> *I shouldn't complain.*
>
> *I don't want to disturb.*
>
> *They won't understand.*
>
> *It won't make a difference.*

In the dialogue below, a patient describes a passive approach to dealing with a situation in which her boyfriend (John) disappointed and upset her:

THERAPIST: So it sounds like you felt really upset when John cancelled the movie plans.
PATIENT: Yeah. He cancelled an hour before the movie, and I was already on my way there. This was the second time in the last week he cancelled our plans.

THERAPIST: Did you talk to him about it?
PATIENT: I didn't want to talk to him after that. I was pretty pissed off. I just texted him: "No worries, we can reschedule next weekend."
THERAPIST: That makes sense. You were pretty irritated with him after that. What happened after you texted him?
PATIENT: To be honest, and this is stupid, I kind of cried.
THERAPIST: So what emotion were you feeling when you were tearing up?
PATIENT: Pretty sad.
THERAPIST: So you were irritated with him, but also really sad and tearing up about what happened.
PATIENT: Yeah. I was really upset.
THERAPIST: I wonder how he would react if he knew how hurt you were and that you were really looking forward to the evening together?
PATIENT: I don't know. It probably wouldn't make a difference.

The patient's passive approach to dealing with the upsetting situation is rooted in her pessimistic prediction of how a more open and assertive interaction would play out (It probably wouldn't make a difference). This type of "why bother?" cognition is common among depressed teens given their negative expectations of the future and low perceived self-efficacy. Therapists can guide their patients through a balanced consideration of the pros and cons of such a passive approach. An important negative consequence to consider is that continued reliance on a more passive interpersonal style can be like a *ticking time bomb* such that frustration simmers initially, but then mounts over time. One could imagine this teen eventually lashing out at her boyfriend and quickly shifting from a passive to an overly aggressive approach. Or perhaps, as irritability simmers, the teen may shift from a passive to a passive-aggressive approach (e.g., being sarcastic, procrastinating, subtly undermining plans with her boyfriend), and then ultimately to an overtly aggressive approach (e.g., a heated verbal argument). In such a case, the therapist can help the teen explore her tendency to repeatedly suppress or *bottle up* her irritability and the negative downstream consequences (e.g., anger boiling over into aggressive behavior). There are most likely other examples of this process in the teen's past that the therapist and patient can explore together. When the teen begins to recognize this habitual negative interpersonal pattern, the therapist can introduce an alternative, healthier approach to dealing with these stressful interactions (see Assertive Communication, below).

Aggressive Communication

Irritability is a common symptom of depression in adolescents, and, when present, it increases the chances that a teen reflexively turns to an aggressive communication style. Aggressive communication can involve a raised voice, a condescending or sarcastic tone, using threats or put-downs, or dominating the interaction and giving others limited time to share their perspective. In contrast to passive communication in which an individual does not give himself and his own perspective enough respect, an aggressive style communicates a lack of respect for others. Examples of negative cognitions that may underlie aggressive communication include:

> *I won't be disrespected.*
>
> *My opinion is more important.*
>
> *I'm right, you're wrong.*
>
> *I'm going to show him/her.*
>
> *I need to look out for number one.*
>
> *It's my way or the highway.*

As described in Table 6.2 individuals with a tendency towards irritability often have NATs revolving around themes of personal injustice and unfairness. From their perspective, they are often being treated unfairly and not receiving what they deserve from others or the world. When present, these cognitive themes can trigger a more aggressive style of communication. In the dialogue below, a teen describes an interaction in which he lashes out at a friend for showing up late to pick him up for a ride to school.

THERAPIST: So what time did he eventually show up?
PATIENT: Oh. A good 10 minutes late . . . again. This is the third time in a row he's been late.
THERAPIST: You were feeling pretty irritated. Even now just talking about it brings up that frustration.
PATIENT: Yeah. I laced into him the second he arrived.
THERAPIST: How did he react?
PATIENT: He got angry back and didn't talk to me all day. But I put him in his place for what he did to me.

The teen in the above dialogue may feel at least a tinge of satisfaction in putting his friend "in his place." Accordingly, when exploring the consequences of an aggressive communication style, it is important that therapists examine the perceived benefits of this style as well as the downside. From the patient's perspective, what are the benefits of this style of interacting with others? Does he view it as something negative, but simply has difficulty controlling his impulses when anger arises? Or does he see benefits in interacting in this way (e.g., You can't let people take advantage of you; People will hurt me unless I protect myself; People get what they deserve; People need to learn their lesson)? Does he fail to consider or see the possible benefits of other approaches, perhaps seeing them as "weak" or ineffective at getting what you want?

With regards to the downside of an aggressive communication style, therapists can explore with their patients possible negative consequences to themselves (e.g., guilt, the distress of holding on to anger) and to their relationship with others (e.g., having to revert to *damage control* after offending a friend). The irony, of course, is that in trying to put the other person down or to *teach them a lesson*, there is a tendency to elicit negative emotions in oneself (e.g., anger, guilt). An adage attributed to the Buddha captures the negative impact of anger on oneself: "Holding on to anger is like grasping a hot coal with the intent of throwing it at someone else; you are the one who gets burned." The best way to minimize the chance that anyone gets burned is through assertive communication. By interacting assertively, we can stand up for ourselves, while at the same time being respectful of others.

Assertive Communication

Assertiveness is commonly conceptualized as lying in the middle of a continuum with passive and aggressive communication on each pole. Assertiveness is characterized by being clear, concise, and honest in communicating one's perspective (unlike passive communication), while at the same time being appropriate and respectful of others (unlike aggressive communication). In addressing a disagreement or difference in perspective, assertiveness involves maintaining a confident but calm tone of voice, using "I" statements (e.g., I felt . . . ; I was upset when . . .), as opposed to criticizing or blaming (e.g., You're disrespectful; You made me feel . . .), and inviting the other person to share her perspective on the situation. Assertiveness is typically (but not always) the best way to communicate because it maximizes an interpersonal interaction, while being respectful of the other person. For teens with a tendency to rely on a more passive communication style, being assertive may feel very uncomfortable and perhaps overly aggressive. Examples of NATs more passive teens may have include: "I'm offending them," "I'm being rude," or "They're going to be mad at me." For those who have a habit of interacting in a more aggressive manner, assertiveness may seem unnatural and perhaps overly passive (e.g., They're going to walk all over me; I look weak). It is important for therapists to explore the concerns that their patients may have regarding trying a more assertive approach to addressing their interpersonal problem. Role-playing can be helpful for teens to: (1) see their therapists modeling assertiveness and (2) "try on" assertiveness and to rehearse their approach before deploying it in the real world. Teens (and therapists) are understandably often uncomfortable about engaging in role-plays. It is important for therapists to openly acknowledge any discomfort, as well as the possible benefits of role plays. To return to the teen who was upset with her boyfriend for cancelling their movie plans:

THERAPIST: I wonder how he would react if he knew how hurt you were and that you were really looking forward to the evening together?
PATIENT: I don't know. It probably wouldn't make a difference.
THERAPIST: It's tough to tell. Have there been other times when you told John you were upset about something he said or did?
PATIENT: Yeah. He was still kind of friends with his ex after we'd been dating for a couple of weeks. I was upset and brought it up.
THERAPIST: How did he react to that?
PATIENT: He was kind of confused at first. But, after hearing how upset I was, he apologized.
THERAPIST: That was nice of him.
PATIENT: Yeah. I guess. But, I shouldn't have had to say anything.
THERAPIST: I totally hear you. But, you did say something. And, it seemed worthwhile. How do you imagine he would respond if you told him that you were upset about the movie?
PATIENT: I don't know. I'm not sure what he'd say, or even what I would say.
THERAPIST: It's always tough to know what to say exactly. Perhaps we can role play and see what you think would be the best approach.
PATIENT: OK . . . [Looks uncomfortable.]
THERAPIST: I know. Acting in therapy is kind of weird. It's weird and uncomfortable for me too, but it might help you figure out what to say. So, to make it a little easier, and since you know John a lot better than I do, why don't I play you and you just play John and react the way you think he would react. [Therapist will first model assertive communication.]
PATIENT: OK.
THERAPIST: How anxious and uncomfortable are you about practicing this with me, on a scale from 1 to 10?
PATIENT: [Nervous laughter.] Honestly, probably an 8.
THERAPIST: OK. I have to admit I'm at about a 7.5 myself – I'm a terrible actor. Having these kinds of conversations can be uncomfortable. But I've found that the best way to prepare is to practice. The more you

practice beforehand, the more comfortable and better prepared you are for the real thing.

PATIENT: That makes sense. OK.

THERAPIST: So let's think about the setting for this conversation. Where would be the best place for this conversation to happen?

PATIENT: Probably in person. We hang out at my place after school pretty much every day. So maybe once we get to my place and relax a bit.

THERAPIST: That sounds great. So, we're at your place after school. I'm you and you're John.

PATIENT: [Smiling.] Still kinda weird, but OK.

THERAPIST [acting as patient]: So what do you feel like doing this weekend?

PATIENT [acting as John]: I dunno. I didn't hear about much going on, right?

THERAPIST [acting as patient]: Yeah, me neither. Do you want to catch a movie Friday?

PATIENT [acting as John]: We still haven't seen [cancelled movie]. It's still playing so we could see that if you want?

THERAPIST [acting as patient]: I'd like that. John, I have to admit, I was really upset when you couldn't make it to the movie last weekend. I was really looking forward to it.

PATIENT [acting as John]: Sorry about that. That was my bad. I know, I was looking forward to it too.

The therapist in the above dialogue begins by modeling for the teen how to be assertive. They can then switch roles and the teen can "try on" assertive communication for herself while the therapist plays the part of the boyfriend. In the latter situation, the therapist uses the following assertive statement: "I have to admit, I was really upset when you couldn't make it to the movie last weekend. I was really looking forward to it." In this statement, the teen clearly expresses how she feels about the situation without criticizing or being disrespectful to her boyfriend.

An overarching point for therapists to highlight in discussing assertive communication with their patients is that we can only control our own behavior, and not that of others. Assertiveness maximizes, but does not guarantee, an optimal reaction from others. It is important for therapists to remind their patients that success should be defined primarily on the basis of *their own* behavior and to feel pride in making the effort to be assertive.

Problem-Solving

Problem-Solving Therapy (PST: D'Zurilla & Nezu, 2007) is an efficacious, stand-alone intervention for a number of psychiatric disorders, including MDD. In adults, it is as effective as other forms of psychotherapy (e.g., CBT) and medications at treating depressive symptoms (Bell & D'Zurilla, 2009). Although there are far fewer clinical trials of stand-alone PST for adolescent depression, training in problem-solving skills is often incorporated into CBT protocols targeting adolescent psychopathology. For example, Dr. David Brent, from the University of Pittsburgh, developed an individual CBT intervention for depressed adolescents that includes a problem-solving module, and results indicated that this treatment was superior to non-directive therapy and a family-based intervention for reducing depressive symptoms among adolescents (Brent et al., 1997). Among treatment-resistant adolescents, adding a variation of this individual CBT intervention to an antidepressant medication also resulted in greater depressive symptom reductions as compared to medication alone (Brent et al., 2008). Taken together, it seems that problem-solving is useful and beneficial to depressed teens, and there is growing evidence that it can be easily incorporated into classic CBT protocols.

Problem-Solving Interventions

There are several reasons why problem-solving may be an important addition to a depressed adolescent's toolbox of CBT skills. First, like all of us, depressed adolescents have concrete problems that necessitate direct action. Although cognitive restructuring is undoubtedly helpful in these situations, this skill may only get the patient part of the way there. For example, an adolescent who is a week late in turning in a term paper may be successful at reappraising her self-critical NATs about her behavior, but she still needs to develop a concrete strategy to avoid failing the assignment. Second, depressed adolescents experience higher levels of acute and chronic stressors that are at least partly dependent on their own behavior (i.e., dependent stress) than non-depressed adolescents (Harkness & Stewart, 2009; Rudolph et al., 2000). These issues, which include conflicts with parents, teachers, and peers, perpetuate depressive symptoms. Developing and applying *real solutions* to these problems is critical for interrupting the cycle of stress and depression. Last, problem-solving may be more easily mastered early on in treatment, particularly for younger adolescent patients. If problem-solving is introduced in the first few sessions, depressed teens have a tool to tackle pressing issues while they practice and become more comfortable with cognitive restructuring.

When PST is integrated into CBT, adolescents are encouraged to use a structured approach to their problems as an adjunct to cognitive restructuring and other behavioral interventions. Most problem-solving protocols enumerate five steps to effective problem-solving. Below we adapt the 5 Ps, a mnemonic used in the ACTION treatment program (see Stark, Streusand, Krumholz, & Patel, 2010), and we add "Proceed" as an additional step. We have added this step for clarity's sake, as the original model includes reasoning about a list of potential solutions, choosing among them, and trying out the chosen solution in the same step. Parsing the action of testing the chosen solution into its own step allows us to highlight the trial-and-error spirit of problem-solving. To illustrate the six steps, consider a depressed adolescent patient who is struggling with specific concepts in his math class. Below, we follow this patient through each of the problem-solving steps.

Problem (Problem Definition)

In this first step, the therapist and patient collaboratively spell out the dimensions of the problem in specific, concrete terms. In our example, the patient defines his problem concretely by using specific indicators (i.e., failing exams, low grades, length spent on homework) of the difficulties he is having in math. In contrast, a non-concrete description of the problem might be, "I suck at trigonometry." It is important to ensure that the problem is indeed solvable and is defined in a way that the outcome is within the patient's control. Focusing exclusively on changeable problems and framing these in concrete ways enhances the likelihood that patients will view their problems as solvable, and consequently, increases their likelihood of benefiting from the intervention.

Purpose (Goal Definition)

This step involves delineating exactly what would have to happen or change for the patient to consider the problem solved. The principles we described for setting goals in therapy (see Chapter 5) can also be applied to goals for specific problems. A patient may articulate and define the central goal as, "I want to try and get a 'B' on the next math test," or alternatively, "It's important for me to get a passing grade so that I don't repeat the class." At this stage, therapists also may take the opportunity to gauge and, if needed, enhance patients' resolve to address the problem (e.g., Why is it important for you to solve this problem? How would your life change for the better if you were able to solve this problem?).

Plans (Solution Generation)

The therapist and patient next work together to brainstorm an exhaustive list of potential solutions to the identified problem. This should be a *no judgment* activity – all possibilities are welcome during this step. Therapists may need to model this process by adding their own ideas. For adolescents who struggle with perfectionism surrounding brainstorming (e.g., I can only list really good possibilities), we recommend using some humor, if appropriate, and suggesting a potential solution that is so *out there* that it is funny. With respect to improving a math grade, a patient may generate a varied list of plans: (1) Spend more time on the homework; (2) Get help from mom or dad; (3) Ask math teacher for help after school; (4) Study with a classmate.

Predict and Pick (Consequential Thinking)

This step can be accomplished in a number of different ways and can be adjusted to suit the patient's developmental stage and his degree of concrete versus abstract thinking. A younger adolescent and/or more concrete thinker might benefit from simply predicting and writing down one potential negative and positive outcome for each brainstormed solution. Older adolescents and/or more abstract thinkers may benefit from completing a formal pros-and-cons list for each option. During this exercise, adolescents may benefit from being prompted to think of several short- *and* long-term consequences; ideally, the chosen solution is optimal both immediately and over time.

Once the list has been generated, therapists may challenge their patients to weigh the relative importance of each item on the pros-and-cons list. Numerical weights (e.g., How important is this pro on a scale from 0 (not important at all) to 10 (extremely important)?) can even be assigned to each item when problems are particularly complicated. No matter the chosen approach, it is important for adolescent patients to practice identifying potential barriers to their brainstormed solutions, determining whether or not these can be managed, and incorporating this determination into their final choice. For example, in exploring the pros and cons of "spending more time on the homework," pros may be that the patient could figure it out himself and develop mastery. Cons, however, may be that he continues to struggle, which results in more frustration.

Proceed (Implement Chosen Solution)

We recommend that the therapist and patient discuss and role play each element involved in implementing the selected solution. Then, any necessary modifications to the plan can be made based on these role plays.

The therapist should ensure that the patient has scheduled a specific time and place to carry out the solution, and that he has a feasible *Plan B* ready in case the initial plan falls through. For example, a patient may decide that getting help after school from the math teacher is the best option. Thus, the therapist and patient would map out a course of action:

THERAPIST: OK, let's hear the plan one more time.
PATIENT: I'll get help from Mr. Green after school on Thursday because that is when he sees students for extra help. To be sure, I will ask him in advance, on Tuesday, about seeing him Thursday.
THERAPIST: What happens if Thursday isn't an option?
PATIENT: If he can't see me Thursday, I will ask him if another day is possible. When I ask, I will make good eye contact, tell him that I really want to bring my grades up, and make sure I say how thankful I am for the extra help.
THERAPIST: It sounds like you have a good plan. You'll do great!
PATIENT: If I get nervous, I will remind myself that my friends John and Mark asked him for math help and that it went fine for them.

Pat on the Back (Self-Evaluation)

Like any homework assignment, it is very important to review the outcome of an implemented solution at the next meeting. Adolescents can be encouraged to describe what they did, providing the results in detail, point by point, so as to minimize the effect of NATs on their evaluation of the attempted solution. Regardless of outcome, it is important to *cheerlead* adolescents for approaching a problem and experimenting with a solution (e.g., Trying something new takes a lot of guts – way to go!) and encourage them to internalize this same point of view. Implemented solutions that did not produce hoped-for outcomes may be altered to address shortcomings and then re-implemented, or may be replaced in favor of trying a different brainstormed solution.

Addressing Common Barriers to Problem-Solving

As we highlight in this chapter and elsewhere, a hallmark characteristic of depression is the presence of negative beliefs and attitudes about oneself, the future, and the world. These cognitions can present obstacles to the effective application of problem-solving. For example, a teen might have hopeless beliefs such as, "My problems never get better" or helpless beliefs such as, "No matter what I do, I can't change things." Additionally, patients may have unhelpful, perfectionistic beliefs about potential solutions to their problems. If patients believe that the chosen solution *must* be optimal, or if they believe that they should only try out desirable solutions, they are likely to remain mired in their most difficult problems. Indeed, one of the most important skills depressed adolescents glean from problem-solving practice is how to choose among unattractive or suboptimal options.

Clearly, there are a number of ways in which cognitions about one's problems (e.g., hopeless and helpless beliefs) or about the problem-solving process (e.g., perfectionist thoughts) can interfere with problem-solving. One approach to these cognitions is to tackle them head-on by identifying and challenging the relevant NATs. This can be explicitly built into the first step (problem definition) of formal problem-solving; for instance, the patient might fill out a thought record on the thoughts and emotions that come up as he describes the problem. Identifying and challenging NATs is most effective if the adolescent already has some practice with these skills. A second, more indirect approach to these cognitions is to help adolescents collect observable evidence contradicting typical depressotypic beliefs. Essentially, if adolescent patients are willing to *try* problem-solving, they have an opportunity to see it working for them, which will ultimately build confidence in their ability to solve future problems. This approach hinges on therapists setting adolescents up for success by focusing on a smaller, less daunting problem at the outset (i.e., we often refer to this as a *digestible bite*). Having success with a smaller problem may directly contradict the patient's expectations, and in doing so, may make it easier for adolescents to engage their next, potentially larger problem.

Depressotypic cognitions also can create a sticking point when it comes to brainstorming solutions to the problem; specifically, adolescents may reflexively *shoot down* potential options, which may thwart the brainstorming phase. In these cases, we find it helpful to encourage adolescents to adopt the perspective of someone they admire and list potential solutions *that person* might suggest.

THERAPIST: So now we've defined the problem we'll be working on: your friends are taking a trip over the weekend and you'd like to join them, but you don't have enough money. Your parents have said that they won't pay for you to go. Let's make a list of possible solutions. At this stage, anything can go on the list – also, let's avoid the temptation of labeling these as good or bad ideas. Let's just jot down all the ideas we can think of.
PATIENT: I dunno. It seems like I've tried everything. I guess I just can't go.
THERAPIST: I guess one possibility might be to sell your guitar – do you think the rest of the band would notice? [Using levity to encourage brainstorming.]
PATIENT: Not a chance.

THERAPIST: Let's step back a moment. Is there someone in your life that seems to be good at solving problems?
PATIENT: Yeah. My friend Chelsea is super smart and always seems to have things figured out.
THERAPIST: OK. What kinds of things might Chelsea suggest in this situation?
PATIENT: Well, she might ask her boss if she could work an extra shift to make up some more money. Or maybe ask a friend to borrow the money. She told me once that she made a deal with her parents that she would pay half of something that she wanted if they would cover the other half until she could pay them back.
THERAPIST: Those sound good. Could we add any of those ideas to our list of possible solutions?

In the example above, when the patient takes her friend Chelsea's perspective on the problem, she is able to distance herself from the associated affect, which leaves room for brainstorming some creative solutions.

In our work with adolescents, we have found it especially helpful to *prime* a problem-solving mode. To this end, short passages (e.g., short stories, TED Talks[9]) that feature individuals who struggle through difficult situations and overcome obstacles may prove to be very powerful for patients and could be suggested as a weekly assignment. These passages often act as a launching point for discussing how people have managed problems across different aspects of their lives, which may eventually allow patients to translate these lessons into their own lives. We often use Ajahn Brahm's (2005) *Who Ordered This Truckload of Dung?*, a book of very short stories speaking from a Buddhist tradition, to illustrate important concepts in problem-solving. We find this book particularly helpful because (1) the stories are exceptionally engaging and easy to relate to one's life and (2) the majority of stories are quite brief, so they generally are not burdensome for patients. For instance, in one story, a man is being chased through the jungle by a hungry tiger intent on eating him. Knowing that he could never outrun the tiger (it's a tiger, after all), he desperately jumps into a well. As soon as the man jumps, he notices a large black snake coiled up at the bottom of the well. Knowing that the snake will surely poison him should he fall to the bottom, the man reflexively grabs a tree root and hangs, caught between the tiger pawing at him from above and the snake striking at him from below. Eventually, the tiger slips while trying to attack the man, tumbles into the well, crushes the snake, and dies in the process. Improbably, the man is saved.

---

9 TED Talks are available at www.ted.com/talks.

The story of the tiger and the snake highlights some important points about problem-solving. First, the man did not *deserve* to be chased by a hungry tiger – he was in the wrong part of the jungle at the wrong time. Our problems can sometimes be like that; we may not have done anything to cause them, but it is still up to us to find solutions. Second, the man jumped into the well to escape the tiger because this was the best of a set of bad options. Finding solutions to problems can be like this; sometimes we need to choose from limited, unattractive options and do the best we can with the choices we have. Last, although the man was remarkably unsuccessful in his initial attempts to escape the tiger, he hung on (literally) and this strength and determination carried him to safety. Problem-solving also can proceed in this manner; particularly for complex problems, adolescent patients may need to exhibit abundant resolve.

Benefits of Problem-Solving in CBT

Blending formal problem-solving into CBT for adolescent patients has the dual effect of potentially augmenting cognitive strategies and adding another tool to patients' coping arsenal. In regard to the former, during problem-solving adolescents are asked to take multiple perspectives and see a problem from several viewpoints. Thus, problem-solving gives adolescents practice with cognitive flexibility in a format that is more accessible than working directly with their thoughts. As we have discussed, cognitive flexibility is a key ingredient in cognitive restructuring and other CBT skills, thus problem-solving may lay a foundation for more complex cognitive (e.g., thought records) and behavioral (e.g., planning pleasurable activities) interventions.

Problem-solving also may be a particularly useful tool to help adolescents maintain treatment gains. As described in Chapter 2, major stressful life events are robust triggers of depressive episodes. Further, life stress is an important risk factor for relapse and recurrence following successful efficacious CBT (Harkness, Theriault, Stewart, & Bagby, 2014). One goal of problem-solving is to help adolescents develop a *positive problem orientation*. Adolescents with a positive problem orientation view problems as solvable challenges and believe that they can overcome them. Further, they are able to see possible positive side effects of working through difficult problems. A positive problem-solving orientation is a hallmark of an effective problem solver, and there is now a substantial body of evidence that problem-solving ability moderates the association between stressful life events and later distress. Specifically, individuals with greater problem-solving skills are buffered from the negative effects of stress, including symptoms of depression and anxiety (see Nezu, 2005, for a review). Taken together, improving problem-solving may have both indirect (through enhancing cognitive interventions) and direct effects on acute treatment and sustained remission in CBT for depressed adolescents.

Summary

In this chapter, we reviewed a variety of strategies from which therapists can select to identify the NATs (and deeper cognitions) that are underlying their patient's depressive symptoms and maladaptive behavioral/interpersonal patterns. In addition, we reviewed strategies to help patients challenge and change their negative patterns of thinking. It is important to highlight that this work can be difficult and requires patience. Although behavioral strategies may be relatively more simple to deliver, successful cognitive work can have a profound therapeutic impact and can provide patients with a set of principles and skills to track and modify their own negative cognitive patterns in their day-to-day lives. Also, we discussed the difference between passive, aggressive, and assertive communication styles, and the negative cognitions that often underlie these different approaches to interacting with others. Finally, as a useful adjunct to cognitive techniques, we reviewed a structured problem-solving approach that may be helpful when teens need to develop plans of action for concrete problems.

7 Maintaining Gains and Relapse Prevention

At any given time, an estimated 15–35% of Americans are attempting to lose weight. Weight loss, as anyone who has attempted knows, is quite the challenge. Unfortunately, research indicates that the majority of individuals who achieve weight loss fail to maintain it (Wing & Phelan, 2005). Those who successfully maintain weight loss typically report having a disciplined regimen of healthy daily habits, including regular exercise, eating a low-calorie, low-fat diet, and monitoring their weight. Like weight loss, recovering from a depressive episode and maintaining gains following treatment termination is no easy feat. It is not uncommon for teens to assume that, once their depressive symptoms have abated, they no longer need to practice the antidepressant skills (e.g., cognitive, behavioral, and interpersonal strategies) they acquired in treatment. However, depression relapse is common among adolescents, as approximately 40–70% experience a recurrence (Rutter, Kim-Cohen, & Maughan, 2006). In this chapter, we review a range of strategies therapists may wish to implement with their adolescent patients to reduce the risk of depression relapse following treatment termination.

Preparing for Treatment Termination

The preparation for treatment termination begins in Session 1. As discussed in Chapter 5, it is important for therapists to gauge their patients' goals and expectations at the beginning of treatment, including their expectations for the course of symptom change. These discussions provide the therapist and patient (and also ideally the parent/guardian) with a shared understanding of the focus and process of therapy, as well as the end state that the patient seeks to achieve by the end of treatment. As treatment progresses and symptoms subside, therapists and patients continually refine therapeutic goals to address remaining problems or new issues that may have emerged (for cases in which symptoms do not sufficiently subside, see Addressing Residual Symptoms and Additional Treatment, below). CBT is intended to be a time-limited treatment and, ultimately, is aimed at providing patients with the coping and emotion regulation skills to manage their own moods and stressors. The end goal is for patients to become *their own cognitive behavioral therapist* and to no longer require therapy.

As treatment goals are achieved, therapists and patients discuss a timeline for final sessions. As noted previously, the length of therapy varies substantially between patients, and should not be based on an arbitrary length of time (e.g., 12 weeks), but rather on treatment goals being achieved to the mutual satisfaction of patient and therapist. On average, however, the acute phase of treatment lasts approximately 3–4 months. During this phase, sessions are once or, if needed, twice per week. Rather than abruptly terminating weekly sessions, we often recommend tapering to biweekly or monthly sessions in order to assess the stability of a patient's symptom remission and, critically, the patient's ability to independently and effectively integrate CBT skills into her life. When patient and therapist are confident that treatment is no longer needed, a final session is scheduled. In the collaborative spirit of CBT, it is important for therapists to inquire about their patient's perspective and feelings about treatment termination as it approaches. In particular, is the patient experiencing substantial anxiety, or perhaps some sadness or anger, at the prospect of terminating treatment? Are there NATs arising that may impede progress in the final sessions (e.g., I'm going to get depressed again; I'm not ready; He's tired of working with me)? These thoughts and feelings are not uncommon, and therapists should guide their patients in using their acquired cognitive skills to identify and to challenge any termination-related NATs.

Reassessing Treatment Goals

As discussed in Chapter 5, the initial treatment session typically involves a discussion of treatment goals to help guide the direction of therapy. Although the initial set of goals may be generated at the beginning of therapy, they are often refined as treatment progresses. It is helpful for therapists and patients to explicitly review progress on treatment goals, as well as any changes patients wish to make to the list. Therapists often include this as an agenda item at the halfway point in treatment, as well as when the final few sessions are approaching. For example, and related to the discussion below regarding addressing residual symptoms, patients may have experienced significant improvement in certain symptoms (e.g., depressed mood, anhedonia) or life domains (e.g., improved grades), but wish to turn increased attention to other lingering symptoms (e.g., insomnia, low self-esteem) or problems in their lives (e.g., lack of friends, conflict with parents). Revisiting treatment goals provides patients with an opportunity to refine existing goals and even introduce new treatment targets that are important to them. There are times when a patient may not be aware that raising new treatment goals is an option, and therefore, when working with adolescents, it is important to continually probe whether goals have shifted and/or changed. This provides the optimal chance to help a teenager maximize the therapeutic experience.

THERAPIST: [Following a discussion on progress made on initial treatment goals.] At this point in treatment I always like to check in to see if we should add or make changes to the goal list. [Hands patient list of goals.] What goals do you think we're missing on this list that are important to add?
PATIENT: I don't know. It looks pretty good, I guess.
THERAPIST: OK. But just for fun, let's imagine I could snap my fingers and all the goals you listed were achieved. What else would be you be struggling with? How else would you want your day-to-day life to be different?
PATIENT: I don't know. I would be feeling a lot better. But I guess I would still like to have more people to hang out with. I don't really know many people at my new school. I'd like to have some more friends and not stay home so much on the weekends.
THERAPIST: I think that's a great goal. How many new friends? Like one or two, or ten?
PATIENT: No, like one, maybe two, would be great, I guess.
THERAPIST: So should we call this goal: "Make one or two new friends?" We can get more specific in how to go about this next week.
PATIENT: Yeah. Sounds good.

Post-Treatment Goals

As treatment progresses and nears termination, it also is important to discuss post-treatment goals (see discussion of *long-term goals* in Chapter 5). As depression subsides, there are likely new goals patients wish to pursue going forward. These post-treatment goals may be interpersonal (e.g., make new friends, fight less with parents), intrapersonal (e.g., feel more confident, worry less), and/or academic (e.g., improve grades if they have slipped during the depressive episode). Irrespective of the domain, steering patients toward goals with intrinsic value may increase the likelihood that they dedicate the necessary motivation, structure, and direction to maximize change. Critically, this also may lower the risk of patients slipping back into maladaptive habits of behavior (e.g., withdrawal, isolation) and thinking (e.g., pessimism, self-criticism), which increase their risk of relapse. Similar to the process of generating treatment goals at the start of therapy, therapists should guide patients in refining overly abstract goals (e.g., I want to be better at school) into ones that are more concrete and measurable (e.g., I want to raise my average from a C to a B in the next year). Moreover, larger goals can be broken down into "mini-goals" or successive steps that gradually lead to the larger goal (e.g., weekly or daily goals for homework completion).

Post-Treatment Competency in CBT Skills

Although depression relapse rates are high, research indicates that CBT significantly reduces the risk of relapse relative to antidepressant medications (for reviews, see Bockting, Hollon, Jarrett, Kuyken, & Dobson, in press; Cuijpers et al., 2013). These findings raise the obvious question: *What accounts for the reduced risk of relapse following CBT?* One logical possibility is that, within competently delivered CBT, patients acquire a set of antidepressant skills that they carry into their daily lives. In short, the cognitive and behavioral skills encouraged in CBT may help reduce the risk of relapse. Indeed, research indicates that those patients who exhibit greater acquisition and regular use of CBT skills at the end of treatment are at a reduced risk of relapse following therapy (Strunk, DeRubeis, Chiu, & Alvarez, 2007). These findings suggest that the cognitive and behavioral skills delivered in CBT may help individuals cope more adaptively with the stressors they will inevitably experience in their day-to-day lives after they leave treatment. Stressors and negative life events are an inevitable part of life during the tumultuous adolescent years, and a growing body of research indicates that the emotion regulation and coping skills introduced in CBT help patients better cope with these stressors. Thus, therapists should pay careful attention to the extent to which patients internalize CBT skills and use them on a daily basis. Accordingly, we suggest therapists carefully review and assess their patients' comfort level with CBT skills. Some questions that therapists may want to consider are listed in Table 7.1.

Realistically, the goal is not for patients to gain mastery across the wide array of cognitive and behavioral skills discussed in this book. Some strategies will undoubtedly be more helpful than others for any given patient. It is important for therapists to gauge the usefulness of different strategies for their patients. As treatment nears termination, patients can be encouraged to review the notes they took in therapy, including their completed homework assignments, to summarize what they found most useful in treatment. Such a review also allows the therapist to provide his or her perspective on the most helpful skills for the patient. For example, a teen with a tendency to withdraw and isolate following interpersonal stressors may find behavioral activation to be the most helpful *go-to* strategy in times of stress. For this patient, a relapse prevention plan might include specific behavioral activation strategies (e.g., Go for a 40-minute run every other day. Play guitar for 30 minutes a day. Get out of house and see a friend

Table 7.1 Questions to Assess Relevant Cognitive Behavior Therapy Skills

Question	Relevant CBT skill
Is the patient able to identify his/her NATs as they arise, or shortly thereafter?	Identifying NATs
Is the patient adept at noticing the link between his/her NATs and negative emotions and behaviors?	Identifying association between thoughts, feelings, and behavior
Does the patient regularly evaluate the evidence for and against his/her NATs?	Evaluating validity of NATs (i.e., reality testing)
Is the patient adept at judging the usefulness of his/her NATs?	Evaluating the utility of NATs
Does the patient generate alternative, more balanced thoughts following the identification of NATs?	Generating realistic/healthy alternatives to NATs
Is the patient able to see his or her thoughts or problems from another person's perspective?	Perspective taking
Does the patient engage in activities that boost a sense of pleasure and mastery (even if s/he does not feel like it)?	Behavioral activation
Did the patient exhibit the ability to plan, practice, and engage in healthy behaviors?	Behavioral activation

at least twice a week), followed by other strategies (e.g., Nightly thought record for 15 minutes). For structure, we recommend therapists use the Personal Relapse Prevention Plan worksheet below to guide and summarize these discussions. The form allows patients to jot down notes on: (1) the cognitive, behavioral, and interpersonal skills they found most useful in treatment; (2) their most important goals for the upcoming year; (3) common depression triggers and warning signs; and (4) relapse prevention strategies to practice regularly.

Mental models for psychological treatment are often largely shaped by experiences with previous medical treatments. Headaches and other acute bodily pains are treated with pain relievers. Bacterial infections (e.g., strep throat, bronchitis, pneumonia) are treated with antibiotics. These treatments eliminate the pain or infection and, in most cases, no further treatment is required. Generally, this is the case for the treatment of common *acute* medical issues. However, depression is more akin to *chronic* (e.g., diabetes, asthma, migraines) rather than acute (e.g., headache, strep throat) medical problems. For chronic asthma, for example, patients not only use an inhaler for asthma attacks, but must also be vigilant in avoiding exposure to triggers – such as dust, smoke, and other allergens – that might cause flare-ups. Similarly, an important point for therapists to highlight

Personal Relapse Prevention Plan

1. The most helpful *behavioral* skills/ideas I've learned are:
   a. _____
   b. _____
   c. _____

2. The most helpful *cognitive* skills/ideas I've learned are:
   a. _____
   b. _____
   c. _____

3. The most helpful *interpersonal* skills/ideas I've learned are:
   a. _____
   b. _____
   c. _____

4. My most important goals for the next year are:
   a. _____
   b. _____
   c. _____

5. The events and situations that might trigger a relapse are:
   a. _____
   b. _____
   c. _____

6. The signs that signal that my mood is starting to slip are:
   a. _____
   b. _____
   c. _____

7. If I notice my mood starting to slip, I will help myself by:
   a. _____
   b. _____
   c. _____

8. What are the early-warning signs that I might be getting depressed again?
   a. _____
   b. _____
   c. _____

9. In order to reinforce my skills and prevent depression relapse, I'll do the following regularly:
   a. _____
   b. _____
   c. _____
   d. _____

is the need for patients to be vigilant about fluctuations in their symptoms and to *regularly* practice CBT skills, even in the absence of depressive symptoms. In particular, teens are encouraged to regularly engage those skills that they personally found most therapeutically beneficial over the course of treatment. Relapse prevention for depression is similar to the management of chronic medical issues. Like these chronic medical issues, depression can be effectively managed, and it is possible for teens to lead perfectly healthy, happy, and productive lives. To maintain wellness and reduce the risk of relapse it is critical that patients maintain a healthy lifestyle, including regularly practicing the skills they have learned in therapy.

In sum, relapse prevention work involves deciding what are the most useful set of skills for a particular patient, when these skills will be practiced (e.g., daily thought records, regularly scheduling activities to boost mood and sense of accomplishment), as well as planning for, and coping more adaptively with, anticipated depression triggers. With regard to skill acquisition, it is important for teens to become increasingly adept at personalizing their preferred CBT strategies and to utilize them across increasingly varied situations in their lives.

Anticipating and Addressing Depression Triggers

As discussed in Chapter 2, diathesis-stress models of depression posit that acute negative life events or stressors interact with existing vulnerability factors to trigger depressive episodes. Accordingly, cognitive behavioral therapists help patients anticipate and better cope with likely future stressors, which often begins with a careful review of the stressors that may have contributed to the onset and/or maintenance of previous depressive episodes. For example, a therapist can conduct a *play-by-play* chain analysis of the sequence of events, cognitions, behaviors, and emotions that triggered the most recent depressive episode, and then discuss with the patient how she might approach the stressor differently going forward (given the coping skills she found helpful in treatment). Further, the Personal Relapse Prevention Plan worksheet provides room for listing events and stressors that the patient anticipates may trigger a relapse in the future, as well as what coping strategies to potentially utilize when confronted with a given stressor.

During these discussions, a metaphor we frequently use with teens is that of *proactive* versus *reactive* driving. In contrast to reactive drivers, proactive drivers anticipate and take steps to prepare for possible obstacles ahead. In bad weather, for example, they may drive more slowly, be more vigilant for erratic drivers, or take an alternate route to avoid dangerous roads. Similarly, taking a proactive approach to one's depression involves anticipating and preparing for possible upcoming triggering events. For example, in an effort to create a buffer against stress, a teen may proactively schedule weekly activities that are known to boost his mood and surround himself with supportive friends. Of course, teens cannot realistically anticipate every stressor that may trigger a depressive event. However, the bottom line is that if we carefully consider the likely stressors in our environment, we will be better prepared to face potential negative emotional consequences.

In addition to anticipating and preparing for depression triggers, becoming attuned to *early-warning signs* that signal the possible onset of a new depressive episode is important for relapse prevention. Indeed, the Personal Relapse Prevention Plan worksheet differentiates between *depression triggers* and *early-warning signs*. The worksheet provides room for listing signs that signal that one's mood is starting to slip (e.g., increased tearfulness, decreased interest in socializing, sleep problems), as well as space for strategies to address these early signs and symptoms to *nip depression in the bud*. Over the course of therapy, in particular the early sessions in which previous depressive episodes are discussed in detail, therapists and patients may have gained an understanding of the early emotional, behavioral, cognitive, and interpersonal symptoms and signs that precede the full onset of a depressive episode. Data on early-warning signs of depression also can be gathered prospectively (e.g., daily tracking of selected symptoms) as a means to monitor depression risk.

Common early-warning signs and symptoms include decreased interest and pleasure in daily activities, spending more time in one's room (e.g., due to anhedonia or fatigue), tearfulness, irritability, insomnia, and rumination. Keeping a daily diary of key symptoms can help patients to track fluctuations in relevant domains that may signal that they are starting to slip. Following the identification of early-warning signs, and as also reflected on the Personal Relapse Prevention Plan, therapists and patients should brainstorm strategies to target these different signs and symptoms when they arise. Strategies can be organized into a hierarchy of approaches based on the severity of symptoms. For example, teens may decide to first implement their preferred behavioral or cognitive skills when they notice their mood begin to slip, and if they struggle in using these strategies they can reach out to their parents or school counselors, who can in turn schedule a session with a therapist if needed (see Booster Sessions section, below).

Addressing Residual Symptoms

It may come as no surprise that among the strongest predictors of depression recurrence is the presence of residual symptoms at post-treatment. One of the mechanisms through which residual symptoms may increase the risk of depression relapse is stress generation (Harkness et al., 2014). In other words, individuals who leave treatment with residual depressive symptoms are more likely to experience stressors that are at least partly dependent on their own behaviors or characteristics, which in turn may trigger increases in depressive symptoms. Reiterating our discussion in Chapter 3, these findings highlight the importance of therapists tracking – ideally on a session-by-session basis – their patients' depressive symptoms. Self-report depressive symptom measures, such as the relatively brief Beck Depression Inventory-II (BDI-II), can be used to track symptoms at each session (see Chapter 3). In addition to providing an assessment of overall depression severity, such measures allow therapists to gauge the presence of particular subsets of symptoms. It is important for therapists to have a sense of the specific residual symptoms that continue to linger as therapy progresses. For example, a teen may have experienced substantial reduction in overall levels of depression, including the cardinal symptoms of depressed mood and anhedonia, but little change in fatigue and insomnia. The therapist then can initiate a discussion regarding the patient's own experience with these remaining symptoms and then work collaboratively to identify factors that may sustain them as well as devise a plan to address them (e.g., via renewed focus on sleep hygiene).

Some residual depressive symptoms require heightened treatment focus due to their severity or relatively strong association with relapse. Anhedonia, for example, may be an especially important treatment target given that this symptom is a relatively strong predictor of subsequent increases in other symptoms (Bringmann, Lemmens, Huibers, Borsboom, & Tuerlinckx, 2014). Therapists can explore the cognitive (e.g., negative self-judgments, distraction), behavioral (e.g., avoidance), and other interfering symptoms (e.g., fatigue, poor concentration) that could possibly be contributing to residual anhedonia.

THERAPIST: So, looking over your depression scores for the week, it seems like you continue to be doing really well. You're at an 8 this week, which is similar to where you've been the last 3 weeks. As I mentioned, that's right in the normal range. But it looks like you're still struggling with a few symptoms.
PATIENT: I don't know. I'm feeling pretty good, I guess.
THERAPIST: You've made great progress. You experience very little sadness, but the last few weeks you mentioned that you're not really enjoying things. Can you say a little more about that?
PATIENT: I've had volleyball practice, or a game, pretty much every day the past week. I don't know. It's just "blah." I'm not into it.
THERAPIST: Gotcha. So you're kind of going through the motions, but not really enjoying it. When you're in a game or practice, what's different about your state of mind now compared to when you weren't depressed?
PATIENT: I'm just really not comfortable. I'm not in the game.

THERAPIST: What are you thinking about? It sounds like you're not focused on the next play or drill.
PATIENT: Ha! Definitely not! Coach told me to get my head out of the clouds on Tuesday. But I'm still playing OK.
THERAPIST: OK. So your coach may have noticed, too. Sounds like you're pretty distracted. What are you thinking about?
PATIENT: I'm just not confident any more. I'm thinking about the mechanics and not screwing up in front of everyone.

In the above example, the therapist guided the patient in exploring the nature and cause of her anhedonia. In the end, the patient revealed specific NATs related to fears of "screwing up" and being judged by her teammates, coach, and perhaps fans. These NATs were interfering with her ability to immerse herself in the practices and games. Without first clarifying exactly what the patient meant by endorsing, "I get very little pleasure from the things I used to enjoy" on the BDI-II, it would be near impossible to address the symptom. In our experience, it is not uncommon for teens to misinterpret and misreport symptoms. For example, and related to anhedonia, teens may endorse, "I can't get any pleasure from the things I used to enjoy," when in fact they do experience some pleasure. However, when completing the anhedonia item they are selectively focusing on activities or instances in which they derived little or no pleasure. Similarly, a teen may endorse high levels of fatigue or psychomotor retardation, when in fact she is referring to lack of interest. Thus, as we illustrate above, it is important for therapists to take the time to clarify what teens mean when they report struggling with specific symptoms and problems.

Other particularly concerning residual symptoms, such as persistent non-suicidal self-injury (NSSI) or suicidal ideation, require heightened attention from therapists. Therapists should explore the factors sustaining these symptoms and behaviors, which may be present even in the absence of clinically significant levels of depressive symptoms. For example, a chain analysis on the specific instances of NSSI may uncover that, despite an overall improvement in depressive symptoms, the patient continues to report surges in negative affect between sessions that trigger NSSI (e.g., cutting). This highlights that certain problematic behaviors and emotions (e.g., brief, yet distressing, spikes in negative affect) may not be adequately captured by weekly assessment measures. Second, certain maladaptive behaviors may persist long after the depression has abated, and thus, it is critical to unpack the situational antecedents that contribute to NSSI urges (and perhaps suicidality more generally). Overall, therapists should be vigilant for persistent symptoms and engage their patients in discussions regarding any remaining emotional, cognitive, behavioral, or interpersonal issues that they wish to target during their remaining time in treatment. Addressing these issues may make the difference between sustained remission and relapse.

Addressing Underlying Vulnerability Factors

Even patients who have experienced substantial symptom improvement and exhibit little or no residual depressive symptoms may be at risk of relapse due to underlying vulnerability factors. These factors likely contributed to the onset of the depressive episode for which they originally sought treatment. Vulnerability factors include cognitive (e.g., rumination, self-criticism, core beliefs), interpersonal (e.g., dependency, excessive reassurance seeking), and personality (e.g., neuroticism) vulnerability factors, as well as residual environmental stressors (e.g., significant problems at home or at school; Harkness et al., 2014). The vigilant CBT therapist will likely have identified relevant vulnerability factors in their case conceptualization. It is critical for therapists to identify and target these factors in treatment, and to examine the ways in which they may have contributed to the onset of previous depressive episodes, as well as the extent to which they continue to represent risk factors for future episodes.

In some cases, further or more specialized treatment will be indicated, as in the case of vulnerability factors linked to personality pathology (Beck, Davis, & Freeman, 2014). The presence of comorbid personality disorders in MDD is exceedingly common, estimated at approximately 45% in a recent meta-analysis (Friborg et al., 2014). Cluster C personality disorder diagnoses (i.e., avoidant, dependent, and obsessive-compulsive) and borderline personality disorder are the most commonly observed in depression. These findings suggest that approximately half of the adolescents walking into our clinics seeking depression treatment are likely suffering from a personality disorder or in the midst of developing one (i.e., exhibit some personality disorder traits). The implications for treatment are important, as personality pathology is associated with poor treatment prognosis in CBT (Fournier et al., 2008), as well as an increased risk of relapse (Grilo et al., 2010). Of course, given current *Diagnostic and statistical manual of mental disorders* (DSM-5) criteria (American Psychiatric Association, 2013), personality disorders are infrequently diagnosed prior to adulthood. Nevertheless, the maladaptive interpersonal, cognitive, behavioral, and emotional features that define personality pathology very often emerge during adolescence. Thus, given their strikingly high comorbidities with MDD, therapists should consider whether their patient's presenting problems (e.g., emotion regulation deficits, interpersonal struggles, avoidance behaviors) are temporary features of depressive episodes, or rather, reflect emerging personality pathology or traits. If it seems like the latter, specialized treatment may be indicated to treat the personality disorder; doing so may reduce the risk of depression relapse (see Beck et al., 2014; Miller, Rathus, & Linehan, 2006; Young, Klosko, & Weishaar, 2003).

Additional Treatment

Of course, the presence of budding personality pathology is not the only instance in which additional treatment is recommended. A patient may have completed 3–4 months of weekly CBT with little improvement in symptoms despite the therapist's and patient's best efforts. In discussion with the patient and parents, it may be decided to try an alternative treatment (e.g., antidepressant medications) or a combination of therapy and medications, which for some patients may lead to more rapid response and symptom remission than either treatment alone (Brent et al., 2011). In addition, as treatment progresses, the presence of other Axis I comorbidities may be revealed that require further treatment. For example, when depressive symptoms remit, it is not uncommon for anxiety symptoms (e.g., social anxiety) to emerge. For these situations, it will be important to shift treatment targets, and address these new presenting symptoms through additional psychotherapy. Moreover, some teens live in homes within which there is substantial interpersonal conflict and turmoil. A stressful home environment increases the risk of relapse, yet typically cannot be adequately addressed in individual CBT. In these cases, we discuss with the teen and parent(s) the possible benefits of seeking family therapy and provide a list of local treatment options.

In addition to stress at home, stress at school can interfere with treatment progress and increase the risk of relapse. Teens struggling with depression frequently experience problems at school and academic difficulties. As symptoms subside, teens may continue to experience school-related issues (e.g., school refusal, poor academic performance, bullying). In these instances, we typically work with the teen, the parents, and if appropriate, school administrators and guidance/counseling staff, to address the problem. Laws vary by state, but schools are typically required to provide accommodations for struggling teens. Overall, with any of the above issues, we recommend that therapists seek consultation with colleagues if they are unsure of the most appropriate approach, while, of course, protecting patient confidentiality.

Parental Depression

Untreated parental depression is a well-established risk factor for depression in youth (Perloe, Esposito-Smythers, Curby, & Renshaw, 2014). Having a depressed parent can interfere with a teen's treatment progress, and increase the risk of relapse following termination. Researchers have explored a wide array of factors that may account for why children of depressed parents are at high risk for developing depression themselves (e.g., genetic contributions, modeling the depressed parent's negative cognitions and maladaptive coping strategies, increased family conflict and stress). In addition to helping themselves, reducing parental depressive symptoms may have a direct and positive impact on their children's symptoms and psychosocial functioning. Indeed, the successful treatment of parental depression has been associated with improved mental health in children, as well as reduced marital and parenting-related distress (Cuijpers, Weitz, Karyotaki, Garber, & Andersson, 2015).

Discussing the importance of receiving treatment for their own depression can understandably be an anxiety-provoking and delicate topic to broach with a patient's parents. Therapists may have their own NATs that are triggering their anxiety about initiating such a conversation (e.g., Who am I to tell my patient's mother that she's depressed and needs help? What if she gets irritated with me or thinks I'm overstepping my bounds?). However, given the dual benefits of improving both parental and child mental health, we recommend that therapists discuss this issue – in private (i.e., without the patient present) – with parents, despite the discomfort they may feel about having such a conversation. Below we provide a sample dialogue between a therapist and parent.

THERAPIST: Mrs. Foster, thanks for speaking with me. I wanted to touch base with you about a few things, including Liz's progress in treatment. What's your perspective on how Liz is doing?
PARENT: I think she's really doing a lot better. But she still gets moody at times, and her temper can flare up.
THERAPIST: That's right. She's definitely doing quite a bit better than when she started 2 months ago. Her depressive symptoms have improved, but she still reports bouts of sadness and irritability a couple times a week. We'll continue to work on that. Anything else you think would be helpful?
PARENT: I think that's the main thing. Getting her feeling better and less moody.
THERAPIST: I know in our initial assessment you mentioned that depression runs in the family, and you've had some depression in the past.
PARENT: Um. Yes. On my side of the family, but not her dad's side.
THERAPIST: And I know you received treatment in the past.
PARENT: Yes, I was on antidepressant medications for a while but I didn't like how they made me feel, and so I eventually stopped.
THERAPIST: How are you feeling now?
PARENT: It's been really stressful lately. And, I've just wanted to focus on helping Liz deal with her problems.
THERAPIST: The reason I'm bringing this up is that many of the teens I work with have parents with a history of depression. And, interestingly,

I've learned that one of the best ways to maximize the teen's benefit in treatment and reduce the likelihood of significant symptoms returning is to ensure that her parents are getting the treatment they need for their depression.

PARENT: I'm just not sure I want to be on medications again.

THERAPIST: That's good to know. Would you be comfortable if we discussed other treatment options?

In the above exchange, the therapist provided some psychoeducation about the tendency for depression to run in families and the benefit that both parent and teen can derive from the parent seeking treatment for her depression. Understandably, parents who struggle with depression may be hesitant to raise their own depression as a topic for discussion. They may consider it inappropriate to discuss and irrelevant to their child's treatment. With limited resources available, they may reasonably assume that they should devote their time and money to their child's, rather than their own, treatment. Their decision may be driven by the belief, "I should sacrifice for the good of my child." Thus, it can be beneficial to discuss the growing body of research that highlights the therapeutic benefits that teens may enjoy when a parent is receiving effective treatment. Therefore, it is often helpful for therapists to have depression treatment resources available for parents to review (e.g., contact information for clinics that specialize in the treatment of adult depression).

Booster Sessions

Even following treatment termination, patients are encouraged to schedule *booster sessions* if they find themselves struggling to cope with life stressors or symptoms begin to re-emerge. As teens encounter stressors in their daily lives, they may find themselves slipping into dysfunctional behavioral patterns (e.g., avoidance) or experiencing elevated levels of negative emotions and accompanying NATs. A booster session typically involves a single therapy session in which patients can address recent struggles or spikes in their symptoms. Sessions also can be proactively scheduled around the time of anticipated stressors as a means to prevent relapse (Beck, 1995). For example, a formerly depressed teen in the midst of completing a successful course of CBT may anticipate that the start of the school year will be particularly challenging for him and could result in a spike in his depressive symptoms. Prior to treatment termination, the therapist and patient can schedule a booster session to take place either immediately prior to the start of the school year, or within the first week or two, to assess the patient's ability to independently utilize his CBT skills to manage school-related stressors.

During the booster session, the therapist and patient can conduct a chain analysis of a recent stressor, review what went well for the patient, as well as areas in which he struggled and which are in need of fine-tuning. The booster session can provide a helpful *tune-up* to refresh and refine the cognitive, behavioral, and interpersonal skills initially learned in treatment. Additional important booster session agenda topics include: (1) discussing anticipated triggers; (2) progress and roadblocks towards goals; (3) plans for practicing cognitive, behavioral, and interpersonal skills; and (4) reviewing and revising relapse prevention strategies. Booster sessions provide a useful middle ground between no treatment and beginning CBT sessions anew, and may serve as a very helpful tool to reduce the risk of relapse.

Mindfulness-Based Interventions for Relapse Prevention

The Mind's Default Setting

To define the concept of mindfulness, it is helpful to first describe the mind in its natural state. The human mind's default is to wander. Our minds are highly active and characterized by a near-constant stream of thoughts, including subtle judgments, commentary, plans, expectations, desires, fantasies, worries, and memories. These thoughts are often focused on the imagined future (e.g., planning, anticipating, worrying) or past (e.g., revisiting a recent conversation or event), rather than attending to the *here and now*. Within the Buddhist tradition, the term *monkey mind* has been used to describe the natural, restless state of our minds "swinging" from one thought to the next (Smith, 2007). Indeed, beginner meditators instructed to engage in a *mindfulness of the breath* exercise (see below) often report first noticing how active and easily distracted their minds are, and how challenging it is to keep their attention anchored to their breath. There is nothing inherently wrong with an occupied mind; in fact, we rely on it to organize and get through our busy days. However, mindfulness emphasizes the fact that our thinking is so often *unintentional* and occurs outside of our awareness. In an important sense, the mind, left to its own devices, has a mind of its own. It runs on autopilot unless we intentionally take over the controls.

Researchers have attempted to quantify the amount of time we spend mind wandering as opposed to attending to the here and now. In a large study that included over 2,000 participants, Harvard researchers found that we spend approximately *half* of our waking hours absorbed in mind wandering (Killingsworth & Gilbert, 2010).[10] Importantly, and consistent

---

10 To assess mind wandering, the study employed Ecological Momentary Assessment (EMA) involving smartphone alerts triggered at multiple time points throughout the day, which signaled participants to complete questions on their phone regarding their current thoughts and emotional state. For a detailed description of EMA, see Chapter 9.

with the Buddhist claim that a wandering mind comes at an emotional cost, participants reported lower levels of happiness during those times in which their mind was wandering. In fact, even when participants reported mind wandering to a pleasant topic, they were no happier than when their minds were focused on the present moment. Not surprisingly, mind wandering to negative topics was associated with the lowest mood.

What is Mindfulness?

The concept and practice of mindfulness have their roots in Buddhist and related contemplative traditions concerned with cultivating attention and awareness (Brown & Ryan, 2003). Mindfulness gained traction in the medical and psychiatric fields as a result of research indicating that stress reduction programs integrating mindfulness (in particular, Mindfulness-Based Stress Reduction: MBSR) were associated with significant improvements in physical and psychological distress (for reviews, see Goyal et al., 2014; Hofmann, Sawyer, Witt, & Oh, 2010; Khoury et al., 2013). One of the most commonly cited definitions of mindfulness was introduced by the father of MBSR, Jon Kabat-Zinn (1994): "Mindfulness means paying attention in a particular way: on purpose, in the present moment, and nonjudgmentally" (p. 3). In other words, mindfulness means intentionally turning the "spotlight" of attention towards whatever is occurring and most salient in the present moment, including any ongoing thoughts, feelings, and body sensations. For example, while eating a meal we may have a tendency to be absorbed in thought (e.g., related to work that needs to get done, upcoming appointments and plans, the TV show we are watching). In contrast, in a mindful state we might intentionally bring our attention to the moment-to-moment taste experience and notice the different flavors, textures, and aromas that arise. Similarly, when a negative emotion such as anxiety emerges, we may have a tendency to try and suppress the feeling, distract or reassure ourselves, or perhaps challenge the NAT underlying the negative emotion. In contrast, mindfulness would involve turning our attention to the salient bodily sensations (e.g., increased heart rate, knot in stomach, sweaty palms) and thoughts (e.g., Not again. I hate this feeling) that constitute our moment-to-moment experience of anxiety. The goal is not to change or escape these thoughts and feelings, but to observe them for what they are: *events in the mind* (and/or body) that arise and inevitably dissipate.

It is important to highlight that mindfulness involves more than simply directing attention to the present moment, but prescribes *how* we should pay attention. As noted in the above definition by Kabat-Zinn (1994), mindfulness involves paying attention non-judgmentally. Similarly, Bishop et al. (2004) operationalized mindfulness as consisting of two components: (1) the self-regulation of attention (i.e., towards the present moment) and (2) adopting an open and non-judgmental attitude towards internal experience. Shapiro, Carlson, Astin, and Freedman (2006) delineated three aspects to mindfulness: *intention, attention,* and *attitude* (i.e., a non-judgmental one). Specifically, the mind reflexively judges or evaluates internal experiences (i.e., thoughts, feelings, and bodily sensations) by automatically labeling them as good/bad, right/wrong, or like/dislike. Mindfulness training involves gradually learning to suspend such judgments and to approach internal experiences with an open and accepting attitude. Of course, being non-judgmental towards our internal experiences is easier said than done, especially when confronted with distressing emotions or thoughts. When judgments inevitably arise, we are encouraged to notice them as just another category of thought and thus "grist for the mindfulness mill" (i.e., another opportunity to practice mindful awareness). For example, when noticing an anxious feeling, we may automatically judge the internal experience (e.g., I hate this feeling). Through mindfulness, we are taught to mentally note this thought (There's judgment) and gently bring our attention back to the present. The same process of noting the thought can be applied to judgments that often come up while practicing mindfulness (e.g., This isn't going to help; This isn't for me).

To facilitate the development of a non-judgmental orientation, mindfulness encourages us to cultivate an attitude of curiosity towards whatever arises in the present moment and adopt a "beginner's mind," meaning observing whatever arises in our internal experience as if seeing it for the first time (Bishop et al., 2004).

Why Would Mindfulness be Beneficial for Depressed Teens?

Mindfulness training has been shown to significantly reduce depressive (as well as anxiety) symptoms in adolescents (Biegel, Brown, Shapiro, & Schubert, 2009) and adults (Goyal et al., 2014; Hofmann et al., 2010). What might account for the benefits of mindfulness for depressive symptoms? As discussed above, the mind, in its default state, has a tendency to drift through an ever-changing stream of thoughts. As highlighted in the cognitive model (see Chapter 2), the thought stream of depressed teens is not evenly distributed between positive and negative content. Rather, depressed teens have well-engrained habits of gravitating towards negative patterns of thinking. As they encounter stressful situations in their day-to-day lives, a cascade of NATs (e.g., self-criticism), negative emotions (e.g., sadness), and maladaptive behaviors (e.g., isolation) are often triggered, which in turn fuel more negative thinking and rumination. The depressed mind so often "hijacks" cognition in the face of a stressor and takes it down a habitual, well-worn path of repetitive negative thinking. Depressed individuals do not intend to have these negative thoughts; they just pop up automatically, and often occupy their minds for extended periods of time without them being aware of it.

Mindfulness training for depression is aimed at developing the attentional and cognitive control skills to more quickly notice and interrupt depressogenic cognitive processing.[11] Teens are trained to notice when their minds are fixated on repetitive negative thoughts (i.e., rumination), and to repeatedly bring their attention back to the here and now. The metacognitive process of directing one's attention to one's thought stream is hypothesized to (at least temporarily) interrupt ruminative thinking due to the fact that the former consumes limited cognitive resources that would otherwise be devoted to maintaining repetitive negative thinking (Segal, Williams & Teasdale, 2012). In addition, mindfulness training encourages depressed individuals to cultivate a curious and non-judgmental orientation towards their distressing thoughts and feelings. Individuals are taught to view their thoughts and feelings for what they are: fleeting events in the mind that that do not necessarily reflect reality or inherent aspects of themselves (Bishop et al., 2004).

Mindfulness Training for Depression Relapse Prevention

A variety of modern psychotherapies have incorporated mindfulness training into their therapeutic skill arsenal, including Acceptance and Commitment Therapy (ACT: Hayes, Strosahl, & Wilson, 1999), Dialectical Behavior Therapy (DBT: Miller et al., 2006) and Mindfulness-Based Cognitive Therapy (MBCT: Segal et al., 2012). MBCT deserves special attention given that it is specifically aimed at reducing the risk of depression relapse and integrates elements of CBT with mindfulness training. MBCT is delivered in a group format over the course of eight weekly sessions. The first four sessions of the program involve psychoeducation and experiential exercises that teach patients the extent to which their minds wander and drift toward negative thoughts, in turn triggering negative emotions. Patients are subsequently introduced to basic mindfulness exercises (e.g., attending to one's breathing and bodily sensations) aimed at gradually developing the attentional control skills to notice when their minds wander and to redirect their attention to the present moment. The second phase of MBCT (Sessions 4–8) focuses on teaching patients mindful, non-judgmental awareness of negative thoughts and feelings as they arise through within- and between-session mindfulness exercises. These exercises are intended to give patients the ability to recognize repetitive negative thoughts as they occur, ultimately providing them with the "space" to pause and select the most appropriate strategy to address their

---

11 In fact, Mindfulness-Based Cognitive Therapy was initially labeled Attentional Control Training (Segal, Williams, & Teasdale, 2012).

distress (e.g., just noticing the thoughts/emotions as they arise and dissipate, or taking specific problem-solving steps to resolve the stressor generating the negative thoughts/feelings). The final stages of MBCT incorporate some of the relapse prevention strategies discussed in this chapter (e.g., identifying depression warning signs, scheduling activities to increase pleasure and mastery).

As noted above, mindfulness has been shown to reduce current depressive symptoms. However, MBCT argues that mindfulness training may be most effective for the prevention of depression relapse, in particular for individuals with a history of more depressive episodes. Indeed, research indicates that MBCT may be most effective at reducing the risk of depression relapse among individuals with three or more previous depressive episodes (see Ma & Teasdale, 2004; Teasdale et al., 2000). These findings have been interpreted with reference to the *stress sensitization* theory of depression (see Chapter 2). Briefly, the theory posits that stressful environmental and/or physiological experiences (including depression) produce "memory traces" in the brain that prime the stress response system. Consequently, primed individuals have a lower threshold for stress necessary to trigger subsequent depressive episodes (Monroe & Harkness, 2005; Post, 1992). According to MBCT theory, even relatively mild stressors can reactivate old, habitual patterns of depressogenic information processing and negative thinking in these primed individuals. Once activated, these individuals get stuck in a self-perpetuating cycle of NATs and negative emotions. Mindfulness training is hypothesized to provide individuals with the attentional control skills to notice and to interrupt the early cascade of NATs and negative emotions, thereby "nipping depression in the bud" prior to the onset of a full-blown episode.

Mindfulness may offer additional benefits beyond providing formerly depressed teens with the ability to interrupt NATs and negative emotions. First, mindfulness weakens the association between negative emotions and maladaptive behaviors. For example, a teen who struggles with anger and lashing out may benefit from training in mindfulness to "widen the gap" between the impulse to lash out and the destructive behavior. A therapist can help teens notice the surge of bodily sensations (e.g., tensing of arms and shoulders, sensation of pressure or heat in the chest), emotions (e.g., correctly identifying and labeling the feeling), and NATs (e.g., "Why is she [mom] always trying to control me?") that constitute their experience of anger. Importantly, in addition to these body sensations, emotions, and thoughts the teen can learn to discern the rise (and inevitable fall) of a behavioral *impulse* to lash out verbally or physically. Mindful awareness of this impulse can introduce just enough "space" (e.g., a few critical seconds) to allow the teen to inhibit the destructive behavior (e.g., either through mindful awareness of the rise and fall of the impulse, or by allowing him/her the time to select and utilize other impulse control strategies learned in treatment). The therapist can gradually guide the patient in mindfulness of anger through in-session exercises (e.g., focusing on mild irritability arising when discussing a recent experience with anger), and between-session practice (e.g., mindful awareness of anger as it arises at school or home, beginning with situations eliciting mild irritability).

Second, mindfulness can serve as a grounding technique for instances of intense affect. For example, teens with intense bouts of anxiety can turn to an easily accessible "go-to" mindfulness exercise to bring their attention back to the present moment and defuse her anxiety. These exercises could include *seat/feet mindfulness* (i.e., bringing their attention to the nuanced sensations of their thighs and buttocks on their chair and of their feet on the ground), *walking meditation* (i.e., mindful awareness of the sensations of different parts of one's feet as one is walking) or a *mindfulness of the breath* exercise (see below). Third, given the tendency of depressed individuals to minimize or altogether fail to recognize positive events in their daily lives, mindfulness can be used as a strategy to help attend to and savor (even seemingly minor) daily positive events as they occur. An added benefit of engaging in mindful awareness of positive events is that the objects of mindfulness in these cases are emotionally non-threatening (e.g., a pleasant meal, conversation, or piece of music), yet provide another useful opportunity to practice attentional control and exercise one's mindfulness muscle. Last, some individuals report benefiting from practicing a brief (e.g., 2–5 minutes) mindfulness exercise in the morning to center themselves and set a more relaxed tone for the day, or in the evening prior to bed, to quiet the mind and improve sleep.

Strategies for Introducing Mindfulness to Depressed Adolescents

An extensive discussion of mindfulness-based interventions is beyond the scope of this book. However, below we suggest some strategies for integrating mindfulness into relapse prevention with teens (for more extensive discussions of mindfulness interventions, see Biegel, 2009; Segal et al., 2012). For clinicians considering integrating mindfulness into their clinical work with teens, we strongly suggest developing your own mindfulness practice. Background reading is helpful, but it only goes so far. First-hand experience yields a wealth of knowledge regarding the nuances of mindfulness that simply cannot be acquired through reading and thinking alone. As an analogy, elite sports coaches typically have extensive first-hand experience within the sport they coach. Mindfulness is a subtle and very challenging skill. Patients frequently raise questions and report struggling with their practice that are difficult for clinicians to adequately address without first-hand experience.

Psychoeducation via Experiential Learning

There are several goals in introducing mindfulness to depressed teens, including defining the construct, describing its benefits for managing negative thoughts and emotions, and developing the skill. Rather than introducing the concept and practice of mindfulness though didactic instruction, we find it most helpful to weave experiential mindfulness exercises with didactic psychoeducation. In brief, mindfulness is best grasped through practice.

Like other cognitive strategies to manage NATs and negative emotions, mindfulness is a skill or mental muscle that is only developed through regular practice. A useful way to introduce the concept and practice of mindfulness is through a *mindfulness of the breath* exercise (also known as *meditation on the breath*). Variants of this exercise have been practiced for centuries as a tool for developing mindful awareness. More specifically, a *mindfulness of the breath* exercise offers the opportunity for teens to: (1) notice how active their minds are and the tendency of their thoughts to drift and (2) practice awareness of the present moment. Breathing fortunately occurs in the present moment and thus, is always available as a tool to reorient and anchor the mind in the here and now.

Box 7.1 Mindfulness of the Breath Exercise

- Get yourself into a comfortable position in your chair, with your feet flat on the ground and back relatively straight.[12] Take a couple deep breaths, just to settle in: a deep breath in (*pause*) and breathe out (*pause*). And another breath in (*pause*), and out (pause). Now let yourself just breathe normally (*pause*).

- Now turn your attention to your breathing. Don't force it or try to change your breathing rate. Your body knows exactly what it's doing. Just notice the sensation of the in-breath and out-breath (*pause*). You might focus on the sensation of your stomach rising and falling as you inhale and exhale (*pause*), or, if you're breathing through your nose, the sensation of the breath passing through your nostrils, or the sensation of the breath brushing against your upper lip (*pause*). Just focus on one of these as you breathe in and out (*pause for 30 seconds*).

---

12 Some patients may feel more comfortable sitting cross-legged on the floor, or lying on their backs (provided they don't fall asleep), when practicing at home.

- You'll probably notice that your mind wanders away from the breath. Maybe your thoughts drifted to things you need to do later, or you had some thoughts about this exercise right now. This is completely natural. The mind has a mind of its own. Whenever you notice that your mind has drifted away from your breath, just note that your mind was "thinking" and gently bring your attention back to your breath. Let's do this for a couple minutes (*pause for 1–2 minutes*).
- Note: For adults, this exercise is commonly done for 10–15 minutes, or longer. With depressed teens, we suggest starting with a brief exercise (under 5 minutes) to introduce the concept of mindfulness. Therapists should use their best judgment regarding what length is appropriate for each of their adolescent patients.

Following the exercise, it is important to debrief and get patients' impression of their experience. Did they notice anything in particular during the exercise? Were they able to catch their mind wandering? Did they struggle to maintain their attention on their breath?

THERAPIST: So, I'm curious, what did you notice?

PATIENT: It was OK, I guess.

THERAPIST: I remember when I first did this exercise I thought it was kind of weird. What was your experience?

PATIENT: I found it hard. I didn't know what to do with my hands. And, I wasn't sure if I should shut my eyes.

THERAPIST: You're right. It is hard. What else did you find hard about it?

PATIENT: Well, I was trying to focus on my breathing like you said, but I kept thinking about stuff.

THERAPIST: Interesting. What kind of thoughts popped up? [Modeling curiosity.]

PATIENT: I kept thinking about soccer practice later, and homework I have to get done for tomorrow. Then I brought my mind back to my breathing, like you said. But it kept drifting. I must have done it like 20 times. It was frustrating.

THERAPIST: That's really common. The mind has a tendency to bounce around like that. Imagine what it's doing when you're not paying attention to it! So your mind drifted to thoughts of things you had to do later, like homework and soccer practice. But on top of these thoughts, the feeling of frustration popped up at some point.

PATIENT: Yeah.
THERAPIST: What was so frustrating about it?
PATIENT: I just couldn't keep my mind on my breathing. I kept thinking, "I can't do this."
THERAPIST: So one of the places your mind was bouncing to was the negative automatic thought, "I can't do this," which made you feel frustrated.
PATIENT: Yeah, I guess so.
THERAPIST: So in your day-to-day life, how often do you "check in" to see where your mind is at?
PATIENT: Um. I don't know. Not much. I just kind of go through my day, I guess.
THERAPIST: I wonder what you would notice if you checked where your mind was at during the day. You just said that you caught your mind drifting about 20 times, which included some NATs, and that was just over the course of a 3-minute exercise.
PATIENT: Kind of scary to think about it. Actually, when I was driving yesterday I caught myself thinking and stressing about all the things I had to get done when I got to school. I pulled into the school parking lot and I literally had no memory of driving the last few miles. It was crazy.
THERAPIST: Yep. That happens to me too sometimes. So it sounds like your mind does a lot of thinking and wandering around, even when you're not aware of it. And one of the places it drifts to is to thoughts that stress you out and make you upset.

The therapist in the above dialogue guided the patient in a reflection on her experience with the *mindfulness of the breath* exercise. The patient had the common experience of struggling to maintain her attention on the breath and noticing her mind wandering, occasionally to NATs. The goal of this exercise is not to stop the mind from wandering, but simply to observe and get an impression of the mind in its natural, restless state. Teens often misinterpret the purpose of this exercise as needing to "control" thoughts and stop them from drifting away from the breath. The mind will inevitably drift. The goal is to notice this tendency and for patients to be introduced to the practice of redirecting attention to the present moment.

Other Mindfulness Exercises

Although *mindfulness of the breath* may be the most commonly used exercise to introduce the concept and practice of mindfulness, other popular exercises include the *body scan meditation* and *walking meditation* (also known as *mindful walking*; see Segal et al., 2012). As opposed to attending to the breath, patients engaged in a *body scan meditation* are guided through a systematic exercise in which they attend to sensations throughout their body. This exercise can help teens develop awareness of subtle bodily sensations, which may aid them in noticing changes in their body as they experience negative emotions. In addition, some teens may prefer a walking, as opposed to a seated, meditation (e.g., if they tend to get very restless sitting). A *walking meditation* involves bringing mindful awareness to the changing sensations across one's feet while walking (ideally at a slow pace).

Whatever mindfulness exercise(s) patients prefer, it is important that they practice them regularly outside of therapy. Although challenging, we recommend assigning 10–15 minutes of daily mindfulness practice. Some patients like to record therapist-led in-session mindfulness exercises (e.g., *mindfulness of the breath*) on their smartphones and listen to them outside of therapy to guide their practice. After each mindfulness practice session, patients are encouraged to take notes on their experience during the exercise. Did they gain any insights into the nature of their wandering minds? Did any patterns emerge with regard to where their mind tends to drift? Do they notice that their attentional control skills are gradually improving over repeated mindfulness practice sessions (e.g., they are able to sustain their attention on the breath for longer periods of time, or are able to more quickly catch their minds drifting and reorient their attention to the breath)? Therapists and patients can then review these notes in subsequent sessions.

Using Metaphors to Introduce Mindfulness

Therapists can use a variety of different metaphors to help their patients get a better impression of what the mindfulness process is like (see Table 7.2 for suggestions of mindfulness metaphors).

Below we present a dialogue in which the therapist uses the metaphor of a movie theater to describe the process of mindfulness.

THERAPIST: When you're watching a movie, do you get absorbed in the story?
PATIENT: Yeah. I love movies.
THERAPIST: Me too. And part of what's so interesting about it is that, most of the time, we're not even aware that we're in a movie theater. We get totally absorbed in the drama on screen. The images and sounds suck us into the movie and influence our thoughts and emotions. We feel what the characters feel. If the main character is in a dangerous situation, you might feel anxious. If he/she loses a loved one, you may feel sad. At other times, you might feel angry, happy, excited, and so on. It looks and feels so real that most of the time

Table 7.2 Mindfulness Metaphors

Metaphor	The Mind is Like...	Mindfulness is like...
Monkey mind	...an (untrained) monkey "swinging" from thought to thought throughout the day	...taking a step back and observing the mind swinging from thought to thought
Movie theater	...an internal movie theater "projecting" thoughts/images. We get absorbed in the drama/plot (i.e., we are fully immersed in the thoughts and are often not even aware that they are occurring)	...recognizing that you are in a theater observing projections on a screen. Sometimes we can even become aware that the same movie (e.g., a sad or anxiety-provoking one) plays over and over
Train ride	...a train that grabs our thoughts and carries them away in a variety of directions. We hop aboard a "train of associations not knowing that we have hopped on, and certainly not knowing the destination" (Goldstein, 1994; pp. 59–60)	...recognizing that you are on a train of thoughts and intentionally hopping off
Sky	...a clear sky with many clouds (thoughts) passing by	...observing the clouds passing by. Sometimes we notice that the same dark, depressive clouds pass by over and over
River	...a river with a stream of leaves (thoughts) floating by	...stepping outside the stream and observing the flow of leaves (thoughts)

you're not aware of the fact that you're sitting in a dark room surrounded by 50–100 strangers. But what if you turned around and looked up at the projector in the back? You would see that the movie is nothing more than flickering beams of light (with an audio track), right?

PATIENT: I sat in the front row with my friends once and you could see all the little pixels on the screen. But we hurt our necks having to look straight up. We sat further back next time [laughs].

THERAPIST: I've done that too. And what you realize is that a movie is simply thousands of little pixels flickering on a screen. That's it. The mind is kind of like that. It's really just a fancy internal movie theater, but a really powerful one. We go about our day absorbed in thoughts, and we're not even aware that our mind is like that projector, creating a never-ending stream of thoughts that manipulate our emotions. Often the movie the mind projects is harmless. Other times, we get sucked into a drama that makes us feel anxious, depressed, or maybe angry. And just like turning around in the movie theater and watching the beams of light, mindfulness is the process of "taking a step back" and just watching the movie our mind is creating in that moment.

In the above dialogue, a movie theater serves as a metaphor for both the mind in its natural state, and the process of mindfulness. Like being absorbed in an engaging movie, the mind is incredibly active, drifting from thought to thought, and we are swept up in the process. Similar to recognizing that the movie one is watching is nothing more than a projection of beams of light and sound, mindfulness involves "stepping back" and observing our thought stream in the moment, as if from a third-person perspective. The movie metaphor can be extended further. For example, through CBT or mindfulness practice, patients may discover patterns in their NATs over time (e.g., the same thoughts revolving around the core theme, "I'm a failure"). The therapist can encourage the teen to mindfully note and categorize these NATs when they arise (There's that "I'm a failure" movie/script, again). Similar to the process of repeatedly rewatching the same drama and feeling less sad each time, patients often find that the more they practice catching the same thematically related NATs, the less emotionally charged they seem.

Mindfulness in Everyday Life

A critical point regarding mindfulness practice is that it should not be limited to formal, seated (or walking) meditations. Mindfulness can be practiced at almost any point of the day, regardless of what one is doing. The only requirement is turning one's attention to whatever is most salient in the present moment and to observe it in an open and non-judgmental way. For example, when walking, one can focus on whatever is most salient in the present moment, such as the sensation of one's feet on the ground or certain sounds in one's environment. Similarly, a teen can be encouraged to practice mindful listening of music by focusing on the most salient elements of a song (e.g., the singer's voice, the melody played by a particular instrument, or, for a more challenging exercise, focusing on the background percussion or bass track). Similarly, as in any mindfulness exercise, when the mind wanders (e.g., to memories the song triggers), the patient is encouraged to gently note these thoughts (e.g., Ah. There's a memory) and to redirect attention on to the music. The same can be done for almost any daily activity (e.g., washing dishes, eating, showering, brushing teeth), allowing teens a range of opportunities to train their mindfulness muscle on a daily basis.

Mindfulness of NATs and Negative Emotions

As adolescents begin to gain comfort in practicing mindfulness, their therapist might encourage them to attend to NATs and negative emotions in the same mindful manner. The above exercises are useful starting points as they allow teens to begin developing their mindfulness skills while focusing on emotionally non-threatening objects (i.e., the breath, the body, drifting thoughts). To be sure, mindfulness of distressing NATs and negative emotions is a challenging skill to develop. However, with regular practice, adolescents can gradually learn to engage their mindfulness muscle when NATs arise: that is, to observe their NATs as fleeting objects in the mind that do not necessarily reflect reality or who they really are. This process of practicing mindful awareness of ongoing NATs provides patients with experiential evidence of the core notion, shared within both CBT and mindfulness, that the "observing self" is separate from the thoughts being observed. In other words, through both CBT and mindfulness, depressed individuals learn to reframe NATs such as, "I'm a failure" to "I'm having the thought, I'm a failure."

It is worth highlighting the fact that this "distancing" or "decentering" process of viewing thoughts as "just thoughts" is a core element of both CBT and mindfulness. In his original CBT for depression manual, Beck, Rush et al. (1979) stated, "One of the central advantages of these [cognitive] techniques is that the patient learns to 'distance' himself from his thoughts; that is, he begins to view his thoughts as psychological events" rather than necessarily reflections of reality (p. 157). Similarly, in describing the benefits of practicing mindfulness, Kabat-Zinn (1990) stated:

> It is remarkable how liberating it feels to be able to see that your thoughts are just thoughts and that they are not "you" or "reality" . . . the simple act of recognizing your thoughts as thoughts can free you from the distorted reality they often create and allow for more clear-sightedness and a greater sense of manageability in your life.
>
> (pp. 69–70)

Another overarching similarity between CBT and mindfulness, and Buddhist philosophy more broadly, is that both traditions place cognition, in particular distorted perceptions of reality and the self, at the center of their models of emotional suffering. Of course, CBT and mindfulness ultimately prescribe different strategies to address these distorted thinking patterns. CBT uses distancing only as a means to set the stage for cognitive change techniques (i.e., one cannot challenge the validity of a thought without first recognizing it as just a thought). In contrast, mindfulness can be considered an elaborated form of distancing, wherein the goal, unlike CBT, is not to change the content of thoughts, but instead to change how one *relates* to one's thoughts (i.e., observing thoughts as objects in the mind, and from a non-judgmental and accepting perspective).

Thus, and as highlighted in the above two quotations, the experience of turning one's attention towards one's ongoing thought content and recognizing that thoughts are transient and subjective psychological events in the mind can be quite revelatory for some depressed teens. In Table 7.3 we summarize some of the other therapeutic insights that mindfulness can provide and that therapists can guide their patients in exploring through regular mindfulness practice.

Summary

Relapse rates are strikingly high in depression. In addition to reducing depressive symptoms related to the current depressive episode, a critical goal of treatment is to reduce the risk of subsequent relapse. A growing body of research indicates that a key benefit of CBT is its ability to reduce relapse rates in depression. Similarly, the integration

Table 7.3 Possible Insights Gained Through Mindfulness Practice

Insight	*Explanation*
Monkey mind	The mind is incredibly active, streaming with thoughts throughout the day. (For depressed individuals, the mind has a tendency to drift to negative thoughts, in particular following stressors)
Mind on autopilot	The mind is usually on autopilot, i.e., we do not *intend* to have the thoughts we have. They simply pop into our minds. Moreover, we are typically not even *aware* of what is going on in the mind. (However, through mindfulness we can observe and interrupt our thought stream, thereby "regaining the controls")
Transience/impermanence of thoughts	Thoughts and feelings are fleeting: they come and go
Thoughts are subjective, not objective.	Thoughts are simply events in the mind. They don't necessarily reflect reality or inherent aspects of self
Observing self	You are separate from your thoughts. You can observe them like objects from a third-person perspective

of mindfulness-based interventions into CBT, in particular MBCT, has shown promise as a strategy to reduce the risk of relapse. In this chapter, we have reviewed a variety of strategies therapists can select from to help patients develop antidepressant skills to carry into their day-to-day lives and to foster resilience against relapse. We also reviewed important issues to address as treatment nears termination. We hope that the approaches and techniques presented in this chapter will inspire readers to incorporate them into their relapse prevention efforts. It is important to highlight that patients will naturally gravitate more towards certain techniques. For example, mindfulness is a subtle and challenging skill, which for some patients may be unappealing and offer limited benefit. It is important for therapists and patients to work collaboratively to explore which interventions may be most appealing and ultimately therapeutically helpful for a given individual.

8 Therapeutic Challenges and Comprehensive Care

Delivering CBT to depressed adolescents presents therapeutic challenges, many of which are unique to this developmental period. In order to provide comprehensive care and maximize treatment effectiveness, therapists need to prepare for and navigate these challenges. Below, we present a non-exhaustive discussion of challenges that, in our experience, most commonly arise.

Family Involvement in Treatment

Family conflict and dysfunction are both causes and consequences of adolescent depression. Therefore, resolving family issues and creating a supportive environment for adolescents is an important factor in predicting long-term recovery from depression. Nevertheless, the tension between prioritizing adolescents' autonomy and channeling input from the family may feel akin to walking a tightrope. Below we discuss strategies for working with families, as well as guidelines for managing family involvement.

Setting and Managing Boundaries

As we describe in Chapter 4, boundary setting with parents and other family members begins at the initial meeting. Parents are given a rationale for why it is important that the majority of the session content be kept between the patient and therapist and are disabused of any expectation that the therapist will be *reporting back* to them (except in cases of clinical emergency). The vast majority of parents agree that this is best; however, supportive, well-intentioned parents and family members may nonetheless challenge boundaries throughout the course of therapy. For example, consider the following exchange from the end of a session.

PARENT: So, Dr. Auerbach, how did things go with Cassie today?
THERAPIST: I think that we had a productive session.

PARENT: Because she really had a tough day today. She had a lot of trouble at school and was crying on the way over. Did she talk about any of that in session?
THERAPIST: I'd be more comfortable if Cassie spoke with you about our session directly. Not only do I want to respect her privacy, but I also think it would be best if she shared her experiences in her own words. Does that sound OK?
PARENT: Sure. We usually talk about her sessions in the car, anyway.

While the exchange may seem rather benign and the adolescent may not be concerned with the therapist sharing non-specific session content, it is an opportunity to reinforce the principle that the patient's privacy is respected. This may go a long way to building trust and rapport with many adolescent patients who are often wary that their privacy will, in fact, be prioritized. Although much less common in our experience, some adolescents may request that therapists have *no contact* with their parents. This creates a complex therapeutic dynamic, especially if the patient is a minor. Therefore, it is recommended that clear guidelines are established prior to the first session among the therapist, patient, and parents, as there may be instances when it would be very appropriate to contact the family (e.g., scheduling, problematic behaviors) or times when it is clinically necessary to do so (e.g., suicidality, maltreatment).

Out of concern for their child, parents may contact therapists over phone or email with updates about a patient's symptoms and functioning. This is unquestionably useful information, but we recommend bringing these between-session updates back to the adolescent.

THERAPIST: I got an email from your mom about how your weekend went.
PATIENT: Yeah, she was really worried about me and was trying to get me up and out of bed.
THERAPIST: Yes, I got that sense from her email. I appreciated her perspective, but I really wanted to hear your side of things and see if it would be something to add to our agenda. How would you feel about discussing it today?
PATIENT: Yeah, I think that would be good. I wanted to mention it anyway.

This type of conversation reinforces the patient's autonomy and again underscores the notion that the therapist is primarily concerned about her unique perspective. In cases where the parent raises major issues, we recommend that the therapist propose a family meeting and involve the adolescent directly in the decision to do so (see below). Finally, when possible, therapists should consider fully transparent communication with parents. For example, a therapist might suggest that adolescents be copied on any and all email communication, and that any concerns or questions from parents be addressed in person with the adolescent present, before or after sessions, rather than over the phone.

Increasing Family Involvement

Sometimes situations arise where involvement of family members might facilitate or enhance interventions for adolescent patients. At these times, we've found it most helpful to work collaboratively with patients to explore potential pros and cons:

PATIENT: It would be great to plan more fun activities with my friends, but my parents don't let me go out when I want to, or can't drive me places.
THERAPIST: Hmm, that sounds like a tough situation. Would it be worth discussing this as a group? You, me, and your parents all together?
PATIENT: I dunno. I'd be worried that they would just say "no" anyway.
THERAPIST: That's definitely a possibility. Are there any advantages of bringing them in?
PATIENT: Well, they might understand. And with you there, they might see it's important.
THERAPIST: And if they understood and saw that it's important, what then?
PATIENT: They might drive me to friends' houses more often. I'd have more fun on the weekend.
THERAPIST: OK, that sounds good. Are there other things you worry about with asking them?
PATIENT: Just that I wouldn't be able to say things right.
THERAPIST: That's understandable. Would it be helpful for us to practice how to say it today?

Depending on the circumstances, the therapist can apply a range of cognitive and behavioral techniques to facilitate family involvement. Problem-solving and role-playing may help patients feel more confident about expressing their needs to family members. In some cases, adolescents may have NATs or negative intermediate beliefs about family involvement (e.g., It's pointless to ask for help; They never understand anyway). Here, therapists may use restructuring techniques to address these cognitions, or even to frame family involvement as a behavioral experiment to test out the patient's beliefs. Ultimately, though, therapists should avoid pushing family involvement; adolescents should feel as though they are behind the wheel of their therapy, and, in our experience, respecting the limits patients draw in regards to family will strengthen the therapeutic alliance.

When to Increase Family Engagement

A common indicator for increased family engagement is when the patient's symptoms are clearly rooted in, and best explained by, a central family issue. In these cases, early monitoring and conceptualization might reveal that moods and symptoms are yoked to family interactions. Individual CBT is unlikely to be effective until the family conflict is resolved. This might involve scheduling separate problem-solving sessions with the patient and parents, or even making an agreement to put an issue aside for a specified period of time and return to it once the adolescent's symptoms have remitted (Brent et al., 2011). Another reason to increase family involvement is when there are signs of a lack of engagement with treatment (e.g., frequent missed sessions or late arrivals). Adolescents often rely on their parents to get to sessions; thus, low parent commitment to treatment can interfere with successful interventions. In these instances, family meetings might focus on eliciting and addressing parents' beliefs about treatment (e.g., She needs medications because her problems are serious) or debunking general myths about CBT (e.g., Therapists just teach you to think happy thoughts). Although less common, there are times when improvements in the patient's functioning may have adverse consequences for the family. For example, an adolescent who becomes less socially withdrawn and more active may have less time to devote to caring for a parent with a medical problem. In these cases, family meetings geared to problem solving the consequences of the patient's positive changes and weighing the pros and cons are warranted. Finally, family involvement is central to managing suicidality, as we describe below.

When to Decrease Family Engagement

Family engagement is an important ingredient to effective treatment of adolescent MDD. However, there are specific circumstances wherein formally involving family in an extensive manner can impede progress. One important factor to consider is the characteristics and/or functioning of a specific family member or members. For instance, if a family member has abused, or is currently abusing, the patient, including the abuser creates a therapeutic environment that is unsafe for the patient, which compromises trust and rapport.[13] Another example is when a family member suffers from serious psychiatric and/or cognitive impairment, which also might create a situation where involvement comes with

---

13 In cases of ongoing abuse, duty-to-report protocols consistent with state and/or federal legislation should be followed and the appropriate documentation should be filed.

more costs than benefits. As we describe in Chapter 9, depression and related mental illnesses run in families, and therapists can affect positive change for both the adolescent patient and parent by discussing the issue directly and encouraging the parent to seek his or her own, independent treatment. The therapist should also consider broader family dynamics that impact the choice to involve family. There are some family systems wherein personal boundaries are very blurred, members are overly involved in one another's lives, and/or there is a great deal of implicit or explicit pressure to conform with the family. At milder levels, even very well-intentioned family members may infringe on their child's autonomy out of concern. In these cases, we recommend that therapists support adolescents' autonomy from their family by limiting family involvement; this may be crucial in eliciting these adolescents' personal feelings, challenges, and goals.

Cultural Considerations

The most recent American Psychological Association (APA) guidelines encourage practitioners to adopt a *culture-centered* approach with all patients. *Culture* is defined as, "the belief systems and value orientations that influence customs, norms, practices and social institutions" (American Psychological Association, 2003, p. 380), and the APA guidelines assume that all people have a cultural, racial, and ethnic heritage. Thus, culture is a broad term that subsumes a number of domains of diversity, including, but not limited to, race, ethnicity, socioeconomic status, religion, gender identity, and sexual orientation. Currently, there is a striking disparity between the population potentially seeking psychological services in the USA and the individuals providing these services. Specifically, the diversity (e.g., ethnicity, socioeconomic status) within the USA is substantial and expanding, while psychologists and other allied mental health practitioners remain, by and large, a culturally homogeneous group of primarily middle-class individuals of European American descent (see Pantalone, Iwamasa, & Martell, 2009 and American Psychological Association, 2003, for reviews).

Adopting a culture-centered approach with depressed adolescent patients is critical. First, automatic or implicit biases and stereotypic attitudes about people from an "out-group" (i.e., people who are different from oneself on any number of cultural factors) are very common. Given the over-representation of cultural majorities among therapists, individuals from racial and/or ethnic minorities are an out-group for most practitioners. Culture-centered therapists recognize this reality and strive to put strategies in place (some of which we describe below) to reduce the negative impact of implicit biases and attitudes on therapy. Second, research indicates that treatment access and efficacy may vary as a function of culture. For example, one large survey found that Mexican and African Americans diagnosed with MDD had lower odds of receiving any treatment than other ethnic groups surveyed (Gonzalez et al., 2010). Further, ethnic minorities receiving treatment for depression show slower improvement and poorer overall outcomes than non-ethnic minorities (Cooper et al., 2003). Using a culturally sensitive approach in CBT may increase patient engagement in therapy and therapeutic alliance, thus, potentially improving retention and overall outcomes.

Below, we list and discuss several general principles that may be helpful for practitioners working with culturally diverse youth. The intention is not to provide hard-and-fast guidelines to apply to specific minority groups. Instead, we hope that the non-exhaustive list can be flexibly adapted to work with youth from a variety of cultural backgrounds. Next, we briefly describe some ways in which cultural factors can color CBT interventions for depressed youth, and how practitioners might incorporate cultural factors into their CBT interventions.

General Principles

The principles below are presented in no particular order and are meant to be a helpful starting point for therapists working with culturally diverse depressed youth. For a more in-depth treatment of cultural diversity in CBT for youth, please refer to Ford-Paz and Iwamasa (2012) and/or the relevant APA guidelines (e.g., American Psychological Association, 2003, 2012).

Self-Evaluation

Codes of ethics for mental health practitioners often explicitly indicate that we have a responsibility to monitor our cultural biases and to eliminate their negative impact on our interventions (e.g., American Psychological Association, 2003). Everyone has biases and gaps in their understanding of cultural diversity, most of which are benign and simply reflect a naiveté stemming from a lack of exposure to minority groups. Nonetheless, such biases may contribute to ineffective treatment for cultural minorities (e.g., Cooper et al., 2003; Gonzalez et al., 2010; Van Ryn, 2002). Being a culturally competent practitioner is a career-long commitment to continuously reflecting on one's biases, working with people from diverse cultural backgrounds, and educating oneself on cultural differences. On a case-by-case basis, therapists also may find it helpful to reflect on the questions below to assess any relevant cultural biases prior to beginning their work with depressed adolescents.

1. What are my experiences (positive and negative) with people of this/these culture(s)?
2. What generalizations do I tend to make about people of this/these culture(s)?
3. How comfortable am I with asking this person about his or her culture(s)?
4. How comfortable am I with the practices and/or beliefs typically attributed to people of this/these culture(s)?
5. Do I diagnose certain psychiatric disorders more frequently in people from this/these culture(s)?
6. Am I more likely to attribute ambiguous symptoms to an underlying psychiatric condition for people from this/these cultures?
7. How much do I know about the potential cultural disadvantages (e.g., effects of stereotyping and prejudice) faced by people of this/these cultures living in my community?
8. How would I adapt treatment to suit the needs of a person from this/these culture(s)?
9. Would I be willing to adapt my therapeutic approach to be more sensitive to a person from this/these culture(s)?

Answering these questions can be uncomfortable. As mental health practitioners, there is a great deal of social desirability and pressure associated with being unbiased. However, burying one's head in the sand with respect to cultural biases and knowledge gaps has potential negative downstream effects on our adolescent patients, particular those from cultural minorities. Following an honest self-assessment, therapists can take steps to address identified biases, which may include seeking supervision from colleagues, making a referral to practitioners with more experience working with culturally diverse patients, and/or self-guided education (see below).

Self-Guided Education[14]

As practitioners, we are responsible for developing a reasonable knowledge base about the cultural groups to which our patients belong. Much of this

---

14 The American Psychological Association's (2003) guidelines on culture-centered practice include a relatively comprehensive list of references regarding psychological theories and information from a variety of cultures. The American Academy of Child and Adolescent Psychiatry has comparable published guidelines specific to pediatric populations (Pumariega et al., 2013). Other helpful places to start include Sue, Zane, Nagayama Hall, and Berger (2009), Hays (2008) and Ford-Paz and Iwamasa (2012). Further information is also available from the US Department of Health and Human Services Office of Minority Health (http://minorityhealth.hhs.gov).

knowledge can be accrued by consulting relevant books and published articles (scientific, popular press) and by familiarizing ourselves with relevant practice guidelines (see note 14 for a list of helpful resources). Longer-term approaches like attending continuing education workshops on cultural diversity, travel, and becoming involved in cultural activities in our community can also help practitioners build greater cultural competence.

Two important points bear highlighting in regard to education about patients' culture(s). First, practitioners should not seek basic education about an adolescent's culture from the patient. On the surface, relying on the patient for this information seems to fit the spirit of collaborative empiricism in that the patients provide expertise on their own experience. However, the process of educating people about the basic characteristics of one's cultural group(s) can be a source of stress for some cultural minorities (Meyer, 2003). Furthermore, having to inform a therapist about one's culture might be profoundly uncomfortable for many teens, might damage the alliance, and lead to thoughts like, "My therapist will never really understand me." Second, general knowledge regarding the cultural group(s) to which an adolescent belongs is not a substitute for a deeper understanding of the patient's experience within that cultural group. Put another way, practitioners should ensure that they do not use newly acquired knowledge of a particular cultural group to inadvertently stereotype adolescent patients. Thus, we encourage therapists to both amass a general background about the patient's culture(s) and conduct a more fine-grained, idiographic assessment of her life within the relevant cultural context(s) (see below).

Direct Assessment of Cultural Factors

At this point, we hope that it is clear that patients' cultural diversity is important to consider in CBT for depressed adolescents. However, asking adolescents direct questions about cultural diversity can make practitioners feel anxious and uncomfortable. These feelings may even be accompanied by NATs like, "I will come off as racist or bigoted," "They will be very uncomfortable," "They will notice *my* discomfort," and/or "It's not my business to ask about this." These types of concerns contribute to the fact that most practitioners rarely initiate a frank discussion of cultural diversity with adolescent patients unless it is directly related to the client's presenting issue (Harper & Iwamasa, 2000). This practice is costly. Although unintended, not asking adolescent patients about their cultural identities can send a message that the therapist is uncomfortable, uninterested, and/or unwilling to discuss the patient's minority status in therapy. Furthermore, patients might develop the impression that the therapist does not value their culture, which could further reinforce the discrimination and prejudice that the patient may already be experiencing. To assist

168 *Therapeutic Challenges and Comprehensive Care*

with this process, we present examples of non-ideal approaches to asking about cultural factors, followed by dialogues assessing the same factors in a more effective manner.

Box 8.1 Example dialogues illustrating different approaches to culture

Ineffective Approach

THERAPIST: Where are you originally from?
PATIENT: Uh, I grew up in Somerville, just outside of Boston.
THERAPIST: I mean, where are your parents originally from, or your ancestors?
PATIENT: Oh [pausing]. Well my grandparents lived in Pakistan before they moved to the USA.

Effective Approach

THERAPIST: What are the aspects of your race or ethnicity that are important for me to know as we work together?
PATIENT: Well, my dad's side of the family is Pakistani. My mom's great-great-grandparents were originally from Ireland but her family has been living in the USA for a long time. My mom wanted me to be raised Catholic, so we go to church and everything.

Ineffective Approach

THERAPIST: When it comes to your sexual orientation, do you identify as heterosexual or homosexual?
PATIENT: Umm, I'm not really sure.
THERAPIST: That's OK. It's quite common to be unsure in adolescence.

Effective Approach

THERAPIST: How would you describe your sexual orientation?
PATIENT: [Pauses and blushes.] I like people of all different genders; I think of myself as pansexual.
THERAPIST: What is it like identifying as pansexual in the context of your school life?

In the first example above, the therapist was able to gather a much richer understanding of the patient's culture using a direct, open approach compared to the tentative, indirect line of questioning. In the second example, the overly narrow approach imposed a binary categorization of sexual orientation on to the adolescent that did not resonate with the person's experience and may have created an empathic break between the therapist and the patient.

As we highlighted above, culture is a broad term that includes a number of domains across which our patients may differ. With this in mind, what cultures should be assessed? Even if time is restricted, we recommend striving to at least briefly query multiple domains of cultural diversity. To this end, Hays (2008) provides a useful acronym (ADDRESSING) that lists areas to consider when assessing culture with adolescent patients:

A – Age and generation

D – Developmental and

D – acquired Disabilities

R – Religion or spiritual orientation

E – Ethnicity

S – Social status

S – Sexual orientation

I – Indigenous heritage

N – National origin

G – Gender

In sum, we encourage therapists to assess adolescents' culture in a direct, open-ended manner that allows them to express the cultural categories and/or identities that fit best for them. Thoroughly and systematically discussing cultural factors *right out of the gate* makes it far easier to query the effect that cultural context may have on patients' thoughts, feelings, and behaviors.

Attend to Heterogeneity within Cultural Groups

Understanding individual differences *within* specific cultural groups is equally important as developing knowledge of between-group differences. Adolescent patients vary substantially in the degree to which they identify with their culture. For some, a cultural factor like ethnicity is the primary lens through which they view themselves while, for others, the same cultural factor could be secondary to other components of identity (e.g., soccer player; movie lover). Below is an example of how a therapist might explore cultural identification.

THERAPIST: What are the aspects of your race or ethnicity that are important for me to know as we work together?
PATIENT: I am a Mexican American. My parents were both born in Mexico, but I was born here.
THERAPIST: What parts of being Mexican American do you most identify with?
PATIENT: I really like how our family is a lot closer than a lot of kids I know. Like, I know a lot about my grandparents and all my aunts and uncles. We all talk a lot and support each other.
THERAPIST: It sounds like you really appreciate your close family ties. Are there parts of your Mexican American culture that you don't identify with as much?
PATIENT: Yeah. My mom really gives into my dad, to the point where it is kind of embarrassing if we are out in public. It's more normal in Mexico. I just wish it weren't so.

In the dialogue above, the patient discusses her different identification with traditional Latino values of *familismo* (i.e., the ideal of family as a major source of identity, support, and protection) and *marianismo* (i.e., the ideal that women should be emotional and kind, and also docile, unassertive, and generally submissive to men). By asking an open-ended question about the patient's experience in relation to her culture, the therapist learned about sources of potential stress (e.g., feeling embarrassed in public) that may be relevant to her depressive symptoms.

Contextual factors also have a strong impact on how much adolescents may emphasize or identify with particular aspects of their culture. For example, the patient from the dialogue above may emphasize her Mexican American culture most strongly when interacting with family, but not express the same values and attitudes with her friends at school. Instead, other aspects of her identity (e.g., editor of the school newspaper) might predominate in these contexts. It also is worth noting that the interaction between two or more cultural factors may compound some of the difficulties that adolescents from cultural minorities face. Working with adolescents to conceptualize the connection between their expressions of their cultural identity and their life contexts is critical for two reasons. First, expressing an appreciation for the variable role that cultural identity may play in an adolescent's life may strengthen therapeutic alliance, particularly with cultural-minority adolescents. Second, identifying situations wherein adolescents feel they need to censor or betray their cultural identity may be central to understanding the manifestation of depressive symptoms.

Incorporating Culture into CBT Interventions

A principal advantage of thoroughly assessing cultural factors is the opportunity to enrich conceptualization and treatment by incorporating these factors. Below, we describe ways in which cultural factors may influence therapeutic process and interventions, and how these factors can be harnessed to maximize outcomes for minority adolescents.

Communication and Therapeutic Process

The majority of therapists who have grown up and trained in North America are accustomed to a certain style of communicating. For instance, we show interest by looking our patients in the eyes, nodding, smiling, and leaning forward. The focus of our sessions is typically client-centered; we ask questions directed at eliciting the client's experience and expect to stay with the client's experience for the majority of our working time. Many of us are explicitly taught to avoid sharing our own experiences with our clients, or to do so in very small, appropriate doses.

However, customary styles of communication vary across cultures and may be substantially different than the North American blueprint. For example, Japanese adolescent patients may be accustomed to very structured, hierarchical environments in which obedience to parents, higher-status individuals (e.g., teachers, doctors), and even older children (called *sempai*) is highly valued. Thus, adolescents from this culture may expect to receive direct advice from the authority figure (i.e., the therapist) and then make the recommended changes. For Japanese adolescents, pleasing one's therapist may be viewed as paying the respect they feel the position deserves and focusing on themselves may be thought of as selfish or a sign of disrespect. In these situations, it can be tempting for therapists to abandon a Socratic approach and fall into a trap of being overly didactic. Although this may seem like one is meeting the patient's needs (i.e., giving them the direct advice they expect), this obviously comes at the expense of delivering effective CBT. Instead of departing from the spirit of CBT (i.e., Socratic questioning and collaborative empiricism), therapists may need to change more subtle aspects of their approach to effectively navigate cultural differences in communication. For example, when working with adolescents with strong collectivist cultural identities, it may be necessary to model disclosing personal information before expecting the patient to do the same, and to place more emphasis on non-verbal and other forms of indirect communication (see Tseng & Streltzer, 2008, for examples of communication styles across several cultures).

Case Conceptualization

As Kuyken and colleagues (2009) describe, incorporating cultural factors into collaborative case conceptualizions can substantially strengthen this process. Indeed, the lens of patients' culture(s) may pervade each major element of the cognitive case conceptualization. For instance, stressors associated with immigration, like living apart from family members for extended periods of time, or parental unemployment due to language barriers, may act as important *predisposing* factors among cultural-minority youth. Relatedly, adolescents from cultural minorities may experience *minority stress* (i.e., the excess stress to which individuals are exposed by virtue of their minority position), which includes oppression in its various of forms (e.g., antisemitism, heterosexism). Sadly, being victimized by peers and adults on the basis of one's cultural identity is a common experience for minority youth beginning at a young age. For example, studies of lesbian, gay, and bisexual youth indicate that approximately 70% (Saewyc et al., 2007) experience discrimination at school and victimization tends to happen across multiple contexts (e.g., schools, places of worship, malls, online; Mishna, Newman, Daley, & Solomon, 2009). Minority stress is very common and may act as a central *precipitating* factor for youth from cultural-minority groups.

Along with conceptualizing how cultural factors contribute to the development of depression in youth, it is critical to consider culturally based strengths. Asking about resilience stemming from cultural identity sends the message that the therapist does not expect minority status to *only* be an impediment to the patient. An adolescent's culture(s) can act as strengths or resilience factors in tangible, instrumental ways. For instance, collectivist cultures (e.g., many Asian and South American cultures) value affiliation more than individualist cultures, which may translate into adolescents receiving more support from nuclear and extended family, as well as from their broader cultural community. Cultural strengths also may exist in the form of culture-specific beliefs. For example, consider a 17-year-old depressed Hispanic adolescent who was frequently tormented by peers for spending a great deal of time helping his mother and embracing her publicly. In response to this bullying, he felt frustrated and sad. He found it useful to frame his experience in the context of the ideal of *machismo* (i.e., a strong sense of masculine pride associated with protecting and caring for one's family) and challenged his NATs with the reframe, "In my culture, it is manly and strong to take care of your family." Capitalizing on cultural strengths like the above can be a critical treatment step, particularly for adolescents experiencing pronounced discrimination.

Cognitive Restructuring

We have discussed how culture is an important lens through which depressed adolescents view events and experiences. When cultural identity is explicitly assessed in therapy, practitioners can later query important aspects of the patient's culture to identify and challenge relevant NATs. In some cases, asking follow-up questions about a teen's culture can operate in a fashion similar to the *downward-arrow technique* (see Chapter 6). Specifically, after a patient identifies surface-level cognitions, the therapist might say, "Earlier in our sessions, you discussed certain cultures that you identify with and view as very important in your life. I'm wondering if any of these cultures affected your thinking, emotions, or reactions in this situation?" In our experience, there are times when an adolescent's cultural identity shapes intermediate beliefs and schemas. Thus, explicitly discussing cultural context during cognitive restructuring presents a unique opportunity for adolescents to enrich their understanding of their present problems.

Adolescents from cultural minorities also may have NATs and/or intermediate beliefs directly related to their minority status. Given the centrality of cultural identity in many adolescents' lives, negative cognitions and/or ambivalence about this identity can be immensely distressing and may perpetuate depressive symptoms. For example, many sexual-minority adolescents (e.g., gay, lesbian, transgendered, queer) are bombarded with negative messages regarding their sexual identity from a young age, and these may be internalized, contributing to worry, low self-esteem, and self-denigration. These adolescents may have thoughts such as, "I'm disgusting," "Something is wrong with me," or "People will reject me if they know I am gay." These thoughts and beliefs may be deeply ingrained and reinforced by current experiences and contexts (e.g., victimization and discrimination at school). Nonetheless, applying cognitive restructuring techniques directly to these thoughts and beliefs may drive cognitive change that is essential to the remission of depressive symptoms and general improvement in self-worth.

Involving the Family

Earlier in this chapter, we highlighted the importance of family involvement in CBT for adolescent depression regardless of cultural identity. It also is important to note that "family" (broadly defined as nuclear and extended biological family, as well as close family friends in some cases) may play a much stronger role for adolescents from certain cultural minorities. In general, people from collectivist cultures view the needs of the collective (i.e., the "family," broadly defined) as superseding their individual needs. Thus, "extended family involvement may be the only acceptable model of addressing emotional and mental health" (Pumariega et al., 2013, p. 1108) for many adolescents from these cultures. Where adolescent clients view family members as a source of support, rather than stress, therapists are encouraged to involve extended family members as much as possible in all stages of therapy, from assessment and conceptualization through termination and relapse prevention. Indeed, research on CBT for both Puerto Rican (Rossello & Bernal, 1999) and African American (Sweeney, Robins, Ruberu, & Jones, 2005) youth indicates that involving family members in a culturally sensitive manner improves treatment engagement and effectiveness.

Increased family involvement also offers an opportunity for adolescents to work directly with family members on culturally bound issues. For instance, acculturation (i.e., the process of adopting social traits from another culture) often creates tension in culturally diverse families. Minority adolescents may experience significant pressure from two opposing forces. On the one hand, they feel pressure to *fit in* with the mainstream culture from friends, at school or even from media, while on the other hand, the more traditional cultural environment at home (e.g., parents, extended family, community) may exert pressure or even punishment for straying from cultural ideals and values. This tension can be further compounded by the fact that children and adolescents tend to acculturate more seamlessly and rapidly than their parents, which can create discrepant values and, ultimately, intergenerational conflict and stress at home (Pumariega et al., 2013). Recognizing this, family involvement in CBT for depressed adolescents provides a forum for communication about acculturation issues, which may reduce misunderstandings and tensions. The ultimate goal is to assist adolescents and their family in converting the family environment from a source of psychological stress back to a source of support and strength.

Summary

Attending to cultural diversity is critical in CBT with depressed adolescents, as doing so effectively increases patient engagement, strengthens the therapeutic alliance, and improves treatment outcomes. Above, we have provided some information regarding specific issues and considerations for work with culturally diverse adolescents, and shared some approaches that we find helpful. Comprehensive coverage of this important topic, however, was not possible in the context of this book, and we strongly encourage practitioners to consult the resources we have cited within this section for their work with culturally diverse patients.

Sleep

Sleep problems, particularly insomnia, are highly comorbid with MDD among youth; approximately three out of every four depressed adolescents also has sleep disturbances. Sleep difficulties are associated with increased symptom severity and poorer treatment response among depressed patients, and they are among the most common residual symptoms following treatment (see Clarke & Harvey, 2012, for a review). Critically, sleep disturbance also is a robust risk factor for future suicidality among adolescents (Goldstein, Bridge, & Brent, 2008). Fortunately, efficacious treatments targeting insomnia and other sleep problems have been developed. CBT for insomnia (CBT-I) is the gold-standard for treating primary sleep difficulties and produces response in 70–80% of insomnia patients, while approximately 40% achieve full remission of their symptoms (Morin, 2010). Among adults with MDD, adding CBT-I to antidepressant medication (ADM) monotherapy leads to improved remission of depressive symptoms relative to ADM alone (Manber et al., 2008).

For depressed youth presenting with pronounced sleep symptoms, it may therefore be beneficial to add elements borrowed from CBT-I to enhance a typical course of CBT. Below, we highlight some helpful psychoeducation, behavioral, and cognitive techniques from CBT-I that could be used to augment the interventions we describe in Chapters 3–7. For a more detailed description of the elements of CBT-I, please see Hood, Rogojanski, and Moss (2014), Clarke and Harvey (2012), and/or Bootzin and Stevens (2005).

Psychoeducation

The psychoeducation component of CBT-I focuses on *sleep hygiene*, defined as a set of practices that are conducive to healthy sleep patterns. Commonly discussed sleep hygiene practices are listed in Table 8.1, and a rationale is provided for each. In the context of CBT for depression, therapists may provide adolescents with relevant sleep hygiene information, and then collaboratively plan changes to carry out between sessions. Therapist and patient may frame larger-scale changes (e.g., establishing more regular daily routines) in a behavioral experiment format (see Chapter 6) and test out whether these changes have beneficial effects on sleep and daytime wakefulness.

Behavioral Interventions

Treatments for sleep problems typically include both *stimulus control* and *sleep restriction* interventions. Stimulus control focuses on re-establishing a strong association between a patient's bedroom/bed and sleepiness, and extinguishing any associations between the sleep environment and wakeful activities (e.g., videogames, television, homework). Essentially, the patient's bed and bedroom become strong cues to fall asleep. Consequently, the following behavioral changes could be implemented with a depressed adolescent: (1) Only engage in non-sleep activities away from the sleep environment; (2) Wake up and get out of bed at similar times each day (including weekends); (3) Lie down in bed only when

Table 8.1 Summary of Potential Sleep Hygiene Interventions for Cognitive Behavior Therapy with Depressed Adolescents

Category	Intervention	Rationale
Diet	Reduce caffeine intake	Caffeine extends wakefulness, increases the length of time it takes to fall asleep, and reduces the amount of deep sleep
	Reduce alcohol use	Alcohol can worsen sleep quality, particularly in large quantities. As alcohol is metabolized, it results in sympathetic arousal and accompanying somatic symptoms (e.g., sweating, headaches)
	Reduce nicotine use	Nicotine is a stimulant that causes wakefulness and reduces the percentage of time spent in deep sleep
	Small snack before bedtime	Hunger can disrupt sleep, but eating a large amount before sleep can also increase wakefulness. A small amount of a tryptophan-containing food (e.g., yogurt, turkey) can increase sleepiness
Daily lifestyle	Establish regular daily routines	Establishing a set regimen of daily activities (e.g., consistent meal times) may improve sleep by calibrating circadian rhythms
	Increase exercise	Exercise helps regulate circadian rhythms, is associated with greater deep sleep, and may reduce sleepiness during the day
	Reduce or eliminate naps	Sleeping during the day, especially in the afternoon, increases wakefulness and disrupts nighttime sleepiness
Nighttime behaviors	Create quiet, dark comfortable sleep environment	Create an environment where sleep is unlikely to be disrupted by external factors (e.g., street/house noise; room temperature)
	Eliminate "screen time" 1 hour before bed	The blue light emitted from computer, tablet, and smartphone screens increases wakefulness
	Reduce stimulating activities 1 hour before bed	High-energy (e.g., exercise) and/or engaging activities (e.g., homework, phone conversations) may increase wakefulness and prevent one's mind from "shutting off" (i.e., increase worry/rumination)
	Establish and follow a "bedtime routine"	Engaging in the same activities each night can "train" your body to "expect" sleep under certain conditions. Activities are paired with sleepiness through classical conditioning

feeling sleepy and ready to sleep; and (4) Restrict time awake in bed to 20 minutes or less; get up if sleep is not coming, engage in a low-energy and/or boring activity (e.g., read a dictionary) and return to bed when sleepy. Many of these interventions can be seamlessly incorporated into behavioral interventions for depressive symptoms (i.e., activity monitoring and scheduling; see Chapter 5). The goal of sleep restriction is to match the time the patient sleeps each night as closely as possible to the presumed sleep requirement. To accomplish this, therapist and client monitor weekly sleep duration and quality and determine the adolescent's average sleep time. The patient and therapist gradually work towards a regular daily sleep–wake schedule that maps on to the patient's average total sleep time. Typically, patient and therapist set an initial bedtime and wake-time goal. This is then adjusted up or down by 15-minute increments based on documented sleep quality, duration, and daytime wakefulness/energy, until an ideal sleep and wake time are established.

Cognitive models of insomnia propose that pre-sleep worry and rumination play a central role in sleep disturbances, as they contribute to heightened physiological arousal. Thus, CBT-I protocols sometimes include scheduling *worry time* several hours before bed (e.g., in the mid-afternoon). This is a planned opportunity for adolescents to write down and process their worries; adolescent patients are encouraged to save their worries for worry time, which may build a feeling of control over these worries. Other patients may simply benefit from having a notebook at their bedside that they may use to write down worries that arise pre-sleep. Finally, some CBT-I packages include formal relaxation strategies like progressive muscle relaxation and diaphragmatic breathing to reduce physiological arousal that may disrupt sleep. Where needed, therapists working with depressed adolescents may incorporate regular relaxation practice, both as homework and in session. Creating a regular relaxation routine makes these skills more accessible and likely to be effective for adolescents trying to fall asleep.

Cognitive Interventions

The cognitive model of insomnia (Harvey, 2002) proposes that chronic sleep disturbances are rooted in intrusive cognitions, worry, and rumination that occur prior to falling asleep. This "excessive negatively toned cognitive activity" (Harvey, 2002, p. 871) contributes to anxiety and sympathetic arousal, as well as selective attention to internal and external cues that threaten sleep (e.g., monitoring muscle tension or heart rate; checking the clock). Upon waking, the model proposes that individuals suffering from insomnia overestimate: (1) how poorly they slept and (2) the impact of the perceived sleep deficit on daytime functioning. Critically, similar to the cognitive model of depression (Beck, 1976), pre-sleep negative cognitions are a product of adolescents' distorted beliefs about sleep (e.g., I need at least 8 hours of sleep to function) and/or the benefits of worry (Worrying is the only way I will be ready and organized for tomorrow). Beliefs about sleep and worry are proposed to maintain and exacerbate sleep disturbances over time (Harvey, 2002).

Given the model above, cognitive interventions for sleep disturbances can begin by identifying and challenging NATs that adolescent patients may have about sleep, both during the day and in the pre-sleep period (e.g., I'm so stressed, there's no way I'll get to sleep tonight) using thought records. CBT-I protocols for adolescents (Clarke & Harvey, 2012) emphasize the use of behavioral experiments to test the validity of intermediate beliefs surrounding sleep. For example, an adolescent patient who has the belief "I must have 9 hours of sleep or I can't think straight" might design an experiment where she researches the effects of sleep deprivation on cognition. Alternatively, she might poll her classmates to see how much sleep they get on average. Adolescent patients with catastrophic beliefs about the impact of sleep loss on their daytime functioning can also collect objective data on their school performance (e.g., textbook pages read; number of homework problems completed) and examine these data as a function of sleep duration and subjective quality from the night before.

Comorbidity

When it comes to depression in adolescence, comorbidity is the rule, rather than the exception. Comorbidity complicates case conceptualizations, the selection of appropriate interventions, and the delivery of treatment to depressed youth. Furthermore, it is associated with poorer treatment response both in CBT (Curry et al., 2006) and other interventions (Young, Mufson, & Davies, 2006). Despite these data, there are few explicit, empirically-supported guidelines for treating depressed adolescents who meet diagnostic criteria for one or more additional psychiatric conditions. Below, we first discuss considerations when the therapist decides to treat comorbid conditions *sequentially* (i.e., treating one diagnosis to remission before addressing a second). Next, we discuss how CBT interventions for depression can be flexibly adapted so as to treat comorbid conditions *simultaneously*. We focus on anxiety and substance use disorders (SUDs), as these are among the most common and detrimental comorbid conditions in adolescent MDD.

Sequential Treatment of Comorbidity

We recommend that decisions regarding how to handle comorbidity, in general, be informed by a detailed assessment and case formulation. Ideally, assessments of complex cases include some form of structured clinical interview, which will provide comprehensive background information regarding the onset and maintenance of comorbid disorders. Where possible, therapists also should obtain information pertaining to the symptom severity of comorbid conditions, using self- and parent-report questionnaires and/or clinician-administered symptom interviews. For example, the Screen for Child Anxiety Related Disorders (Birmaher et al., 1999) has child and parent versions, and is available for free at: www.psychiatry.pitt.edu/research. Choosing treatment priorities is done on a case-by-case basis; below, we enumerate several guidelines for making these challenging decisions.

1 *Life-threatening symptoms.* As we discussed in Chapter 5, life-threatening symptoms should be prioritized and rigorously addressed in treatment. In many cases, this means prioritizing depressive symptoms. For example, suicidality is often rooted in depressive symptoms and related cognitions (e.g., hopelessness, worthlessness) and so the choice to target depression may be clear. However, at other times, comorbid diagnoses can present the most acute threat. For instance, withdrawal from substances (e.g., alcohol) can be life-threatening; medically supervised detoxification should be prioritized ahead of depression treatment in these cases.
2 *Functional impairment.* When deciding how to order interventions, therapists should incorporate information about the symptom severity of each diagnosis, and the extent to which each type of symptom impacts the adolescent's academic, occupational (where applicable), and interpersonal (i.e., family, peer, and romantic relationships) functioning. To illustrate this point, consider two adolescents, both reporting symptoms of depression and social anxiety, and both routinely missing school. One adolescent misses school because she oversleeps and cannot will herself to rise from bed, and has the thought, "There's no point, I'm going to fail anyway." The other adolescent reports severe anxiety and panic while packing his bag for school and has the thoughts, "What if I forget something I need?" and "The teacher will yell at me in front of the class." For the first adolescent, the therapist might prioritize treating depressive symptoms, while for the second, it may be more effective to address the patient's social anxiety prior to explicitly working on depression.
3 *Lifetime temporal sequence of comorbid disorders.* The order of onset of MDD and comorbid conditions provides the therapist with vital information about how the patient's overall psychopathology developed. These data may reveal important contingencies between earlier- and later-developing symptom clusters that can guide treatment decisions. For example, Cummings, Caporino, and Kendall (2014) recently proposed a *multiple pathways* model of comorbid depression

and anxiety. In Pathway 1, youth have a general diathesis for anxiety disorders and, initially, develop these symptoms. These youth are characterized by more severe anxiety symptoms and milder depression, and over time, anxiety-related impairment (e.g., avoidance of pleasant social situations) is thought to contribute to the development of depression. In contrast, Pathway 3 describes youth who have depressotypic vulnerability and develop MDD prior to the onset of anxiety disorders. The functional consequences of depressive symptoms fuel anxiety in these cases (e.g., poor assertiveness contributes to social anxiety).[15] Pathway 1 youth may benefit most from treatment for anxiety followed by interventions targeting any remaining depressive symptoms while Pathway 3 youth might be best served using the opposite sequence.

4 *Existing evidence.* Studies indicate that depressive symptoms reduce the efficacy of CBT for anxiety, but that comorbid anxiety does not consistently negatively impact CBT for depression (see Cummings et al., 2014). Further, meta-analyses show that CBT for depression significantly reduces symptoms of depression *and* anxiety (Weisz, McCarty, & Valeri, 2006). If none of the issues above (1–3) are present, a practitioner might generally choose a depression-focused intervention for an adolescent with depression–anxiety comorbidity. In a recent study, researchers compared the efficacy of three treatment sequences for youth with comorbid depression and substance abuse: (1) family-focused substance abuse treatment followed by group CBT for depression; (2) group CBT followed by the family intervention; and (3) the two interventions simultaneously. The authors found no differences in the rate at which depressive symptoms reduced across conditions, but the group receiving substance abuse treatment *first* showed the greatest remission of these symptoms (Rohde, Waldron, Turner, Brody, & Jorgensen, 2014). These results provide some rationale for prioritizing substance-related problems when they co-occur with MDD in adolescent patients.

Simultaneous Treatment of Comorbidity: Flexible Adaptation of a Single-Target Intervention

We do not view treatment manuals as step-by-step recipes to successfully treat psychopathology. Instead, when addressing comorbid conditions simultaneously in CBT for depression, we recommend *flexibility within fidelity* (Kendall & Beidas, 2007; Nock, Goldman, Wang, & Albano, 2004).

---

15 Cummings et al. (2014) propose three Pathways in their model. Pathway 2 describes youth with a shared diathesis for both anxiety disorders and MDD. These adolescents are proposed to develop these comorbid conditions simultaneously.

That is, therapists should use their clinical judgment (under appropriate supervision, where necessary) to adapt single-target interventions to best address the unique problems and needs of their adolescent patients. Research with youth indicates that treatments can be altered in creative ways while still maintaining a high level of fidelity (Chu & Kendall, 2009), although this work has been confined to primary anxiety disorders. Below we provide some recommendations for adapting manualized CBT for adolescent depression for comorbid cases.

Anxiety Disorders

Although depression and anxiety disorders share several core features, including trait neuroticism, negative affectivity, and rumination (Cummings et al., 2014), they also have distinct, discriminable cognitive content (Lerner et al., 1999). Depressotypic cognitions focus on loss, hopelessness, and self-denigration, while anxiety disorders are characterized by themes of threat, danger, and vulnerability. The cognitive content of anxiety is more often future-oriented, while depression is more often characterized by fixating on the negative content of past events (i.e., depressive rumination). We find it helpful to highlight the cognitive content that typifies anxiety (e.g., probability overestimation; catastrophic predictions) in the psychoeducation phase of CBT treatment of comorbid cases. In addition, therapists may need to spend more time discussing the connection between physiology and affect, as this is more central to understanding the development of certain anxiety disorders (e.g., Craske & Barlow, 2007). As in adolescent depression, avoidance is common in anxiety disorders, and it is one mechanism that maintains anxious thoughts and beliefs (e.g., Zinbarg, Craske & Barlow, 2006). With this in mind, the therapist and patient may collaboratively conceptualize differences between *depressive avoidance* (e.g., Not going to a party because you predict it will not be fun) and *anxious avoidance* (e.g., Not going to the dance because you are certain other students will laugh at you). Finally, connections between depression and anxiety symptoms should be highlighted during psychoeducation collaborative case conceptualization.

The general framework of behavioral activation (BA) can be used to address symptoms of depression and anxiety. Exposure to feared and/or previously avoided stimuli is a cornerstone of treatments for anxiety disorders. For adolescents with comorbid symptoms, behavioral scheduling can involve equal doses of pleasurable activities and activities that place the patient into avoided situations. Unlike BA for depression, scheduling *exposure activation* may require thoroughly discussing feared outcomes and developing strategies to cope. For instance, patients could practice and plan to use deep breaths and/or pleasant imagery when attending a social event they typically avoid. Adolescents with comorbid anxiety and depression also may benefit from scheduling a regular relaxation routine that may include techniques like progressive muscle relaxation (Zinbarg et al., 2006), diaphragmatic breathing (Craske & Barlow, 2007), and meditation/visualization (Bourne, 2010). Finally, behavioral interventions that are more unique to treating anxiety disorders also can be introduced seamlessly into CBT for depression. For instance, the application of guided discovery (Chapter 3) is common across cognitive therapies; an *in vivo* exposure (Craske & Barlow, 2007) designed to elicit panic-like physiological symptoms could be framed as an experiment, where patient and therapist test hypotheses about the consequences of body symptoms.

The basic principles of cognitive restructuring apply to identifying and challenging thoughts linked to both anxiety and depression. We recommend that therapists impart a generic cognitive restructuring *process* to their patients (e.g., teaching patients to ask themselves, "what went through my mind when I noticed a shift in mood?"; encouraging patients to treat their thoughts as hypotheses and examine evidence that supports and refutes them) that can be flexibly applied to different types of thought *content*. Cognitive interventions for anxiety disorders aim to: (1) reduce the perceived probability and severity of threat and/or danger; (2) increase confidence in adaptive coping abilities; and (3) establish a sense of personal safety. To this end, Table 8.2 presents common cognitive themes found in anxiety-related cognitions and strategies for challenging these thoughts. When working with adolescents struggling with comorbid depression and anxiety, these strategies may be used to augment the interventions discussed in Chapter 6. We also have found that anxiety-specific worksheets from other protocols (e.g., realistic odds pie chart; Craske & Barlow, 2007, p. 104) can be easily be woven into depression-focused CBT protocols when patients have a solid understanding of the common elements of cognitive restructuring.

Substance Use Disorders

Comorbid SUDs are relatively common in adolescent MDD. SUDs are associated with a 6.0–8.5 times greater risk of suicide among adolescents (Esposito-Smythers & Spirito, 2004), and the psychiatric consequences of even subclinical substance use may be heightened for depressed youth. Because of the impact of comorbid SUDs, the goal of treatment is generally *dual recovery*, wherein both depression and the SUD are considered central problems. Standard outpatient CBT for these patients is almost always supplemented with pharmacotherapy, family therapy, and/or group therapy interventions. Existing evidence regarding treatment of comorbid MDD and SUD suggests that intensive, multi-modal treatments are most likely to be successful (Esposito-Smythers, Spirito, Kahler, Hunt, & Monti, 2011; Rohde et al., 2014). Adolescents also may benefit from attending

Table 8.2 Common Cognitive Distortions in Anxiety Disorders

Cognitive Theme	Example(s)	Restructuring Strategy
Catastrophic thinking	"I'm going to pass out in front of the whole class" "I will completely fail the exam"	*Engage the worst-case scenario.* "What's the worst thing that could happen if your fear came true?" "Could you live through it?" "What's the most likely scenario?"
Probability overestimation	"I will get so nervous I will have a heart attack"	*Generate estimates of true odds.* "How common is the feared event generally, e.g., how many are affected?" "Has it ever happened to you?" "What are other possibilities?" "How likely are the other possibilities?"
Emotions and sensations as evidence	"My heart is racing – this must be dangerous"	*Decouple emotion/sensation and outcome.* "Have there been situations where you felt this way and there was no danger?" "How about the opposite – times where there was some danger, but you didn't feel this way?"
Inability to cope	"If the teacher calls on me I will fall apart" "I can't handle conflict"	*Build awareness of past coping and current options.* "Have similar things happened before?" "How did those go?" "What helped you get through?" "What have you learned that could be helpful to you now?"
Vulnerability and/or lack of safety	"I can't be outside alone" "I could be mugged at any moment"	*Probe utility of the thought; build awareness of strength.* "How does having this thought help you, e.g., does it make you feel more prepared?" "What have you done in times where you thought you wouldn't make it through something?" "What characteristics would your friends say make you strong?"

community-based support meetings (e.g., Alcoholics Anonymous; SMART Recovery) while in treatment. These offer a source of social support and combat the stigma associated with SUDs.

Building a strong therapeutic alliance may be particularly difficult with patients with comorbid MDD and SUDs. It's not uncommon for these patients to be adamantly resistant to including substance use as a problem and/or treatment target, and they may even view substances as their primary means of coping with depression. It is unwise to rush rapport building in these cases; instead, we recommend staying collaborative and meeting patients *where they are at*. If they do not see their substance use as an issue, explore the symptoms and associated behaviors in a non-judgmental way (e.g., Help me understand how you currently manage your depression; What are some of the concerns your parents and friends have about your marijuana use? What have you noticed has changed in your pattern of substance use since you became depressed? How would your life be different if you were not drinking most days?). Changes in substance use behaviors may come in the form of fortuitous side effects to achieving other goals. For example, a patient whose goal is "fight less with my parents" might need to reduce his substance use in service of this goal. Standard CBT can also be supplemented with motivational enhancement techniques (Miller & Rollnick, 2012). For example, therapists might work collaboratively with their patients on the pros and cons of their substance use, or on listing things that the patient could do in the future if he made changes versus if he maintained the status quo.

For dually diagnosed adolescents, outpatient CBT may include some SUD-specific psychoeducation. Where possible, this should highlight the substance's effects on mood and/or the symptoms of depression that the participant is experiencing. With alcohol, for example, a therapist might present information on how this substance reduces deep sleep (Table 8.1), disrupts the functioning of GABAergic receptors, which contributes to irritability and agitation, and, over time, reduces serotonin levels in the brain, which may worsen depression. We have found it especially useful to supplement *information giving* with *information gathering*; an adolescent patient may be willing to monitor his substance use along with his moods (anxiety, depression, irritability) and/or sleep for several weeks and examine the connections among these variables. Alternatively, a patient could research information on typical substance use habits for adolescents his age and bring his findings back into session.

Behavioral interventions for dually diagnosed patients may require a greater focus on *crisis survival skills*. In early sessions, therapist and patient may use detailed chain analyses (Chapter 6) of substance binges or intense cravings to identify a list of *warning signs* that can alert the patient in the future. Effective treatments for adolescent SUDs target the skill deficits these patients present with by building and practicing effective coping strategies (Esposito-Smythers et al., 2011). Thus, treatment for dually diagnosed adolescents may involve creating elaborate, portable *coping toolboxes*; these could include patient's audio-recorded instructions or encouraging words for himself, written reminders of reasons not to use, important phone numbers, and/or materials for distraction (e.g., music; a favorite picture or poem).

Along with the depressotypic beliefs we describe throughout this book, adolescents with comorbid SUDs also may possess the following beliefs directly related to substance use: (1) *Anticipatory beliefs* (e.g., Alcohol helps me socialize better); (2) *Relief-oriented beliefs* (e.g., This sadness won't stop unless I use); and (3) *Permissive beliefs* (e.g., I've had a hard day at school so I deserve to relax) (Beck, Wright, Newman, & Liese, 1993). Once identified, these beliefs and the automatic thoughts they generate can be challenged using thought records (e.g., What evidence do you have that alcohol reduces sadness? Is there any evidence against this?), behavioral experiments (e.g., plan to hang out with friends without using substances), and developing and testing new, more adaptive beliefs (e.g., I can relax in a bunch of ways like exercising, playing video games, or doing my relaxation tape). The process of identifying, challenging, and restructuring distorted, SUD-related cognitions can be mixed in with concurrent cognitive strategies directed at depression.

Pharmacotherapy

To date, 16 ADMs have received approval from the US Food and Drug Administration (FDA) to treat adult depression, and there is evidence to support their efficacy in treating MDD in randomized controlled trials (RCTs) (Khan, Faucett, Lichtenberg, Kirsch, & Brown, 2012). By contrast, RCTs of ADMs for child and adolescent depression are mixed. Meta-analyses of these treatment trials have concluded that ADMs, as a whole, show limited benefits over and above placebo effects in treating depressive symptoms in youth (Spielmans & Gerwig, 2014; Tsapakis, Soldani, Tondo, & Baldessarini, 2008). Fluoxetine (Prozac) may be the sole exception to these findings; at the time of writing, fluoxetine is the only FDA-approved ADM for adolescent depression.

Despite the empirical status of ADMs, they are commonly prescribed to treat depression in youth and are useful in many cases. A closer examination of the data reveals that depressed adolescents have good response rates (40–70%) to ADMs. However, somewhat surprisingly, adolescents also show a very strong response to placebos (30–60%). While there is no evidence that CBT and ADMs are differentially effective in treating adolescent depression (Cox et al., 2014), some evidence suggests that the combination (CBT + ADM) may be more effective than either alone (March et al., 2004).

Types of Medication

Selective serotonin reuptake inhibitors (SSRIs), such as fluoxetine, sertraline (Zoloft), and citalopram (Celexa), are the first- and second-choice ADMs according to existing practice guidelines (Birmaher et al., 2007; Hughes et al., 2007; Taurines, Gerlach, Warnke, Thome, & Wewetzer, 2011). These guidelines recommend beginning with a trial of fluoxetine because of its authorization by the FDA, and switching to an alternative, off-label SSRI in the event of non-response. Off-label refers to a medication that is prescribed without official approval; adolescents and parents using off-label medications should have an explanatory discussion with their prescriber about using these medications and provide their informed consent (Taurines et al., 2011). Counterintuitively, the doses of SSRIs used for treating adolescent depression are equivalent to adult patients, but adolescents may need to be monitored more carefully than adults. Adolescents absorb and metabolize faster than adults, and so SSRIs may have shorter half-lives for these patients (Bridge et al., 2007). Consequently, some adolescents may actually require *higher* doses of SSRIs than adults.

Other classes of medications are considered as third-line options and are rarely prescribed in adolescents (Birmaher et al., 2007; Hughes et al., 2007). The serotonin and norepinephrine inhibitor (SNRI) venlafaxine (Effexor) has shown the most promise (Bridge et al., 2007) and has a relatively benign side-effect profile. Other SNRIs (e.g., duloxetine), however, have failed to demonstrate efficacy in RCTs (Atkinson et al., 2014). Tricyclic antidepressants (TCAs; e.g., clomipramine) and monoamine oxidase inhibitors (MAOIs; e.g., phenelzine) are very seldom used because of their undesirable side effects (e.g., drug–food interactions) and lethality in overdose. Patients taking TCAs should be monitored especially carefully for suicidality, as many of these ADMs are life-threatening at only three times the recommended dose (Taurines et al., 2011).

Side Effects

Generally, SSRIs are well tolerated by adolescents and have relatively few, mild side effects that may subside over time (Safer & Zito, 2006). Most commonly, adolescents experience gastrointestinal symptoms (e.g., nausea, changes in appetite and/or weight), headaches, restlessness, sleep changes, and/or sexual dysfunction (e.g., anorgasmia). A minority (<8%) of adolescents experience increased impulsivity, irritability, and drive in response to SSRI use; these symptoms should be carefully assessed and differentiated from symptoms of mania, particularly for adolescents with a family history of bipolar disorder (Birmaher et al., 2007). Therapists working with adolescents taking ADMs may explicitly target side effects using cognitive behavioral strategies (e.g., sleep hygiene for insomnia) and can help their patients challenge NATs (e.g., I can't handle these side effects) or beliefs (e.g., Only weak people take medications) that might impact medication compliance.

ADMs and Suicidality

In 2004, the FDA issued a black box warning stating that ADMs may increase suicidality in children and adolescents. An initial meta-analysis supported this warning; a study evaluating trials of nine medications suggested that ADMs increased risk for suicide attempts by nearly two-fold (Hammad, Laughren, & Racoosin, 2006). However, an updated, more thorough analysis concluded that ADMs do not increase risk for suicidality among depressed children and adolescents. The authors demonstrated that one adverse event (i.e., increased suicidal ideation or suicide attempt attributable to medication) would be expected for every 112 treated patients (Bridge et al., 2007). Notably, there were no *completed* suicides in any of the trials included in either meta-analysis. With these data in mind, most guidelines recommend that SSRIs continue to play a central role in the treatment of adolescent MDD. Specifically, they emphasize a favorable risk/benefit ratio for SSRIs: "nearly 11 times more depressed patients may respond favorably to antidepressants than may spontaneously report suicidality" (Birmaher et al., 2007, p. 1516). Risks associated with taking ADMs can be addressed by building routine assessments of suicidality into therapy sessions (see Chapter 3). Indeed, adding psychotherapy to medication interventions has been shown to reduce risk for suicidality (March et al., 2007).

Summary

Working with depressed adolescents comes with many potential challenges. Above, we listed some suggestions for how a therapist's approach and interventions may be adjusted to address common issues that can arise in therapy. Along with these recommendations, therapists should keep in mind that referring patients to practitioners with more expertise in specific problem areas and/or gathering additional treatment support is always a viable option. Although adolescent work comes with unique and sometimes taxing wrinkles, these challenges afford the opportunity for therapy to have an important impact on a teen and potentially alter her mental health trajectory going forward.

9 Addressing Suicidality

Suicide is the second leading cause of death among adolescents ages 13–18 (Centers for Disease Control and Prevention (CDC), 2013), and depressive disorders increase the risk for suicidal thoughts, planning, and actions. Specifically, depressed adolescents have a sixfold greater likelihood of making a suicide attempt as compared to non-depressed youth (Nock et al., 2013); however, only one third of adolescent ideators make an attempt (Nock et al., 2013). Few studies have identified mechanisms that explain how depression may contribute to the transition from ideation to attempt (for exception, see Auerbach, Millner, Stewart, & Esposito, 2015). Epidemiological data show that more people are now receiving treatment for suicidality but increasing utilization of these services has not led to an accompanying reduction of the occurrence of suicidal behaviors (Kessler, Berglund, Borges, Nock, & Wang, 2005). Reviews of the adolescent treatment literature (Brent et al., 2013; Glenn, Franklin, & Nock, 2015) have underscored two important points: (1) treating depressive symptoms alone is not sufficient to reduce adolescent suicidality and (2) few interventions have demonstrated efficacy at reducing risk for suicidal behaviors. Therefore, careful assessment of and improved treatment for suicidality in youth are critical.

Assessing Suicidality

As discussed briefly in Chapter 3, suicide assessment should be integrated and documented from the outset of treatment. Assessing suicide minimizes risk of adolescent patients, and it informs treatment planning and management. Berman et al. (2006) indicate that a thorough suicide risk assessment probes four primary domains: (1) predisposing vulnerability factors; (2) precipitating events (triggers); (3) mental status across affective, cognitive, and behavioral states; and (4) contraindications: coping resources versus failed protections. The resulting clinical information obtained should be viewed in the context of an adolescent's suicidal intent, motivation, and lethality as well as the level of compliance exhibited in the context of assessment and treatment to ascertain an adolescent's suicide risk (for complete review of suicide assessment and treatment in adolescents, see Berman et al., 2006).

Predisposing Vulnerability Factors

There is a wide range of vulnerability factors that increase suicidal behaviors among adolescents, including: (1) mental health disorder diagnoses; (2) personality traits; (3) family history; (4) trauma, abuse, and maltreatment; and (5) history of suicidality. First, it is estimated that approximately 90% of adolescents who die by suicide report acute psychiatric symptoms (Berman et al., 2006), and the most common diagnoses, which are often comorbid, are mood disorders, substance use disorders, impulsive disorders, and conduct disorders (Nock et al., 2013). Second, many suicidal youth endorse pronounced pathological personality traits (e.g., *narcissistic-perfectionistic*: lack of ability to tolerate imperfection; *impulsive-aggressive*: sensitivity to stress resulting in anger; *hopelessness*: inability to identify how or why life may change for the better) (see Apter, 2000). Personality traits are particularly pernicious; they are challenging to treat and often result in alienation from peers and family. Third, a family history of both mental illness and suicidality places youth at greater risk for suicide (Gould & Kramer, 2001), and approximately half of all adolescents who complete suicide have a family history of psychiatric illness (Houston, Hawton, & Shepperd, 2001). Fourth, exposure to early life stress (i.e., trauma, abuse, maltreatment) is a robust predictor of suicidal behaviors. Although all forms of abuse increase risk for suicide, sexual abuse, in particular, may predispose youth to greater risk for suicidality (e.g., Brent, Baugher, Bridge, Chen, & Beery, 1999; Miller, Esposito-Smythers, Weismoore, & Renshaw, 2013; Stewart et al., 2015). Last, past behavior is a strong predictor of future behavior, and accordingly, past suicide attempts are strong predictors of future attempts (e.g., Rudd, Joiner, & Rajab, 1996). Specifically, approximately one-third of people who complete suicide have made at least one known prior attempt (Brent et al., 1999; Shaffer et al., 1996).

Precipitating Events (Triggers)

As discussed in detail in Chapter 2, stress – particularly relational stressors involving "targeted rejection" – confers risk for MDD as well as increased suicidality. In younger adolescents, interpersonal tension with parents often is a trigger for suicidal behaviors, and in older teens, suicidality may stem from romance-related problems (e.g., break-ups, loss) (Brent et al., 1999). In fact, in a study by Brent and colleagues (1988), as many as 70% of suicide attempts and completions were precipitated by interpersonal conflict. Other common triggers of suicidal behaviors in adolescents include incarceration, embarrassment, humiliation, and threat (particularly to status). As we underscored earlier in this book, it is crucial for clinicians to explore stressors that may precede suicidality, as doing so may provide important insights into whether teens transition from ideating to attempting.

Mental Status

Broadly speaking, this refers to the need for clinicians to continually assess key affective, cognitive, and behavioral states. First, suicidal adolescents often exhibit worsening sadness, anxiety, fearfulness, anger, shame, and guilt. Shifts, especially acute spikes in these states, may be a signal for a therapist to spend more time understanding how these symptoms may be influencing an adolescent's suicidality. At times, suicidal adolescents describe an intense emotional pain that seems ceaseless. Often this pain is viewed as intolerable, and for some, suicide is considered as the only way to end the suffering. Another promising marker of suicide risk may be anhedonia (i.e., a reduced ability to experience pleasure). In both children (Nock & Kazdin, 2002) and adolescents (Auerbach, Millner, Stewart, & Esposito, 2015), suicide attempters reported more severe anhedonia as compared to suicide ideators even after controlling for current depressive symptoms. For many, the experience of anhedonia (or feeling "numb," as some patients describe it) is unbearable, especially as it tends to be stable over time (Clark, Fawcett, Salazar-Grueso, & Fawcett, 1984). Across these situations, it is important to have adolescents identify the emotions they are feeling. Talking about these feelings may reduce distress and provide a "gap" to begin exploring more specific strategies to reduce suicidality.

Second, suicidal adolescents often report intractable hopelessness and cognitive rigidity. Research has demonstrated that hopelessness is a strong predictor of suicide completions above and beyond mental disorders (Beck, Steer, Kovacs, & Garrison, 1985; Kerfoot, Dyer, Harrington, Woodham, & Harrington, 1996). Youth may view their troubles as "unsolvable," and thus, suicide may seem like a viable option for escape. Whereas some teens may have difficulty identifying possible solutions to their existing troubles, other teens can become fixated on suicide and view this as the only feasible solution to a given problem. Suicide also may have different meanings across patients: (1) an escape from the pain of everyday living; (2) an exercise of power and control; (3) self-punishment in response to shame and failure; or (4) an effort to reunite with loved ones. When probing an adolescent's suicidal ideation, assessing the reasons for wanting to end one's life may provide key information about the patient's motivations and overall mindset (Berman et al., 2006).

Last, the presentation of adolescent suicidality may be quite heterogeneous. A subset of suicide attempts is "impulsive," and thus, poor impulse control or aggression may be important predictors. Indeed, the majority of suicide attempts and completions are carefully planned; however, there are a significant percentage of attempts characterized by a brief lag time (i.e., less than 5 minutes) between thinking about suicide and attempting suicide (Simon et al., 2001). These attempts may stem from poor impulse control and aggression (or intoxication). When poor impulse control and aggression co-occur within youth, there is an increased risk for suicidal behaviors (Berman et al., 2006). For other attempts there may be behaviors and symptoms that act as red flags for an impending attempt. Adolescents may exhibit a preoccupation with suicide. This may surface in the form of discussing death and dying more than usual, writing about suicide (e.g., poems, stories, diary entries), and drawing suicide-related imagery. Similarly, adolescents may make preparations for their death (e.g., giving their things away to friends, family). From a symptomatic perspective, suicidal teens also may become more agitated in light of greater sleeplessness, anxiety sensitivity (i.e., agitation), and diminished concentration.

Contraindications

Perhaps the most challenging aspect of completing a suicide assessment is that risk does not exist in a vacuum. Although certain teens will endorse a range of factors closely linked to suicidality (e.g., predisposing vulnerability factors, cognitive rigidity, agitation), these patients also may possess a range of coping strategies (e.g., internal and external resources) that buffers them from suicidal thoughts and actions. Internal resources may hinge on the ability of a teen to use problem-solving or interpersonal effectiveness strategies across challenging situations. Conversely, high-risk teens may have a strong support network. This includes, but is not limited to, parents, siblings, and peers. Many teens receive enormous support from teachers, guidance counselors, as well as therapists, and collectively, this external support helps teens navigate through choppy waters. On the flip side, there also are intrapersonal risk factors that may increase risk for suicide. Notable factors are low self-esteem and self-efficacy, diminished attachment to others, lack of control (i.e., external versus internal locus of control over important life events). Additionally, environmental factors such as peer victimization (e.g., physical bullying, online bullying) have received widespread national attention, and have been strongly linked with suicidal behaviors among teens (Hinduja & Patchin, 2010). Clear assessment of these protective and vulnerability factors is essential when ascertaining a teen's level of suicide risk.

Risk Assessment

There is no universal consensus for operationalizing suicide risk; however, in day-to-day practice, most clinicians have developed an idiosyncratic rating system – often based on previous experience and consultation with allied health professionals – that identifies whether a teen is an imminent threat to suicide. Perhaps as a response to this non-standardized risk assessment, Berman and colleagues (2006) outlined a three-tier screening system which provides a framework to unpack an adolescent's level of suicide risk. Although no system is perfect, we believe that it provides a *workable heuristic* to obtain key insights into at-risk patients (for more detail, see Berman et al., 2006).

Level I Risk

The first tier represents the lowest risk level. An adolescent patient may present with one or more predisposing vulnerability factors (examples described above). At Level I, adolescents will have a current diagnosis (e.g., depression), behavioral problems that typify suicidal teens (e.g., irritability), and acute interpersonal stress (e.g., romantic conflict, family-related discord). When these factors co-occur, the clinician should probe for underlying suicidality (ideation versus plans versus attempts).

On the surface, lower levels of risk may seem "easier" to assess. However, adolescents are not always forthright with describing their level of suicidality, and, importantly, they may not even have a clear sense of their own level of risk. Issues pertaining to suicidality may arise at any point within treatment, and if it emerges in the earlier sessions, therapists may not have had an opportunity to obtain sufficient information across relevant domains (i.e., predisposing vulnerability factors, precipitating events, mental states, contraindications) and may feel ill equipped to correctly ascertain risk level. Addressing suicidality in these initial sessions can be extraordinarily challenging. There are different safety (e.g., imminent threat) and therapeutic (e.g., alliance rupture, erosion of trust) considerations, and these issues will profoundly impact the course of therapy. The following exchange reflects a therapist attempting to ascertain risk level with an uncommunicative teen in the early phases of treatment:

Box 9.1 Level I Risk: Challenging Patient

THERAPIST: Tim, reviewing your weekly questionnaires, it looks like the depression and hopelessness seem more severe as compared to our first session last week, and you also indicated that you've been thinking more about suicide over the past week.
TIM: Eh. [shrugs shoulders]
THERAPIST: What happened during the past week that may have made you feel worse and think about suicide?
TIM: Nothing.
THERAPIST: Can I ask you some questions about your suicidal thoughts?

> TIM: I guess.
> THERAPIST: What types of suicidal thoughts are you having?
> TIM: I don't know.
> THERAPIST: Sorry, I was not particularly clear. Let's take this one step at a time. Can you tell me about whether you have a plan to hurt yourself?
> TIM: No.
> THERAPIST: If you were going to make a suicide attempt, how do you think you might do it?
> TIM: Not really sure.
> THERAPIST: It may surprise you to learn that most people who don't have any intention of making a suicide attempt often know how they would do it. Has it ever crossed your mind?
> TIM: I guess pills.
> THERAPIST: What type of pills?
> TIM: My meds . . . I guess.
> THERAPIST: I see. What types of steps have you taken with your pills?
> TIM: None.
> THERAPIST: What would need to happen for you to decide to take pills to end your life?
> TIM: Not sure.
> THERAPIST: OK, it sounds like you have a plan, but it doesn't really sound like you've decided that it is necessary to take your life.
> TIM: I guess. But, my life still sucks.
> THERAPIST: I'm sorry. Sounds like you're really struggling. Let's see what we can do today to reduce some of the pain you're feeling.

In the example above, Tim (the adolescent patient) was not particularly forthright about his suicidality, and, as a new patient, the suicide history and possible protections were unclear. Nevertheless, it was essential for the therapist to try to determine whether Tim's suicidal ideation and plans included a clear decision to end his life. As noted in the dialogue, there is no definitive plan to suicide, and the presence of an *inactive plan* – a plan in which there may not be any preparation or intent – is not necessarily an indicator that a teen will make a suicide attempt. In fact, it has been our experience that most non-suicidal patients have a sense of how they *might* end their life (and, in fact, the same can be said of healthy youth who have a sense of *how*, in a very general way, they might make a suicide attempt). In this example, less is known about precipitating events and coping resources, so the therapist can dedicate the remainder of the session to learning more about these key domains without directly discussing

194 *Addressing Suicidality*

suicide (i.e., probing protective mechanisms, reasons for living). This may prove helpful, as Tim may be less reticent to discuss interpersonal stressors (e.g., fights with friends, disagreements with parents), intrapersonal resources, and family issues (and mental illness history). Through these probes a therapist then would be in a better position to judge an adolescent's suicide risk.

Level II Risk

Moving along the risk severity continuum, Level II reflects an increase in suicidal ideation and related behaviors. At this level, adolescents exhibit a preoccupation with suicide, and when this occurs in the context of impulse-related problems and substance use, there is increased cause for concern. It is not uncommon for teens also to exhibit an escalating rigidity in their thinking (e.g., There is no way out of this; Nothing will work for me; No one understands my problems). Berman and colleagues (2006) refer to this as "tunnel vision" or "psychological myopia," and, in many instances, this cognitive rigidity contributes to increased hopelessness (e.g., Nothing is ever going to change in my life; There is nothing to live for any more). Another factor that distinguishes this tier of risk from lower levels is that there tends to be increased social isolation. For example, adolescents may stop attending school, drop out of extracurricular activities, avoid friends, and spend more time in their room. This is even more problematic when the family environment is chaotic (e.g., discord, substance use, violence) or unsupportive (e.g., unavailable, unreliable, neglectful). Similar to the therapeutic exchange in Level I risk, correctly identifying an adolescent's suicide risk in Level II is challenging. To highlight this difficulty, we will continue the dialogue from earlier to underscore more subtle aspects that may increase (or decrease) the level of risk as a given session continues:

Box 9.2   Level II Risk: Challenging Patient

THERAPIST: Tim, thanks for talking with me about your suicidal thoughts. I know this isn't an easy conversation, especially since we're just getting to know one another. If it's OK, I want to switch gears for a moment.
TIM: OK.
THERAPIST: We haven't really talked much about life at home. What's your relationship like with your parents?
TIM: What relationship?
THERAPIST: Sorry, what do you mean?

TIM: My parents are divorced. I see my dad here and there. My mom, well, she's a piece of work.
THERAPIST: Can you tell me a little more about your dad?
TIM: He travels for work, and at this point, I don't really care if I see him.
THERAPIST: And your mom?
TIM: She works a lot. So, I get stuck with taking care of my younger brother.
THERAPIST: That seems like a lot of responsibility.
TIM: It is. But, he's my brother.
THERAPIST: It sounds tough.
TIM: It's whatever. It doesn't really matter 'cause there's nothing I can do.
THERAPIST: What do you mean?
TIM: Someone needs to watch Max – he's only 11. And, it's just the way it is.
THERAPIST: How has taking care of Max affected you?
TIM: It takes a lot of time. I quit my band. Don't have time to see friends.
THERAPIST: I'm sorry to hear that.
TIM: Yeah.
THERAPIST: How else has it affected you?
TIM: I just need to be home – so, I just spend time there.
THERAPIST: What about your friends?
TIM: No time. No interest.
THERAPIST: I see. That seems really tough.
TIM: Like I said, my life sucks.

Although Tim has not made any suicidal gestures, there is an increased suicide risk by virtue of the fact that he: (1) does not have a supportive family system (i.e., infrequent contact with father, busy mother); (2) is isolated from peers; and (3) is expressing increased levels of hopelessness. Tim's situation is objectively challenging, but there may still remain different points of entry to de-escalate any suicidality. For example, based on Tim's identified goals, it might be important to decrease his social isolation through him spending more time with friends and/or rejoining the band. While this may necessitate talking with Tim's mother to explore alternative afterschool care for Max (the younger brother), this may provide immediate benefits. Although there may not be an easy fix, probing the associated domains that influence suicidality provides key insights into what may or may not be feasible for the adolescent patient and family system.

Level III Risk

Level III risk is when adolescents are at acute risk of making a suicide attempt, and in these severe cases, hospitalization may be necessary. In addition to each of the factors described with the lower risk levels, clinicians should clearly ascertain whether: (1) there is availability and accessibility to the means resulting in suicide and (2) a patient's mental status (e.g., substance use, psychotic symptoms, disorganized behavior) is likely to affect judgment. According to the CDC, the most common way for adolescents to die by suicide is firearms (Centers for Disease Control and Prevention, 2013). However, overdosing on medication (or drugs), particularly among female adolescents, also is relatively common. Given the higher prevalence of these methods, it is important for clinicians to work with families to ensure that safety precautions are taken (e.g., storing firearms and medications in a locked cabinet; monitoring use of medication). Not surprisingly, the likelihood of suicide attempts increases when adolescents are in an altered state, which includes substance-induced mood states as well as psychotic and manic episodes. Resulting mood states may increase impulsivity and poor decision making and jeopardize the health and safety of youth. By way of example, we continue our dialogue with Tim to determine his risk status:

Box 9.3   Level III Risk: Challenging Patient

THERAPIST: Tim, I want to summarize what we've discussed just to make sure I have everything straight.

TIM: OK.

THERAPIST: Over the last 2 weeks, you've experienced an uptick in your suicidal thoughts and hopelessness. You don't necessarily want to die, but you do have a plan. Meaning, you indicated that you would likely take your antidepressant medication. At home, you're feeling pretty stuck. Your dad travels quite a bit, and you don't see or talk to him much. Since your mom works a lot you're left to shoulder a great deal of responsibility at home. Right now, you're feeling pretty stuck and hopeless.

TIM: Yup.

THERAPIST: What am I missing here?

TIM: Dunno.

THERAPIST: One thing we discussed briefly last week was your drinking. You said that you don't drink a lot. However, we didn't really get into details. Would you feel comfortable if we returned to this?

TIM: Um. I guess. [Visibly uncomfortable.]

THERAPIST: What do you typically drink, and when would you do so?

TIM: Well, I drink whatever is lying around. I don't really care what it is. Vodka, gin, whatever. My mom sometimes works late. And, so, after my brother goes to sleep, I'll just drink in my room. It helps me shut down a bit . . . .

THERAPIST: So, it helps you calm down.
TIM: Yeah, like it lets me not think about the day.
THERAPIST: Gotcha. How effective is it?
TIM: Most of the time, it's great.
THERAPIST: The other times?
TIM: It just gets me angrier.
THERAPIST: What happens then?
TIM: Usually nothing. But, a few times, I cut myself. It's stupid, I know.
THERAPIST: And other times?
TIM: It doesn't do anything. I just get more and more down.
THERAPIST: Anything else?
TIM: A few times, I've come close to just taking my pills. They're in my bathroom.
THERAPIST: What do you mean by "coming close"?
TIM: I get them. Hold them in my hand. I don't want to die. I just want to go to sleep. Just for a little while.
THERAPIST: When was the last time this happened?
TIM: A couple of weeks ago.
THERAPIST: It sounds like things are really tough for you.

As demonstrated above, Tim is at very high risk. He may not be an imminent threat to himself, but it seems possible that in an altered state (i.e., after drinking alcohol), he may make an impulsive decision to take his pills. Although Tim does not express an explicit desire to die, the unintended consequence of taking pills and going to sleep may be suicide. For this reason, coupled with the other risks highlighted in the previous dialogues, it might be beneficial to provide a targeted plan of action. For example, in light of the depression severity, unsupportive family environment, access to substances, and suicidality (i.e., ideation and plans), it may be important to talk with the parent about a short-term hospital stay. These stays are critical to ensure that adolescents do not hurt themselves (either intentionally or accidentally). This is, however, a challenging conversation. We encourage therapists to speak openly about safety concerns, and further, discuss with the patient the pros and cons of parent involvement. As discussed in Chapter 4, respecting a patient's autonomy is key.

Box 9.4   Level III Risk: Challenging Patient

THERAPIST: Tim, thanks for being so open with me about what's going on with you and at home. In light of everything we've discussed, I'm worried about your safety.
TIM: You are?

> THERAPIST: I am. On the one hand, you don't want to die. On the other hand, you are drinking alone and, at times, coming dangerously close to taking medication to go to sleep.
>
> TIM: I haven't, though.
>
> THERAPIST: I know. I'm worried that your depression and suicidal thoughts and behaviors seem to be escalating. And, drinking has become less effective as a means of coping with the pain you're going through. I'm also concerned that if you're home alone with your brother and under the influence, then he may not be receiving the attention he needs.
>
> TIM: OK.
>
> THERAPIST: In these cases, there are options. I wonder if you'd be willing to hear about a couple?
>
> TIM: OK.
>
> THERAPIST: In the past, I've often recommended short-term hospital programs. This is an excellent opportunity to receive an evaluation for your medication. And, there also is more treatment provided, which I think might be incredibly helpful for you to relieve your distress.
>
> TIM: I'm not going to a hospital.
>
> THERAPIST: Can you help me understand your concerns?
>
> TIM: I just don't want to do it.
>
> THERAPIST: It's a big decision – there's no doubt. I wonder if we can walk through some of the pros and cons together.

Our experience is that most teens will be resistant to the idea of hospitalization. This is understandable. We recommend using a motivational interviewing approach when discussing hospitalization, and, in a similar fashion, including parents in this process. For Level III risk, hospitalization may be inevitable. However, we believe the hospitalization and the associated treatment will be more effective if the adolescent is involved in the decision process to be admitted. While this is ideal, adolescents' *buy-in* or *approval* may not be obtained, and it still may be necessary to move forward with the hospitalization to ensure safety.

Imminent Risk

In contrast to the risk levels described above, imminent risk describes a situation when an adolescent is not safe and will likely make an attempt within the next 24 hours. An immediate response is needed, and, for many youth, this may necessitate a visit to the emergency room or psychiatric hospitalization. Although these situations are uncommon, it is important for clinicians to have a clear plan in place. We recommend that therapists have a standard operating procedure, which provides clear instruction to parents with respect to: (1) where a parent should bring a teen when there is an imminent risk to suicide (both in the office and in the patient's home); (2) what a parent needs to bring to the emergency room or hospital when imminent risk is present (e.g., insurance information, clothes for teen); and (3) what to do when a teen refuses to go to the emergency room or hospital. Understandably, managing an actively suicidal adolescent will be distressing for parents. Therefore, it will be essential for a clinician to have clear answers (and directives). Namely, if there is an imminent risk, a clinician should have a list of the nearby hospitals that will be receptive to an actively suicidal teen. Alternatively, if a teen refuses and is a risk to suicide, it is always possible to dial 911, and emergency services will assist with the hospitalization. While tackling the acute crisis, parents often will want to know "what's next?" Consequently, it also may be helpful to have a handout for parents, which restates: (1) how to hospitalize the teen and (2) acute treatment options following discharge from emergency services. These options will vary as a function of local resources and providing this information for a parent in an accessible manner will serve as an important guide (or starting place).

In summary, suicide risk is not static. It may change as an adolescent progresses through treatment, and, as demonstrated through the sample dialogues, it can change within a session as more information is obtained. Careful assessment of suicide risk and associated protective mechanisms is essential to ensure the safety of depressed adolescents.

Treatment of Suicidality

As discussed earlier in this chapter, the treatment of depression may not be sufficient to reduce suicidality. Below, we discuss different approaches aimed at reducing suicidality in youth-based populations.

Adjusting the Treatment Approach

The most effective interventions for reducing risk of suicidal behaviors among adolescents are intensive (Glenn et al., 2015). For therapists, this may mean increasing session frequency (i.e., multiple sessions per week) and/or duration of both individual sessions and overall treatment course. Treatments may need to be *front-loaded* (i.e., higher frequency of sessions shortly after an attempt) for recent suicide attempters, as adolescents are at the highest risk for further attempts in the months following hospital discharge (Qin & Nordentoft, 2005).

Furthermore, no therapist should be an island when working with suicidal adolescents. We recommend building a treatment team and integrated treatment structure around patients and their families. Some practitioners work within settings (e.g., specialized hospital-based outpatient services; multidisciplinary outpatient clinics) where the team approach includes regular communication and consultation among members. In other cases, therapists may need to reach out to the patient's psychiatrist, social worker, guidance counselor, or other allied mental health professionals to explicitly build a team. In these cases, regular supervision and structured team consultation are essential for acquiring support in making potentially difficult treatment decisions (e.g., hospitalizing patients expressing suicidal intent). Finally, therapists need to arrange for their patients to have 24-hour access to crisis interventions, which may include paging the therapist and/or psychiatric emergency services (see Brent et al., 2011).

Involving the Family

Nearly all interventions that have successfully reduced adolescent suicidality have included formal modules geared towards improving family functioning (Brent et al., 2013; Glenn et al., 2015). CBT therapists working with depressed, suicidal adolescents should therefore strongly consider making a referral for concurrent family therapy. Family interventions with demonstrated efficacy focus on topics like parent–adolescent communication, consistent discipline, problem-solving during conflict, and increasing positive interactions within the family. For individual CBT with suicidal adolescents, family involvement (with parents, especially) is crucial, particularly in early sessions. Parents are important resources for securing the patient's environment (e.g., restricting access to lethal means like firearms and certain medications) and for monitoring the patient's safety. The ways in which parents carry out these functions can be negotiated collaboratively; for instance, therapists can assist patients and their parents in creating a list of the adolescent's warning signs (e.g., I get really quiet and withdraw) and corresponding steps for the parents to take (e.g., Remind me of my coping playlist). In a similar vein, given the robust link between family conflict and suicide, parents and adolescents might need to negotiate a planned hiatus on discussing *hot-button* issues (e.g., having romantic partners stay the night) in the early stages of therapy to give the adolescent time to develop skills to better address these issues with parents nearer to treatment termination (Brent et al., 2011).

Safety Planning

A safety plan is a detailed, step-by-step list of coping strategies that the patient agrees to employ in the event of an acute suicidal crisis. Safety plans typically include the following elements: (1) triggers to potentially avoid or limit; (2) warning signs (thoughts, feelings, and/or behaviors); (3) coping strategies that the patient can try; (4) people the patient can reach out to for support; and (5) emergency contact information (including phone numbers) for therapists and other health professionals, the closest psychiatric emergency room, and/or a crisis hotline. We provide an example of a completed safety plan below. Safety plans are individually tailored to a patient's previous experiences (e.g., suicidal crises, attempts) and are developed collaboratively with the adolescent and family. In a crisis, potential coping strategies are hierarchically deployed from least to most intensive; patients are encouraged to first use personal skill-based strategies to manage suicidal urges (e.g., deep breathing). If these strategies prove unsuccessful, patients *move up the hierarchy* to external supports (e.g., going to school counselor's office, talking to parents). Where possible, parents should not only be included as *steps* in the safety plan (e.g., call mom), but also be given copies of the plan to support its implementation. Finally, safety plans are working documents; new strategies should be added as the adolescent progresses through therapy, and interventions can be altered based on how helpful they are in navigating crises.

Box 9.5 Sample Safety Plan

Triggers to avoid	1 Movies/pictures with cutting or blood 2 Parties where there's alcohol 3 Looking up ex-girlfriend on Facebook
Warning signs	**Thoughts** 1 "I'm such a loser" 2 "People would be happier if I wasn't here" **Emotions** 1 Despair (8/10 or more) 2 Guilt (7/10 or more) **Behaviors** 1 Staying in my room for hours during the day 2 Not responding to texts from my best friends 3 Cutting my skin with paper clips
Things I can do	1 Go for a short walk 2 Do a breathing exercise 3 Watch a funny YouTube clip (e.g., laughing baby) 4 Listen to my motivation playlist 5 Do a thought record
Ways I can reach out	1 Call Mike to talk about anything (school, hockey) 2 Call Chris and tell him I'm having a tough time 3 Call my sister and ask her to distract me 4 Call Mom or Dad

What will I do if I still feel unsafe?	I will tell mom or dad that I feel this way and ask for help. If I can't reach them, I will call my therapist (Christian: XXX-XXX-XXXX) or my psychiatrist (Dr. Cook: XXX-XXX-XXXX). In an emergency, I will call 911

Therapist and Psychiatrist Contact Numbers

[Therapist name]	[Psychiatrist name]
[Address]	[Address]
Phone: XXX-XXX-XXXX	Phone: XXX-XXX-XXXX

Emergency Numbers

Emergency Room
XXX-XXX-XXXX or 911

National Suicide Prevention Lifeline
XXX-XXX-XXXX   (24 hours, 7 days/week)

Interpersonal Skills and Social Support

Interpersonal difficulties are among the most common reasons adolescents provide for their suicidal behaviors. Although the exact skills to focus on will vary as a function of patient needs, major areas to consider include: (1) communicating needs calmly and directly (using "I" statements while maintaining consistent eye contact and a steady tone of voice); (2) saying "no" (i.e., being able to refuse a request appropriately, and without *burning bridges*; being aware of boundaries and drawing them firmly but respectfully); (3) making a request or asking for help (stating the facts in a concise manner; accepting "no" for an answer gracefully); and (4) effective socializing (listening actively and expressing interest in others; resisting urges to *over-share*; identifying and building from shared interests and experiences). Role-playing in therapy can be a very effective way to experiment with interpersonal skills in a safe environment, which is crucial as it may help teens navigate interpersonal stressors that trigger increased suicidality.

Box 9.6   Sample Safety Plan

THERAPIST: So, to practice this, why don't you play your teacher, and I'll be you asking for help with the math homework.
PATIENT: Yeah, OK.

> THERAPIST (acting as patient): Excuse me, Mr. Dillon, can I speak with you for a few minutes?
> PATIENT (acting as teacher): Yes, but I'm really busy so make it quick.
> THERAPIST (making consistent eye contact): OK. So, as you know, I've been having some trouble in your class this year. Part of that is because I've gotten behind and missed assignments.
> PATIENT: Yes, I noticed you missed a lot of class in February.
> THERAPIST: You're right, I was dealing with a lot then. And I want you to know that I really want to do well in this class. I think that if I get your help, I can really get back on track. Would you be willing to meet with me after class to answer some of my questions?
> PATIENT (as himself): I think it would be really hard not to get upset if he talks about my absences. I would just want to melt down and leave.
> THERAPIST: That's important to notice. Why don't we work on some skills to help you get through that kind of thing if it comes up?

Doing a reverse role play like the one illustrated above may be especially helpful because it allows the therapist to model interpersonal skills, and adolescents will often play out their *worst-case scenario*, which can then be trouble-shot in session. The therapist and patient can then switch roles to allow the patient to try out interpersonal skills previously modeled by the therapist.

Finally, a supportive interpersonal network is a strong protective factor against future suicidality. Therefore, along with addressing specific interpersonal behaviors at a *micro* level, therapy can focus on how to maximize and/or increase the adolescent's support network. To this end, therapists and patients might collaboratively catalogue the patient's supports (e.g., family, friends, teachers, treatment team) and brainstorm the role that each support plays in the adolescent's long-term wellness. In circumstances where a helpful support is not being used to its fullest potential, the patient can create an action plan for how to draw on the relevant support more extensively in the future.

Summary

Adolescent suicidality is a pressing issue, and the preceding passages provide a framework to assess and treat suicidal youth. Perhaps the most important message to convey is the need to be prepared. Preparation includes a consistent and clear assessment of suicidal ideation and related behaviors and the use of targeted treatment strategies (e.g., building social support, safety planning). Moreover, in situations when depressed adolescents are expressing acute or imminent risk, it is crucial for therapists to have a standard operating procedure to manage crises. Collectively, these strategies will improve outcomes for high-risk, depressed youth.

10 Innovations and Future Directions in CBT

Since its initial development in the 1960s (Beck, 1967), CBT has emerged as among the most widely researched and practiced form of psychotherapy in the world (DeRubeis et al., 2010). It has been refined over the years, with adaptations targeting a wide array of mental disorders (e.g., mood, anxiety, and personality disorders), and it has evolved to incorporate additional techniques in its therapeutic arsenal (e.g., mindfulness- and acceptance-based techniques). However, throughout its history, the delivery format of CBT has remained the same: face-to-face individual or group therapy. The exponential growth of internet-based interventions and smartphone technology has the potential to reshape the landscape of CBT and mental healthcare more broadly. These recent technological developments may serve as important tools in the therapeutic toolkit of current and future clinicians. In this chapter, we review emerging technologies for targeting depression, focusing first on computer- and internet-based treatments, followed by a discussion of innovative mobile mental health interventions.[16]

Computer- and Internet-Based Interventions

Among the most exciting new developments in the field of CBT are computer- and internet-based interventions for depression. The majority of these programs are internet-delivered adaptions of CBT (i.e., iCBT), rather than computer-based programs (i.e., cCBT). Early instantiations of these iCBT programs were offline and computer-based (e.g., delivered via CD-ROM disk). However, the majority of cCBT programs have

---

16 We have no commercial or personal financial interests in the programs reviewed in this chapter. There are a large number of internet-based programs for depression, as well as numerous mobile mental health applications. We highlight the ones that have been most frequently reviewed in the literature and use them as examples of the helpful features that can be found in many available programs.

moved online and are now easily accessed through provider websites. Accordingly, in the section below, we focus primarily on current iCBT programs, with limited discussion of cCBT.

iCBT Programs Targeting Depression

The most commonly used web-based interventions for depression are cognitive behavioral in nature, including *Beating the Blues*[17] (*BTB*: Proudfoot et al., 2004), *MoodGYM*[18] (Christensen, Griffiths, & Korten, 2002), and the *Sadness Program*[19] (Perini, Titov, & Andrews, 2008). These online programs differ in the way in which information is provided, but deliver similar overall CBT content. Specifically, they provide web-based access to a series of modules focused on psychoeducation about the symptoms of depression and the cognitive behavioral model, and critically, they teach users the common cognitive and behavioral skills encouraged in traditional, face-to-face CBT. These programs are typically self-guided, stand-alone interventions; however, to reduce dropout rates, many internet-based interventions have incorporated support coaches who will periodically contact the user to troubleshoot content and increase accountability (Mohr, Cuijpers, & Lehman, 2011).

Among the available programs, *BTB* has been the most frequently tested for the treatment of depression. Briefly, the *BTB* program consists of eight online CBT-based modules, which gradually guide participants in the use of various cognitive (e.g., identifying and challenging NATs) and behavioral (e.g., activity-scheduling, problem-solving, sleep hygiene) techniques. In addition to filmed case studies of individuals modeling common depressive symptoms and the application of CBT techniques, the program provides homework to be completed in between the weekly online sessions (Proudfoot et al., 2004). Similar to *BTB*, the *Sadness Program* involves six web-based modules focused on psychoeducation regarding the symptoms of depression and the cognitive behavioral model, as well as modules providing guidance in common cognitive (e.g., thought record) and behavioral (e.g., activity schedule) symptom management tools. Following each session, participants download a document with homework activities focused on reinforcing the skills learned in that particular session (Perini, Titov, & Andrews, 2008; Titov et al., 2010).

One recently developed iCBT program integrates web-based crowdsourcing technology to target depression. Specifically, *Panoply*, recently renamed *Koko* (Morris, Schueller & Picard, 2015), is a web-based CBT

---

17 http://www.beatingtheblues.co.uk
18 https://moodgym.anu.edu.au/welcome
19 https://thiswayup.org.au

application that leverages a peer-to-peer crowdsourcing platform to aid in the cognitive reappraisal of NATs. Users submit a brief description of a stressor and accompanying NATs through the *Koko* platform, and these are then reviewed by other users who are trained to provide one of three types of responses: (1) support (i.e., empathic emotional support); (2) debug (i.e., identify cognitive distortions in the NAT, such as mind reading or catastrophizing); or (3) reframe (i.e., offer more positive and helpful ways of thinking about the triggering situation). Importantly, responses are vetted by fellow *Koko* peers before being returned to the user who submitted the original post. Thus, *Koko* differs from other iCBT programs in that responses to NATs, including cognitive reframing, are "outsourced" and generated by other users. A recent study indicated that a 3-week *Koko* intervention resulted in significant reductions in depressive symptoms among young adults (Morris et al., 2015). Intriguingly, *Koko* was most effective for those users who began treatment with greater deficits in cognitive reappraisal, suggesting that this process of outsourcing and having cognitive strategies modeled by peers may be particularly helpful for these individuals. In addition, as noted above, another unique aspect of *Koko* is the fact that users not only receive helpful responses (e.g., cognitive reframing, identifying cognitive distortions) from their peers, but also generate such response for others. The practicing of these cognitive techniques, as well as the online social support and interaction, may also be therapeutically beneficial for participants.

The Benefits of iCBT

There are a number of benefits associated with web-based interventions. First, they are convenient as they eliminate travel time to a clinician's office, and individuals in need can access mental health resources from the privacy and comfort of home. Second, costs are substantially reduced, as subscription fees to iCBT programs are typically much lower than face-to-face treatment costs. Third, those reluctant to seek face-to-face treatment (e.g., due to perceived stigma associated with seeing a therapist or psychiatrist) may feel more comfortable accessing a web-based intervention from home. Thus, given their lower costs and ability to reach anyone with internet access, iCBT programs may help bridge the gap in access to mental health services. Indeed, approximately 40% of teens diagnosed with depression in the last year have not received treatment for their episode (Avenevoli et al., 2015); increasing the availability of CBT may help reduce the number of untreated, clinically depressed adolescents. Last, younger populations are becoming more reliant on *being connected* electronically, and while there is certainly an argument to be had about the importance of "unplugging," internet-based services may reach a population that would otherwise go untreated. Given these benefits, and the growing body of research supporting the efficacy of these programs in treating depression (Richards & Richardson, 2012; see section on The Efficacy of iCBT for Depression, below), iCBT is now recommended by the UK National Health Service (NHS) as a treatment option for mild to moderate depression.[20] The NHS recognizes that iCBT could be used as a low-cost strategy to disseminate cognitive behavioral techniques to a large number of individuals, many of whom may not have sought treatment in a face-to-face format.

In addition to the benefits of iCBT, it is important to highlight potential risks associated with online interventions for depression. In particular, current iCBT platforms are not well equipped to manage clinical crises, which are best dealt with through face-to-face treatment. For example, a patient in face-to-face treatment who endorses active suicidal ideation can be evaluated *in person* by the treating clinician, to assess for safety and whether a higher level of care (e.g., hospitalization) may be needed. Online iCBT interventions often include brief self-report depressive symptom assessments (e.g., Patient Health Questionnaire-9 (PHQ-9); Kroenke, Spitzer, & Williams, 2001). However, if patients endorse suicidality on these measures, a more detailed assessment is required to determine the severity of suicidality and whether continued iCBT treatment is appropriate. Although programs differ, existing iCBT programs are typically stand-alone interventions, and there is necessarily a lag between the time a patient endorses suicidality on an online measure and when the patient is contacted by a clinician on the iCBT team. In addition, and relatedly, iCBT users are reporting detailed personal information on their mental health status on these websites. Although websites are increasingly secure, there may be concerns about the security of these servers and privacy of highly personal data.

It is important to note that, although iCBT programs have typically been tested as stand-alone interventions, with no (human) therapist interaction, they can be utilized as an adjunct to face-to-face therapy. For example, instead of providing paper-and-pencil worksheets to teens to practice cognitive (e.g., thought record) or behavioral (e.g., activity schedule) skills in between sessions, a teen may find it more appealing to be assigned access to a relatively engaging online iCBT module. Similarly, within the initial sessions of CBT, one could imagine assigning a teen to online psychoeducational modules focused on common depressive symptoms and the cognitive behavioral model. Moreover, as we describe in Chapter 7, patients who exhibit greater acquisition and regular use of CBT skills at the end of treatment are at a reduced

---

20 http://www.nhs.uk/Conditions/online-mental-health-services/Pages/introduction.aspx

risk of relapse following therapy (Strunk et al., 2007). Thus, to minimize relapse risk, patients with lower levels of skill acquisition could be assigned iCBT modules after completing a course of CBT to shore up their cognitive and behavioral skills. In addition, iCBT could be integrated into a patient's Personal Relapse Prevention Plan; for example, a patient might plan to use iCBT in response to a spike in symptoms following termination of face-to-face treatment.

The Efficacy of iCBT for Depression

The proliferation of iCBT programs raises the critical question: *How effective are these internet-based treatments for depression?* There are now several dozen studies that have tested the efficacy of these programs in reducing depressive symptoms. A recent meta-analysis identified 24 randomized clinical trials of iCBT for depression,[21] and found a moderate post-treatment effect size ($d = 0.56$) favoring iCBT relative to control groups in reducing depressive symptoms (Richards & Richardson, 2012). Importantly, the majority of iCBT studies have used wait-list control groups as comparison conditions (i.e., patients in the wait-list condition receive no treatment during the trial, and are only provided access to the iCBT content following the completion of the study). Thus, the advantage of iCBT programs compared to wait-list control groups could be due to the cognitive and behavioral techniques patients have acquired. However, within such wait-list designs, the influence of other common or "non-specific" factors in driving symptom change (in particular, placebo-related processes) cannot be ruled out. In contrast, face-to-face CBT has been subjected to numerous randomized clinical trials, many of which have employed rigorous control groups (e.g., antidepressant medication or placebo conditions). It will be important for future iCBT studies to test these programs against more rigorous control groups to more adequately assess their efficacy in treating depression.

One control group that is particularly relevant as a comparison condition for iCBT is, of course, face-to-face CBT. Unfortunately, at the time of this writing, data are lacking on the efficacy of iCBT versus face-to-face CBT (Andersson, Cuijpers, Carlbring, Riper, & Hedman, 2014). The few preliminary studies that have compared the two indicate that internet-based CBT is about as efficacious as individual (Wagner, Horn, & Maercker, 2014) or group (Spek et al., 2007) CBT in reducing depressive symptoms. However, to our knowledge, no such study has been conducted in depressed adolescents.

---

21 Two of these studies were computer-based (cCBT), the remainder were delivered over the internet (iCBT).

iCBT Programs Tailored for Teens

Perhaps not surprisingly, the bulk of prior iCBT studies have been tested in adult samples. However, there are an increasing number of internet-based cognitive behavioral interventions targeting depression and anxiety in youth. In their meta-analytic review, Ebert and colleagues (2015) identified 13 randomized clinical trials of iCBT for depression and/or anxiety in youth (four of these studies were exclusively focused on the treatment of depression and two targeted both depression and anxiety symptoms). Although these programs were all CBT-based, they differed widely in program characteristics, including the extent to which parents were involved and delivery format. For example, programs ranged from clinician-facilitated chat room-based interventions adapted from CBT manuals to CBT interventions embedded within a video-game format (e.g., Stasiak, Hatcher, Frampton, & Merry, 2012). On average, these interventions significantly reduced both depressive and anxiety symptoms in adolescents, and there were no significant differences in symptom improvement among programs that incorporated parent involvement (e.g., parents receiving psychoeducation about their child's symptoms; parents learning about the process of cognitive restructuring and graded exposure) and those programs that did not.

There are several important limitations to the current evidence base for iCBT programs for depressed and anxious teens. First, 11 of the 13 studies reviewed by Ebert and colleagues (2015) reported no follow-up assessments, and thus little is known regarding the extent to which adolescents maintain their treatment gains following termination. Second, similar to the adult iCBT literature, only three of the iCBT studies in youth compared their intervention to a placebo control group (the remainder used a wait-list control group). Finally, severely depressed youth often are excluded from these trials, and thus it is not known whether these interventions are effective for severely depressed adolescents. Relatedly, little is known about which adolescents might benefit most from iCBT interventions. Are there certain pretreatment patient characteristics (e.g., demographic, clinical, cognitive factors) that predict better or worse treatment response in iCBT versus face-to-face CBT (or antidepressants)? Addressing this question is essential, as it may determine which teens respond more optimally to this form of treatment (versus more traditional individual and group therapy).

Mobile Depression Interventions (Smartphones and Applications)

Mobile phone subscriptions have reached over 6.6 billion worldwide (International Telecommunications Union, 2013), and the percentage of

American teens who own a smartphone (i.e., mobile phone with advanced operating systems) has increased dramatically in recent years. Only 36% of teens aged 13–17 owned a smartphone in 2011; in 2013, that number had risen to 70% (Nielsen, 2013). Smartphones are an integral part of the daily lives of many teens, and the potential to harness smartphone technology as a helpful therapeutic adjunct to face-to-face therapy is now a reality.

Computer- and internet-based inventions brought CBT out of the therapist's office and into patients' homes. Smartphones place CBT tools *literally* in the patient's pocket and thus can be accessed throughout the patient's day. These therapeutic tools range from using the "Notes" function on a smartphone to record relevant treatment data (e.g., as a replacement for paper-and-pencil activity logs) to utilizing applications (i.e., apps) predicting mood states as a means of alerting teens to when it may be beneficial to engage in interventions to improve their mood. Below we review some of the ways in which smartphones can be integrated into CBT with depressed teens.

Using Built-In Smartphone Functions

Smartphones, such as the popular iPhone and Android platforms, are sold with a variety of existing features, which can be used as tools for between-session self-monitoring and guided interventions. For example, the "Notes" function may be a more appealing and practical means for some teens to record relevant homework data than traditional paper-and-pencil worksheets (e.g., thought record, activity schedule). "Notes" often include time stamps indicating when the entry was completed, which can be helpful for clarifying the timing of events during in-session homework review. In addition, the "Calendar" feature on smartphones can be useful for keeping therapy appointments and for behavioral scheduling (e.g., scheduling activities on specific dates and times over the week to boost mood or sense of accomplishment, or to schedule behavioral experiments). Moreover, alarms can be set on the phone for a variety of therapeutic purposes. For instance, alarms could be used to signal the time to complete scheduled homework activities or to take medications, or for setting bed and wake times to establish healthy sleep habits. Audio recordings made in session on a patient's smartphone also may be useful to listen to outside of therapy (e.g., guided mindfulness practice, progressive muscle relaxation). The potential therapeutic uses of built-in smartphone functions for homework activities are only limited by the therapist's and patient's creativity. In the collaborative spirit of CBT, therapists can engage their adolescent patients in brainstorming ways in which they could use their smartphones to tailor treatment to their unique needs and preferences.

Mental Health Applications (Apps)

A wide array of mobile mental health apps have been developed for smartphones, in particular the iPhone and Android platforms.[22] These apps can be used as helpful therapeutic adjuncts and can be broadly classified into those that offer tools for *self-monitoring* (e.g., mood and symptom tracking) and CBT-based *interventions* (e.g., guided cognitive restructuring and behavioral activation tools).

Self-Monitoring Apps

A critical component of treatment is tracking change in a patient's symptoms, including improvements across affective, behavioral, cognitive, and interpersonal domains. In Chapter 3, we discussed assessment tools to aid in tracking symptom improvement, such as asking teens to complete weekly Beck Depression Inventory (BDI) questionnaires. These weekly assessments are undoubtedly informative; nonetheless, they are not without their limitations. In particular, symptom assessment questionnaires, such as the BDI-II, require *retrospective* recall of symptoms over the past week (or longer). The role of memory or recall biases in distorting the accuracy of self-reports is well documented (see Chapter 2 and Kahneman, 2011). For example, a teen in CBT treatment may have experienced very few depressive symptoms over the course of the past week, but the day prior to her session, her mood plummets due to an argument with a friend. When asked to report on her week, the patient may state that she felt depressed much of the week rather than only on 1 out of 7 days. Although these memory biases may not be completely eliminated, self-monitoring apps that incorporate Ecological Momentary Assessment (EMA) may minimize their occurrence. EMA encompasses a range of different methodologies, but typically requires participants to "report repeatedly on their experiences in real time, in real-world settings, over time and across contexts" (Shiffman, Stone, & Hufford, 2008). The "ecological" aspect of EMA refers to the fact that assessments are completed in *real-world* contexts as individuals go about their daily lives, as opposed to completing questionnaires in the therapist's office. The "momentary" aspect refers to EMA's focus on individuals' *current* experience, thus minimizing memory biases inherent in questionnaires involving retrospective recall.

---

22 The Anxiety and Depression Association of America (ADAA) provides helpful reviews of mobile mental health apps (http://www.adaa.org/finding-help/mobile-apps). In addition, the Quantified-Self website (http://quantifiedself.com/guide) is a helpful resource providing information on a wide array of self-monitoring tools, including mood-monitoring apps.

The number of new apps to track emotional states in real time has flourished recently, including apps to track changes in depressive symptoms and mood (e.g., *Mindful Moods, Track Your Happiness, T2 Mood Tracker*)[23] (Torous et al., 2015). These apps are either free or relatively low-cost (e.g., less than $5) and involve repeated assessments of current emotional states or symptoms that are prompted by smartphone alerts at random intervals throughout the day. By virtue of these repeated assessments embedded within a patient's day-to-day life, these apps can provide a more fine-grained and ecologically valid assessment of symptom change.

The data generated from self-monitoring apps can be used for the benefit of patients (e.g., to allow them to gain a better sense of their emotional patterns), as a tool to highlight weekly stressors or successes to add to the agenda, or for the purpose of tracking treatment progress. In addition to tracking emotional states, these apps often include assessments of current location, social context, behaviors, and cognitions. For example, the *Track Your Happiness* app provides user-friendly graphical summaries of mood ratings and their relation to reported location (e.g., at home versus school), social context (e.g., alone versus with a friend), and activity (e.g., listening to music versus commuting), among other relevant variables. These data can be easily reviewed in session with the therapist to get an overview of the patient's week and relevant emotional and behavioral patterns.

Guided-Intervention Apps

In addition to self-monitoring, a variety of apps have been developed to guide patients in the use of CBT techniques (e.g., *iCBT, ICouchCBT, eCBT, CBT Referee*). Given the speed with which new apps are developed, some of the abovementioned apps may be substantially upgraded, or perhaps obsolete, by the time you read this. In general, these CBT apps provide patients with guidance in identifying NATs, linking them to specific cognitive distortions or thinking traps (e.g., catastrophizing, all-or-nothing thinking) and cognitive restructuring skills. The apps often provide psychoeducational information about the symptoms of depression and the cognitive behavioral model, as well as guidance in behavioral exercises to boost mood and a sense of accomplishment (or mastery). We encourage clinicians who are considering integrating these apps into their treatment to download them and try them out prior to recommending them to their patients. As we note above, ADAA also provides helpful reviews of mental health apps tested by mental health professionals.

---

23 We are not endorsing the use of any specific apps, but rather mention a few to highlight helpful features that can be found in many other current, and likely future, apps.

Passive Data Collection

The above apps require that patients have the discipline to pull out their smartphone and to regularly input information. A recent development in smartphone apps is passive data collection (i.e., no user input required). These newer apps take advantage of built-in smartphone features and embedded sensors (e.g., accelerometer, GPS, Bluetooth, wi-fi) to collect data without the need for user report. For example, *Mobilyze!*, an app which has been shown to significantly reduce depressive symptoms in depressed adults (Burns et al., 2011), passively collects data on a large array of information, including amount of activity (using the smartphone's accelerometer), location (using GPS and Bluetooth recognition of wi-fi devices), amount of light in environment (using ambient light sensors) and recent calls. Along with passive data collection, the app initially requires user-inputted EMA data, including assessments of current mood states. By pairing the EMA and passive data, an algorithm gradually "learns" the user's emotional patterns and builds a model to predict the user's current mood state solely on the basis of the passive data. When *Mobilyze!* predicts that the user is experiencing low mood, it suggests an intervention. For example, if the app senses that the user has spent 6 hours in her bedroom (on the basis of GPS data and Bluetooth recognition of wi-fi devices in the room) with little movement (assessed via accelerometer), it may send a text message predicting the user's low mood (e.g., You are at home and your mood is lower than average) and suggest a behavioral intervention (e.g., Give a friend a call or get out of the house. You'll feel better if you do!; Burns et al., 2011).

To our knowledge, *Mobilyze!* is the first app to incorporate ecological momentary *intervention* on the basis of predicted mood states. Although apps like *Mobilyze!* are far from perfect in their ability to predict subjective states and suggest the most appropriate intervention, they highlight the exciting possibility of developing sophisticated, and easy-to-use, personalized assessment and intervention tools for depressed individuals requiring limited user input.

There are a range of other creative and intriguing new passive data collection strategies under development. These include using small, mobile external sensors to assess heart rate and galvanic skin response as proxy measures of stress or emotional reactivity (Mohr, Burns, Schueller, Clarke, & Klinkman, 2013) and harnessing voice capture technology to assess the emotional tone of speech and text recognition software to measure depressive symptoms (Aguilera & Muench, 2012; De Giacomo, L'Abate, Pennebaker, & Rumbaugh, 2010). In addition, and given growing recognition of the therapeutic benefits of targeting sleep problems in depressed adolescents (Clarke et al., 2015), there are an increasing number of sleep management apps that rely on passive data collection (e.g., *Sleep Cycle*,

Sleep Bot). These apps typically require users to place their smartphone on their bed and use the built-in accelerometer to track movement throughout the night to assess sleep quality. The apps generate graphical summaries of sleep quality throughout the night that can be reviewed in session. These sleep apps can be combined with mood-monitoring apps to examine the relation between poor sleep and mood or depressive symptoms.

Providing CBT via Videoconferencing

Many families have difficulty accessing adequate treatment for their depressed teens (e.g., due to living in rural areas with few mental health resources available). Videoconferencing provides another means to bridge gaps in clinical care by allowing therapists to provide long-distance treatment. In contrast to iCBT or mobile mental health apps, videoconferencing (e.g., Skype, Google Hangouts, FaceTime) allows patients to interact in a face-to-face fashion but through a computer screen. The percentage of therapists providing psychotherapy using videoconferencing has grown steadily in the last several decades, and studies support its efficacy in the treatment of depression (Duncan, Velasquez, & Nelson, 2014; Shore, 2013). Indeed, research indicates that CBT delivered via videoconferencing may be as effective in the treatment of depression as traditional CBT (Gros et al., 2013; Nelson & Duncan, 2015).

Clinicians considering using videoconferencing should be aware of the unique legal, regulatory, and risk management issues involved in delivering treatment from a distance. An exhaustive discussion of these issues is beyond the scope of this book. However, we highlight a few important issues below and refer the reader to more extensive discussions of these challenges (e.g., see Kramer, Mishkind, Luxton, & Shore, 2012; Shore, 2013). Relevant issues include: (1) reimbursement for videotherapy from insurance companies and (2) regulations necessitating that clinicians hold a license within the state the patient is located. One concern frequently raised against videoconferencing as a means to deliver therapy is that a clinician might not be able to effectively manage clinical crises. It is particularly important for therapists to establish a detailed safety plan with their patients at the initiation of treatment (e.g., a local clinician to contact in case of emergency, determining closest emergency room). Another potential issue is whether treatment delivered via a computer screen may limit the therapist's ability to establish a strong therapeutic alliance with patients. Although a reasonable concern, studies suggest that the alliance is as well established in videotherapy relative to face-to-face CBT (Nelson & Duncan, 2015).

As one can gather, the potential benefits of delivering therapy via videoconferencing (e.g., reaching underserved populations) are balanced by a number of unique challenges (e.g., patient safety, cross-state licensing). Clinicians considering integrating videotherapy into their clinical practice should carefully consider these potential challenges when deciding whether it is an appropriate treatment approach for them and their patients.

Summary

A growing body of research supports the efficacy of face-to-face individual and group CBT for depression in youth (Klein, Jacobs, & Reinecke, 2007; Weersing & Gonzalez, 2009; Weisz et al., 2006). The past decade has seen a rapid rise in the development of internet-based adaptions of CBT and advancements in mobile mental health applications. These developments have the potential to reshape the dominant delivery formats of CBT and, more broadly, the landscape of mental healthcare. This new wave of mental health technologies may help bridge the gap between the availability of empirically supported treatments for depression and the large number of individuals, including depressed teens, who fail to receive them (e.g., Avenevoli et al., 2015). Indeed, the National Institute of Mental Health Strategic Plan highlights the promise of iCBT and smartphone apps in increasing access to empirically supported interventions (http://www.nimh.nih.gov/about/strategic-planning-reports/strategic-objective-4.shtml).

In closing, the surge in rates of depression over during adolescence is striking. In addition to the emotional distress and impairment associated with depressive symptoms, a diagnosis of MDD during adolescence is linked to a range of negative downstream emotional, behavioral, interpersonal, academic, and socioeconomic consequences. Effective CBT will alleviate painful, debilitating symptoms of depression and help adolescents re-engage with a healthier developmental trajectory. We hope that this book provides a useful guide to navigate the obstacles that often arise in treatment and, thereby, allows you to help youth in need.

References

Abela, J. R., Aydin, C., & Auerbach, R. P. (2006). Operationalizing the "vulnerability" and "stress" components of the hopelessness theory of depression: A multi-wave longitudinal study. *Behavior Research and Therapy, 44,* 1565–1583.
Abela, J. R., Aydin, C. M., & Auerbach, R. P. (2007). Responses to depression in children: Reconceptualizing the relation among response styles. *Journal of Abnormal Child Psychology, 35,* 913–927.
Abela, J. R., Brozina, K., & Haigh, E. P. (2002). An examination of the response styles theory of depression in third- and seventh-grade children: A short-term longitudinal study. *Journal of Abnormal Child Psychology, 30,* 515–527.
Abela, J. R., & Hankin, B. L. (2009). Cognitive vulnerability to depression in children and adolescents: A developmental psychopathology perspective. In S. Nolen-Hoeksema & L. M. Hilt (Eds.) *Handbook of depression in adolescents* (pp. 335–376). New York, NY: Routledge.
Abela, J. R., & Hankin, B. L. (2011). Rumination as a vulnerability factor to depression during the transition from early to middle adolescence: A multiwave longitudinal study. *Journal of Abnormal Psychology, 120,* 259–271.
Abela, J. R., Parkinson, C., Stolow, D., & Starrs, C. (2009). A test of the integration of the hopelessness and response styles theories of depression in middle adolescence. *Journal of Clinical Child and Adolescent Psychology, 38,* 354–364.
Abela, J. R., Rochon, A., & Vanderbilt, E. (2000). The children's response styles questionnaire. Unpublished questionnaire.
Abela, J. R., & Sarin, S. (2002). Cognitive vulnerability to hopelessness depression: A chain is only as strong as its weakest link. *Cognitive Therapy and Research, 26,* 811–829.
Abela, J. R., & Sullivan, C. (2003). A test of Beck's cognitive diathesis-stress theory of depression in early adolescents. *The Journal of Early Adolescence, 23,* 384–404.
Abramson, L. Y., Metalsky, G. I., & Alloy, L. B. (1989). Hopelessness depression: A theory-based subtype of depression. *Psychological Review, 96,* 358–372.
Abramson, L. Y., Seligman, M. E., & Teasdale, J. D. (1978). Learned helplessness in humans: Critique and reformulation. *Journal of Abnormal Psychology, 87,* 49–74.
Achenbach, T. M. (1991). *Manual for the Child Behavior Checklist/4–18 and 1991 profile.* Burlington, VT: University of Vermont, Department of Psychiatry.
Achenbach, T. M., & Rescorla, L. A. (2001). *Manual for the ASEBA school-age forms and profiles.* Burlington, VT: University of Vermont, Research Center for Children, Youth, and Families.

Addis, M. E., & Jacobson, N. S. (2000). A closer look at the treatment rationale and homework compliance in cognitive-behavioral therapy for depression. *Cognitive Therapy and Research, 24,* 313–326.

Aguilera, A., & Muench, F. (2012). There's an app for that: Information technology applications for cognitive behavioral practitioners. *The Behavior Therapist/AABT, 35*(4), 65.

Alloy, L. B., Abramson, L. Y., Whitehouse, W. G., Hogan, M. E., Panzarella, C., & Rose, D. T. (2006). Prospective incidence of first onsets and recurrences of depression in individuals at high and low cognitive risk for depression. *Journal of Abnormal Psychology, 115,* 145–156.

Alloy, L. B., Black, S. K., Young, M. E., Goldstein, K. E., Shapero, B. G., Stange, J. P. . . . & Abramson, L. Y. (2012). Cognitive vulnerabilities and depression versus other psychopathology symptoms and diagnoses in early adolescence. *Journal of Clinical Child and Adolescent Psychology, 41,* 539–560.

Alloy, L. B., & Clements, C. M. (1998). Hopelessness theory of depression: Tests of the symptom component. *Cognitive Therapy and Research, 22,* 303–335.

Ambrosini, P. J. (2000). Historical development and present status of the Schedule for Affective Disorders and Schizophrenia for School-Age Children (K-SADS). *Journal of the American Academy of Child and Adolescent Psychiatry, 39,* 39–48.

American Psychiatric Association (2000). *Diagnostic and statistical manual of mental disorders* (4th ed., text rev). (DSM-IV-TR). Washington, DC: American Psychiatric Association.

American Psychiatric Association (2013). *Diagnostic and statistical manual of mental disorders: DSM-5™* (5th ed.). (2013). Arlington, VA: American Psychiatric Publishing.

American Psychological Association. (2003). Guidelines on multicultural education, training, research, practice, and organizational change for psychologists. *The American Psychologist, 58,* 377–402.

American Psychological Association. (2012). Guidelines for psychological practice with lesbian, gay, and bisexual clients. *The American Psychologist, 67,* 10–42.

Andersson, G., Cuijpers, P., Carlbring, P., Riper, H., & Hedman, E. (2014). Guided internet-based vs. face-to-face cognitive behavior therapy for psychiatric and somatic disorders: A systematic review and meta-analysis. *World Psychiatry, 13*(3), 288–295.

Angold, A., Costello, E. J., Messer, S. C., Pickles, A., Winder, F., & Silver, D. (1995). The development of a short questionnaire for use in epidemiological studies of depression in children and adolescents. *International Journal of Methods in Psychiatric Research, 5,* 237–249.

Apter, A. (2000). *Personality constellations in suicidal behaviour.* Proceedings of the 5th Annual Conference, Irish Association of Suicidology (pp. 14–25). Castlebar, County Mayo, Ireland: Irish Association of Suicidology.

Armstrong, T., & Olatunji, B. O. (2012). Eye tracking of attention in the affective disorders: A meta-analytic review and synthesis. *Clinical Psychology Review, 32*(8), 704–723.

Atkinson, S. D., Prakash, A., Zhang, Q., Pangallo, B. A., Bangs, M. E., Emslie, G. J., & March, J. S. (2014). A double-blind efficacy and safety study of duloxetine flexible dosing in children and adolescents with major depressive disorder. *Journal of Child and Adolescent Psychopharmacology, 24,* 180–189.

Auerbach, R. P., Admon, R., & Pizzagalli, D. A. (2014). Adolescent depression: Stress and reward dysfunction. *Harvard Review of Psychiatry, 22*(3), 139–148.

Auerbach, R. P., Bigda-Peyton, J. S., Eberhart, N. K., Webb, C. A., & Ho, M. H. (2011). Conceptualizing the prospective relationship between social support, stress, and depressive symptoms among adolescents. *Journal of Abnormal Child Psychology, 39*, 475–487.

Auerbach, R. P., Ho, M. H. R., & Kim, J. C. (2014). Identifying cognitive and interpersonal predictors of adolescent depression. *Journal of Abnormal Child Psychology, 42*, 913–924.

Auerbach, R. P., Millner, A. J., Stewart, J. G., & Esposito E. C. (2015). Identifying differences between depressed adolescent suicide ideators and attempters. *Journal of Affective Disorders, 186*, 127–133.

Auerbach, R. P., Stanton, C. H., Proudfit, G. H., & Pizzagalli, D. A. (2015). Self-referential processing in depressed adolescents: A high-density event-related potential study. *Journal of Abnormal Psychology, 124*, 233–245.

Auerbach, R. P., Stewart, J. G., Stanton, C. H., Mueller, E. M., & Pizzagalli, D. A. (2015). Emotion processing biases and resting EEG activity in depressed adolescents. *Depression and Anxiety, 32*, 693–701.

Avenevoli, S., Knight, E., Kessler, R. C., & Merikangas, K. R. (2008). Epidemiology of depression in children and adolescents. In S. Nolen-Hoeksema & L. M. Hilt (Eds.), *Handbook of depression in children and adolescents* (pp. 6–32). New York: Routledge.

Avenevoli, S., Swendsen, J., He, J. P., Burstein, M., & Merikangas, K. R. (2015). Major depression in the national comorbidity survey-adolescent supplement: Prevalence, correlates, and treatment. *Journal of the American Academy of Child and Adolescent Psychiatry, 54*(1), 37–44 e32.

Bacon, F. (1597/1857). *Meditationes sacrae*. Excusum impensis Humfredi Hooper. Retrieved from: https://scholar.google.com/scholar?q=Meditationes+Sacrae&btnG=&hl=en&as_sdt=0%2C22.

Bandura, A. (1986). *Social foundations of thought and action: A social cognitive theory*. Englewood Cliffs, NJ: Prentice Hall.

Bandura, A. (1999). Social cognitive theory: An agentic perspective. *Asian Journal of Social Psychology, 2*, 21–41.

Bandura, A., Pastorelli, C., Barbaranelli, C., & Caprara, G. V. (1999). Self-efficacy pathways to childhood depression. *Journal of Personality and Social Psychology, 76*, 258–269.

Barnes, G. M., Hoffman, J. H., Welte, J. W., Farrell, M. P., & Dintcheff, B. A. (2007). Adolescents' time use: Effects on substance use, delinquency and sexual activity. *Journal of Youth and Adolescence, 36*, 697–710.

Bastin, M., Mezulis, A. H., Ahles, J., Raes, F., & Bijttebier, P. (2014). Moderating effects of brooding and co-rumination on the relationship between stress and depressive symptoms in early adolescence: A multi-wave study. *Journal of Abnormal Child Psychology*.

Beck, A. T. (1967). *Depression: Causes and treatment*. Philadelphia: University of Pennsylvania Press.

Beck, A. T. (1976). *Cognitive therapy and the emotional disorders*. New York, NY: International Universities Press.

Beck, A. T. (2008). The evolution of the cognitive model of depression and its neurobiological correlates. *American Journal of Psychiatry, 165*, 969–977.

Beck, A. T., Davis, D. D., & Freeman, A. (2014). *Cognitive therapy of personality disorders* (3rd ed.). New York, NY: Guilford Press.

Beck, A. T., & Dozois, D. J. (2011). Cognitive therapy: Current status and future directions. *Annual Review of Medicine, 62*, 397–409.

Beck, A. T., Kovacs, M., & Weissman, A. (1979). Assessment of suicidal intention: TheScale for Suicide Ideation. *Journal of Consulting and Clinical Psychology, 47*, 343–352.

Beck, A. T., Rush, A. J., Shaw, B. F., & Emery, G. (1979). *Cognitive therapy of depression.* New York, NY: Guilford Press.

Beck, A. T., & Steer, R. A. (1987). *BDI, Beck depression inventory: Manual.* San Antonio, TX: Psychological Corporation.

Beck, A. T., & Steer, R. A. (1991). *Manual for Beck scale for suicide ideation.* San Antonio, TX: Psychological Corporation.

Beck, A. T., Steer, R. A., & Brown, G. K. (1996). *Manual for the Beck Depression Inventory – II.* San Antonio, TX: Psychological Corporation.

Beck, A. T., Steer, R. A., Kovacs, M., & Garrison, B. (1985). Hopelessness and eventual suicide: A 10-year prospective study of patients hospitalized with suicidal ideation. *American Journal of Psychaitry, 142*, 559–563.

Beck, A. T., Wright, F. D., Newman, C. F., & Liese, B. S. (1993). *Cognitive therapy of substance abuse.* New York, NY: Guilford Press.

Beck, J. S. (1995). *Cognitive therapy: Basics and beyond.* New York, NY: Guilford Press.

Beck, J. S. (2005). *Cognitive therapy for challenging problems: What to do when the basics don't work.* New York, NY: Guilford Press.

Beck, J. S. (2011). *Cognitive behavior therapy: Basics and beyond* (2nd ed.). New York: Guilford Press.

Bell, A. C., & D'Zurilla, T. J. (2009). Problem-solving therapy for depression: a meta-analysis. *Clinical Psychology Review, 29*, 348–353.

Benassi, V. A., Sweeney, P. D., & Dufour, C. L. (1988). Is there a relation between locus of control orientation and depression? *Journal of Abnormal Psychology, 97*, 357–367.

Berman, A. L., Jobes, D. A., & Silverman, M. M. (2006). *Adolescent suicide assessment and intervention* (2nd ed.). Washington, DC: American Psychological Association.

Biegel, G. M. (2009). *The stress reduction workbook for teens: Mindfulness skills to help you deal with stress.* Oakland, CA: New Harbinger Publications.

Biegel, G. M., Brown, K. W., Shapiro, S. L., & Schubert, C. M. (2009). Mindfulness-based stress reduction for the treatment of adolescent psychiatric outpatients: A randomized clinical trial. *Journal of Consulting and Clinical Psychology, 77*(5), 855.

Birmaher, B., Brent, D. A., Chiappetta, L., Bridge, J., Monga, S., & Baugher, M. (1999). Psychometric properties of the Screen for Child Anxiety Related Emotional Disorders (SCARED): A replication study. *Journal of the American Academy of Child and Adolescent Psychiatry, 38*, 1230–1236.

Birmaher, B., Brent, D., Issues, A. W. G. o. Q., Bernet, W., Bukstein, O., Walter, H., ... & Medicus, J. (2007). Practice parameter for the assessment and treatment of children and adolescents with depressive disorders. *Journal of the American Academy of Child and Adolescent Psychiatry, 46*, 1503–1526.

Bishop, S. R., Lau, M., Shapiro, S., Carlson, L., Anderson, N. D., Carmody, J., ... & Devins, G. (2004). Mindfulness: A proposed operational definition. *Clinical Psychology: Science and Practice, 11*(3), 230–241.

Blazer, D. G., Kessler, R. C., & Swartz, M. S. (1998). Epidemiology of recurrent major and minor depression with a seasonal pattern. The National Comorbidity Survey. *British Journal of Psychiatry, 172,* 164–167.

Bockting, C., Hollon, S. D., Jarrett, R. B., Kuyken, W., & Dobson, K. (in press). A lifetime approach to major depressive disorder: The contributions of psychological interventions in preventing relapse and recurrence. *Clinical Psychology Review, 41,* 16–26.

Boland, R. J., & Keller, M. B. (2009). Course and outcome of depression. In I. H. Gotlib & C. L. Hammen (Eds.), *Handbook of depression* (2nd ed.). (pp. 23–43). New York, NY: Guilford Press.

Bonner, R. L., & Rich, A. R. (1991). Predicting vulnerability to hopelessness: A longitudinal analysis. *Journal of Nervous and Mental Disease, 179,* 29–32.

Bootzin, R. R., & Stevens, S. J. (2005). Adolescents, substance abuse, and the treatment of insomnia and daytime sleepiness. *Clinical Psychology Review, 25,* 629–644.

Bordin, E. S. (1979). The generalizability of the psychoanalytic concept of the working alliance. *Psychotherapy: Theory, Research and Practice, 16*(3), 252–260.

Bourne, E. J. (2010). *The anxiety and phobia workbook.* Oakland, CA: New Harbinger Publications.

Brahm, A. (2005). *Who ordered this truckload of dung? Inspiring stories for welcoming life's difficulties.* Boston, MA: Wisdom Publications.

Brent, D. A., Baugher, M., Bridge, J., Chen, J., & Beery, L. (1999). Age and sex-related factors for adolescent suicide. *Journal of the American Academy of Child and Adolescent Psychiatry, 38,* 1497–1505.

Brent, D. A., Holder, D., Kolko, D., Birmaher, B., Baugher, M., Roth, C., ... & Johnson, B. A. (1997). A clinical psychotherapy trial for adolescent depression comparing cognitive, family, and supportive therapy. *Archives of General Psychiatry, 54,* 877–885.

Brent, D., Emslie, G., Clarke, G., Wagner, K. D., Asarnow, J. R., Keller, M., ... & Zelazny, J. (2008). Switching to another SSRI or to venlafaxine with or without cognitive behavioral therapy for adolescents with SSRI-resistant depression: the TORDIA randomized controlled trial. *JAMA, 299*(8), 901–913.

Brent, D. A., McMakin, D. L., Kennard, B. D., Goldstein, T. R., Mayes, T. L., & Douaihy, A. B. (2013). Protecting adolescents from self-harm: A critical review of intervention studies. *Journal of the American Academy of Child and Adolescent Psychiatry, 52,* 1260–1271.

Brent, D. A., Perper, J. A., Goldstein, C., Kolko, D., Allan, M., Allman, C., et al. (1988). Risk factors for adolescent suicide: A comparison of adolescent suicide victims with suicidal inpatients. *Archives of General Psychiatry, 45,* 581–588.

Brent, D. A., Poling, K. D., & Goldstein, T. R. (2011). *Treating depressed and suicidal adolescents: A clinician's guide.* New York, NY: Guilford Press.

Bridge, J. A., Iyengar, S., Salary, C. B., Barbe, R. P., Birmaher, B., Pincus, H. A., ... & Brent, D. A. (2007). Clinical response and risk for reported suicidal ideation and suicide attempts in pediatric antidepressant treatment: A meta-analysis of randomized controlled trials. *Journal of the American Medical Association, 297,* 1683–1696.

Bringmann, L. F., Lemmens, L. H. J. M., Huibers, M. J. H., Borsboom, D., & Tuerlinckx, F. (2014). Revealing the dynamic network structure of the Beck Depression Inventory-II. *Psychological Medicine*, 1–11.

Brown, G. W., & Harris, T. O. (1978). *Social origins of depression: A study of psychiatric disorder in women*. New York, NY: Free Press.

Brown, K. W., & Ryan, R. M. (2003). The benefits of being present: mindfulness and its role in psychological well-being. *Journal of Personality and Social Psychology, 84*(4), 822.

Bulmash, E., Harkness, K. L., Stewart, J. G., & Bagby, R. M. (2009). Personality, stressful life events, and treatment response in major depression. *Journal of Consulting and Clinical Psychology, 77*, 1067–1077.

Burke, B. L., Arkowitz, H., & Menchola, M. (2003). The efficacy of motivational interviewing: a meta-analysis of controlled clinical trials. *Journal of Consulting and Clinical Psychology, 71*(5), 843–861.

Burns, D. D. (1980). *Feeling good. The new mood therapy*. New York: New American Library.

Burns, D. D. (1999). *The feeling good handbook*. New York: Plume.

Burns, M. N., Begale, M., Duffecy, J., Gergle, D., Karr, C. J., Giangrande, E., & Mohr, D. C. (2011). Harnessing context sensing to develop a mobile intervention for depression. *Journal of Medical Internet Research, 13*(3), e55.

Burton, E., Stice, E., & Seeley, J. R. (2004). A prospective test of the stress-buffering model of depression in adolescent girls: No support once again. *Journal of Consulting and Clinical Psychology, 72*, 689–697.

Burwell, R. A., & Shirk, S. R. (2007). Subtypes of rumination in adolescence: Associations between brooding, reflection, depressive symptoms, and coping. *Journal of Clinical Child and Adolescent Psychology, 36*, 56–65.

Capelli, M. (2011). HEADS-ED. Retrieved from www.heads-ed.com.

Carter, J. S., & Garber, J. (2011). Predictors of the first onset of a major depressive episode and changes in depressive symptoms across adolescence: Stress and negative cognitions. *Journal of Abnormal Psychology, 120*, 779–796.

Carter, J. S., Garber, J., Ciesla, J. A., & Cole, D. A. (2006). Modeling relations between hassles and internalizing and externalizing symptoms in adolescents: A four-year prospective study. *Journal of Abnormal Psychology, 115*, 428–442.

Centers for Disease Control and Prevention (2013). *Web-based injury statistics query and reporting system*. National Center for Injury Prevention and Control, CDC. Retrieved from: http://www.cdc.gov/injury/wisqars/leadingcauses.html.

Cheavens, J. S., Strunk, D. R., Lazarus, S. A., & Goldstein, L. A. (2012). The compensation and capitalization models: a test of two approaches to individualizing the treatment of depression. *Behavior Research and Therapy, 50*, 699–706.

Christensen, H., Griffiths, K. M., & Korten, A. (2002). Web-based cognitive-behaviour therapy: Analysis of site usage and changes in depression and anxiety scores. *Journal of Medical Internet Research, 4*(1), 1–8.

Chu, B. C., & Kendall, P. C. (2009). Therapist responsiveness to child engagement: Flexibility within manual-based CBT for anxious youth. *Journal of Clinical Psychology, 65*, 736–754.

Ciesla, J. A., & Roberts, J. E. (2007). Rumination, negative cognition, and their interactive effects on depressed mood. *Emotion, 7*, 555–565.

Clark, D. C., Fawcett, J., Salazar-Grueso, E., & Fawcett, E. (1984). Seven-month clinical outcome of anhedonic and normally hedonic depressed inpatients. *American Journal of Psychiatry, 141*(10), 1216–1220.

Clarke, G., & Harvey, A. G. (2012). The complex role of sleep in adolescent depression. *Child and Adolescent Psychiatric Clinics of North America, 21*, 385–400.

Clarke, G., McGlinchey, E. L., Hein, K., Gullion, C. M., Dickerson, J. F., Leo, M. C., & Harvey, A. G. (2015). Cognitive-behavioral treatment of insomnia and depression in adolescents: A pilot randomized trial. *Behaviour Research and Therapy, 69*, 111–118.

Cole, D. A. (1989). Validation of the Reasons for Living Inventory in general and delinquent adolescent samples. *Journal of Abnormal Child Psychology, 17*(1), 13–27.

Cole, D. A., Nolen-Hoeksema, S., Girgus, J., & Paul, G. (2006). Stress exposure and stress generation in child and adolescent depression: A latent trait-state-error approach to longitudinal analyses. *Journal of Abnormal Psychology, 115*, 40–51.

Cooper, J. M. (Ed.). (1997). *Plato: Complete works.* Indianapolis: Hackett.

Cooper, L. A., Gonzales, J. J., Gallo, J. J., Rost, K. M., Meredith, L. S., Rubenstein, L. V., . . . & Ford, D. E. (2003). The acceptability of treatment for depression among African-American, Hispanic, and white primary care patients. *Medical Care, 41*, 479–489.

Costello, E. J., Angold, A., Burns, B. J., Stangl, D. K., Tweed, D. L., Erkanli, A., & Worthman, C. M. (1996). The Great Smoky Mountains Study of Youth. Goals, design, methods, and the prevalence of DSM-III-R disorders. *Archives of General Psychiatry, 53*(12), 1129–1136.

Costello, E. J., Farmer, E. M., Angold, A., Burns, B. J., & Erkanli, A. (1997). Psychiatric disorders among American Indian and white youth in Appalachia: the Great Smoky Mountains Study. *American Journal of Public Health, 87*(5), 827–832.

Costello, R. T., Mallet, F., Sainty, D., Maraninchi, D., Gastaut, J. A., & Olive, D. (1998). Regulation of CD80/B7-1 and CD86/B7-2 molecule expression in human primary acute myeloid leukemia and their role in allogenic immune recognition. *European Journal of Immunoly, 28*(1), 90–103.

Cox, G. R., Callahan, P., Churchill, R., Hunot, V., Merry, S. N., Parker, A. G., & Hetrick, S. E. (2014). Psychological therapies versus antidepressant medication, alone and in combination for depression in children and adolescents. *Cochrane Database Systematic Reviews, 11*, CD008324.

Craske, M. G., & Barlow, D. H. (2007). *Mastery of your anxiety and panic: Therapist guide.* New York, NY: Oxford University Press.

Crowe, M., Ward, N., Dunnachie, B., & Roberts, M. (2006). Characteristics of adolescent depression. *International Journal of Mental Health Nursing, 15*(1), 10–18.

Cuijpers, P., Hollon, S. D., van Straten, A., Bockting, C., Berking, M., & Andersson, G. (2013). Does cognitive behaviour therapy have an enduring effect that is superior to keeping patients on continuation pharmacotherapy? A meta-analysis. *BMJ Open, 3*(4), e002542.

Cuijpers, P., Weitz, E., Karyotaki, E., Garber, J., & Andersson, G. (2015). The effects of psychological treatment of maternal depression on children and parental functioning: A meta-analysis. *European Child and Adolescent Psychiatry, 24*, 237–245.

References

Cummings, C. M., Caporino, N. E., & Kendall, P. C. (2014). Comorbidity of anxiety and depression in children and adolescents: 20 years after. *Psychological Bulletin, 140*, 816–845.

Curry, J., Rohde, P., Simons, A., Silva, S., Vitiello, B., Kratochvil, C., . . . & Team, T. (2006). Predictors and moderators of acute outcome in the Treatment for Adolescents with Depression Study (TADS). *Journal of the American Academy of Child and Adolescent Psychiatry, 45*, 1427–1439.

Deci, E. L., & Ryan, R. M. (1985). *Intrinsic motivation and self-determination in human behavior.* New York: Plenum Press.

De Giacomo, P. D., L'Abate, L., Pennebaker, J. W., & Rumbaugh, D. (2010). Amplifications and applications of Pennebaker's analogic to digital model in health psychology promotion, prevention, and psychotherapy. *Clinical Psychology and Psychotherapy, 17*, 355–362.

DeRubeis, R. J., & Feeley, M. (1990). Determinants of change in cognitive therapy for depression. *Cognitive Therapy and Research, 14*(5), 469–482.

DeRubeis, R. J., Webb, C. A., Tang, T. Z., & Beck, A.T. (2010). Cognitive therapy. In K. S. Dobson (Ed.), *Handbook of cognitive-behavioral therapies* (3rd ed.). New York: Guilford.

Dimidjian, S., Hollon, S. D., Dobson, K. S., Schmaling, K. B., Kohlenberg, R. J., Addis, M. E., . . . & Jacobson, N. S. (2006). Randomized trial of behavioral activation, cognitive therapy, and antidepressant medication in the acute treatment of adults with major depression. *Journal of Consulting and Clinical Psychology, 74*, 658–670.

Dinan, T.G., & Scott, L.V. (2005). Anatomy of melancholia: focus on hypothalamic–pituitary–adrenal axis overactivity and the role of vasopressin. *Journal of Anatomy, 207*, 259–264.

Dobson, K. S., Hollon, S. D., Dimidjian, S., Schmaling, K. B., Kohlenberg, R. J., Gallop, R. J., . . . & Jacobson, N. S. (2008). Randomized trial of behavioral activation, cognitive therapy, and antidepressant medication in the prevention of relapse and recurrence in major depression. *Journal of Consulting and Clinical Psychology, 76*, 468–477.

Doran, G. T. (1981). There's a S.M.A.R.T. way to write management's goals and objectives. *Management Review, 70*, 35–36.

Dozois, D. J. (2002). Cognitive organization of self-schematic content in non-dysphoric, mildly dysphoric, and moderately–severely dysphoric individuals. *Cognitive Therapy and Research, 26*, 417–429.

Dozois, D. J., & Dobson, K. S. (2001a). Information processing and cognitive organization in unipolar depression: Specificity and comorbidity issues. *Journal of Abnormal Psychology, 110*, 236–246.

Dozois, D. J., & Dobson, K. S. (2001b). A longitudinal investigation of information processing and cognitive organization in clinical depression: Stability of schematic interconnectedness. *Journal of Consulting and Clinical Psychology, 69*, 914–925.

Dozois, D., & Dobson, K. (2003). The structure of the self-schema in clinical depression: Differences related to episode recurrence. *Cognition and Emotion, 17*, 933–941.

Dozois, D. J., & Frewen, P. A. (2006). Specificity of cognitive structure in depression and social phobia: A comparison of interpersonal and achievement content. *Journal of Affective Disorders, 90*, 101–109.

Duncan, A. B., Velasquez, S. E., & Nelson, E. L. (2014). Using videoconferencing to provide psychological services to rural children and adolescents: A review and case example. *Journal of Clinical Child and Adolescent Psychology, 43*(1), 115–127.

Dunn, D. W., Austin, J. K., & Huster, G. A. (1999). Symptoms of depression in adolescents with epilepsy. *Journal of the American Academy of Child and Adolescent Psychiatry, 38*, 1132–1138.

D'Zurilla, T. J., & Nezu, A. M. (2007). *Problem-solving therapy: A positive approach to clinical intervention* (3rd ed.). New York, NY: Springer.

Ebert, D. D., Zarski, A.-C., Christensen, H., Stikkelbroek, Y., Cuijpers, P., et al. (2015). Internet and computer-based cognitive behavioral therapy for anxiety and depression in youth: A meta-analysis of randomized controlled outcome trials. *PLoS ONE, 10*(3): e0119895.

Eliot, G. (2008). *The Spanish Gypsy (1868)*. Whitefish, MT: Kessinger Publishing.

Esposito-Smythers, C., & Spirito, A. (2004). Adolescent substance use and suicidal behavior: A review with implications for treatment research. *Alcoholism: Clinical and Experimental Research, 28*, 77S–88S.

Esposito-Smythers, C., Spirito, A., Kahler, C. W., Hunt, J., & Monti, P. (2011). Treatment of co-occurring substance abuse and suicidality among adolescents: A randomized trial. *Journal of Consulting and Clinical Psychology, 79*, 728–739.

Essau, C. A. & Ollendick, T. H. (2010). Diagnosis and assessment of adolescent depression. In S. Nolen-Hoeksema & L. M. Hilt (Eds.), *Handbook of depression in adolescents* (pp. 33–52). New York: Routledge.

Ferster, C. B. (1973). A functional anlysis of depression. *American Psychologist, 28*, 857–870.

Flynn, H. A. (2011). Setting the stage for the integration of motivational interviewing with cognitive behavioral therapy in the treatment of depression. *Cognitive and Behavioral Practice, 18*(1), 46–54.

Foland-Ross, L. C., & Gotlib, I. H. (2012). Cognitive and neural aspects of information processing in major depressive disorder: An integrative perspective. *Frontiers in Psychology, 3*, Article 489.

Ford-Paz, R., & Iwamasa, G. Y. (2012). Culturally diverse children and adolescents. In E. Szigethy, J. R. Weisz, & R. L. Findling (Eds.) *Cognitive-behavior therapy for children and adolescents* (pp. 75–118). Arlington, VA: American Psychiatric Association.

Fournier, J. C., DeRubeis, R. J., Hollon, S. D., Gallop, R., Shelton, R. C., & Amsterdam, J. D. (2013). Differential change in specific depressive symptoms during antidepressant medication or cognitive therapy. *Behaviour Research and Therapy, 51*(7), 392–398.

Fournier, J. C., DeRubeis, R. J., Shelton, R. C., Gallop, R., Amsterdam, J. D., & Hollon, S. D. (2008). Antidepressant medications v. cognitive therapy in people with depression with or without personality disorder. *British Journal of Psychiatry, 192*(2), 124–129.

Frank, E., Prien, R. F., Jarrett, R. B., Keller, M. B., Kupfer, D. J., Lavori, P. W., . . . & Weissman, M. M. (1991). Conceptualization and rationale for consensus definitions of terms in major depressive disorder. Remission, recovery, relapse, and recurrence. *Archives of General Psychiatry, 48*(9), 851–855.

Fredrickson, B. L. (2001). The role of positive emotions in positive psychology. The broaden-and-build theory of positive emotions. *American Psychologist, 56,* 218–226.

Fredrickson, B. L. (2013). Positive emotions broaden and build. In P. Devine, & A. Plant (Eds.). *Advances in experimental social psychology* (Vol. 47) (pp. 1–53). Burlington, VA: Academic Press.

Freeman, A., Simon, K. M., Beutler, L., & Arkowitz, H. (Eds.) (1989). *Comprehensive handbook of cognitive therapy.* New York: Plenum Publishers.

Friborg, O., Martinsen, E. W., Martinussen, M., Kaiser, S., Overgard, K. T., & Rosenvinge, J. H. (2014). Comorbidity of personality disorders in mood disorders: A meta-analytic review of 122 studies from 1988 to 2010. *Journal of Affective Disorders, 152–154,* 1–11.

Friedberg, R. D., & McClure, J. M. (2002). *Clinical practice of cognitive therapy with children and adolescents: The nuts and bolts.* New York: Guilford Press.

Frost, R. (1915). Mending wall. *North of Boston* (pp. 11–13). Henry Holt and Company: New York.

Furman, W., & Buhrmester, D. (1992). Age and sex differences in perceptions of networks of personal relationships. *Child Development, 63,* 103–115.

Gaddy, M. A., & Ingram, R. E. (2014). A meta-analytic review of mood-congruent implicit memory in depressed mood. *Clinical Psychology Review, 34,* 402–416.

Garber, J., Keiley, M. K., & Martin, C. (2002). Developmental trajectories of adolescents' depressive symptoms: predictors of change. *Journal of Consulting and Clinical Psychology, 70,* 79–95.

Garber, J., Korelitz, K., & Samanez-Larkin, S. (2012). Translating basic psychopathology research to preventive interventions: A tribute to John R. Z. Abela. *Journal of Clinical Child and Adolescent Psychology, 41,* 666–681.

Garber, J., Webb, C. A., & Horowitz, J. L. (2009). Prevention of depression in adolescents: A review of selective and indicated programs. In S. Nolen-Hoeksema & L. Hilt (Eds.), *Handbook of depression in adolescents* (pp. 619–659). New York, NY: Routledge.

Gardner, E. A. (1968). Depression checklist. Unpublished.

Gaynor, S. T., Lawrence, P. S., & Nelson-Gray, R. O. (2006). Measuring homework compliance in cognitive-behavioral therapy for adolescent depression: review, preliminary findings, and implications for theory and practice. *Behavior Modification, 30,* 647–672.

Gilman, S. E., Kawachi, I., Fitzmaurice, G. M., & Buka, L. (2003). Socio-economic status, family disruption and residential stability in childhood: relation to onset, recurrence and remission of major depression. *Psychological Medicine, 33*(8), 1341–1355.

Glenn, C. R., Franklin, J. C., & Nock, M. K. (2015). Evidence-based psychosocial treatments for self-injurious thoughts and behaviors in youth. *Journal of Clinical Child and Adolescent Psychology, 44,* 1–29.

Goeleven, E., De Raedt, R., Baert, S., & Koster, E. H. (2006). Deficient inhibition of emotional information in depression. *Journal of Affective Disorders, 93,* 149–157.

Goldstein, J. (1994). *Insight meditation.* Boston: Shambhala.

Goldstein, T. R., Bridge, J. A., & Brent, D. A. (2008). Sleep disturbance preceding completed suicide in adolescents. *Journal of Consulting and Clinical Psychology, 76,* 84–91.

Goldston, D. (2003). *Measuring suicidal behaviors and risk among children and adolescents.* Washington, DC: American Psychological Association.

Gonzalez, H. M., Vega, W. A., Williams, D. R., Tarraf, W., West, B. T., & Neighbors, H. W. (2010). Depression care in the United States: too little for too few. *Archives of General Psychiatry, 67,* 37–46.

Gotlib, I. H., & Joormann, J. (2010). Cognition and depression: Current status and future directions. *Annual Review of Clinical Psychology, 6,* 285–312.

Gotlib, I. H., Krasnoperova, E., Yue, D. N., & Joormann, J. (2004). Attentional biases for negative interpersonal stimuli in clinical depression. *Journal of Abnormal Psychology, 113,* 121–135.

Gould, M. S., & Kramer, R. A. (2001). Youth suicide prevention. *Suicide and Life-Threatening Behavior, 31,* 6–31.

Goyal, M., Singh, S., Sibinga, E. M., Gould, N. F., Rowland-Seymour, A., Sharma, R., . . . & Haythornthwaite, J. A. (2014). Meditation programs for psychological stress and well-being: a systematic review and meta-analysis. *JAMA Internal Medicine, 174*(3), 357–368.

Greden, J. F. (2001). The burden of recurrent depression: causes, consequences, and future prospects. *Journal of Clinical Psychiatry, 62* (Suppl. 22), 5–9.

Green, J. G., McLaughlin, K. A., Berglund, P. A., Gruber, M. J., Sampson, N. A., Zaslavsky, A. M., & Kessler, R. C. (2010). Childhood adversities and adult psychiatric disorders in the national comorbidity survey replication I: Associations with first onset of DSM-IV disorders. *Archives of General Psychiatry, 67,* 113–123.

Greenberg, P. E., Kessler, R. C., Birnbaum, H. G., Leong, S. A., Lowe, S. W., Berglund, P. A., & Corey-Lisle, P. K. (2003). The economic burden of depression in the United States: how did it change between 1990 and 2000? *Journal of Clinical Psychiatry, 64*(12), 1465–1475.

Greenberger, D., & Padesky, C. A. (1995). *Mind over mood: Change how you feel by changing the way you think.* New York: Guilford Press.

Grilo, C. M., Stout, R. L., Markowitz, J. C., Sanislow, C. A., Ansell, E. B., Skodol, A. E., . . . & McGlashan, T. H. (2010). Personality disorders predict relapse after remission from an episode of major depressive disorder: a 6-year prospective study. *Journal of Clinical Psychiatry, 71*(12), 1629–1635.

Gros, D. F., Morland, L. A., Greene, C. J., Acierno, R., Strachan, M., Egede, L. E., . . . & Frueh, B. C. (2013). Delivery of evidence-based psychotherapy via video telehealth. *Journal of Psychopathology and Behavioral Assessment, 35*(4), 506–521.

Hafen, C. A., Spilker, A., Chango, J., Marston, E. S., & Allen, J. P. (2014). To accept or reject? The impact of adolescent rejection sensitivity on early adult romantic relationships. *Journal of Research on Adolescence, 24,* 55–64.

Hammad, T. A., Laughren, T., & Racoosin, J. (2006). Suicidality in pediatric patients treated with antidepressant drugs. *Archives of General Psychiatry, 63,* 332–339.

Hammen, C., Henry, R., & Daley, S. E. (2000). Depression and sensitization to stressors among young women as a function of childhood adversity. *Journal of Consulting and Clinical Psychology, 68,* 782–787.

Hankin, B. L. (2008). Cognitive vulnerability-stress model of depression during adolescence: Investigating depressive symptom specificity in a multi-wave prospective study. *Journal of Abnormal Child Psychology, 36,* 999–1014.

Hankin, B. L., Gibb, B. E., Abela, J. R., & Flory, K. (2010). Selective attention to affective stimuli and clinical depression among youths: Role of anxiety and specificity of emotion. *Journal of Abnormal Psychology, 119*, 491–501.

Hankin, B. L., Mermelstein, R., & Roesch, L. (2007). Sex differences in adolescent depression: Stress exposure and reactivity models. *Child Development, 78*(1), 279–295.

Hankin, B. L., Wetter, E., Cheely, C., & Oppenheimer, C. W. (2008). Beck's cognitive theory of depression in adolescence: Specific prediction of depressive symptoms and reciprocal influences in a multi-wave prospective study. *International Journal of Cognitive Therapy, 1*, 313–332.

Harkness, K. L. (2008). Life events and hassles. In K. S. Dobson & D. J. A. Dozois (Eds.), *Risk factors in depression* (pp. 317–341). Burlington, MA: Elsevier.

Harkness, K. L., Alavi, N., Monroe, S. M., Slavich, G. M., Gotlib, I. H., & Bagby, R. M. (2010). Gender differences in life events prior to onset of major depressive disorder: The moderating effect of age. *Journal of Abnormal Psychology, 119*, 791–803.

Harkness, K. L., Bruce, A. E., & Lumley, M. N. (2006). The role of childhood abuse and neglect in the sensitization to stressful life events in adolescent depression. *Journal of Abnormal Psychology, 115*, 730–741.

Harkness, K. L., & Lumley, M. N. (2007). Child abuse and neglect and the development of depression in children and adolescents. In J. R. Abela & B. Hankin (Eds.) *Depression in children and adolescents* (pp. 639–657). New York, NY: Guilford Press.

Harkness, K. L., & Stewart, J. G. (2009). Symptom specificity and the prospective generation of life events in adolescence. *Journal of Abnormal Psychology, 118*(2), 278.

Harkness, K. L., Theriault, J. E., Stewart, J. G., & Bagby, R. M. (2014). Acute and chronic stress exposure predicts 1-year recurrence in adult outpatients with residual depression symptoms following response to treatment. *Depression and Anxiety, 31*(1), 1–8.

Harper, G. W., & Iwamasa, G. Y. (2000). Cognitive-behavioral therapy with ethnic minority adolescents: Therapist perspectives. *Cognitive and Behavioral Practice, 7*, 37–53.

Harrow, M., Hansford, B. G., & Astrachan-Fletcher, E. B. (2009). Locus of control: Relation to schizophrenia, to recovery, and to depression and psychosis – A 15-year longitudinal study. *Psychiatry Research, 168*, 186–192.

Harvey, A. G. (2002). A cognitive model of insomnia. *Behavior Research and Therapy, 40*, 869–893.

Hayes, S. C., Strosahl, K. D., & Wilson, K. G. (1999). *Acceptance and commitment therapy: An experiential approach to behavior change.* New York, NY: Guilford Press.

Hays, P. (2008). *Addressing cultural complexities in practice: Assessment, diagnosis, and therapy* (2nd ed.). Washington, DC: American Psychological Association.

Hettema, J., Steele, J., & Miller, W. R. (2005). Motivational interviewing. *Annual Review of Clinical Psychology, 1*, 91–111.

Hilt, L. M., McLaughlin, K. A., & Nolen-Hoeksema, S. (2010). Examination of the response styles theory in a community sample of young adolescents. *Journal of Abnormal Child Psychology, 38*, 545–556.

Hinduja, S., & Patchin, J. W. (2010). Bullying, cyberbullying, and suicide. *Archives of Suicide Research, 14*(3), 206–221.

Hofmann, S. G., Sawyer, A. T., Witt, A. A., & Oh, D. (2010). The effect of mindfulness-based therapy on anxiety and depression: A meta-analytic review. *Journal of Consulting and Clinical Psychology, 78*(2), 169.

Holahan, C. K., & Holahan, C. J. (1987). Self-efficacy, social support, and depression in aging: A longitudinal analysis. *Journal of Gerontology, 42*, 65–68.

Hood, H. K., Rogojanski, J., & Moss, T. G. (2014). Cognitive-behavioral therapy for chronic insomnia. *Current Treatment Options in Neurology, 16*, 321.

Houston, K., Hawton, K., & Shepperd, R. (2001). Suicide in young people aged 15–24: A psychological autopsy study. *Journal of Affective Disorders, 63*, 159–170.

Hughes, C. W., Emslie, G. J., Crismon, M. L., Posner, K., Birmaher, B., Ryan, N., ... & Texas Consensus Conference Panel on Medication Treatment of Childhood Major Depressive, Disorder (2007). Texas children's medication algorithm project: Update from Texas consensus conference panel on medication treatment of childhood major depressive disorder. *Journal of the American Academy of Child and Adolescent Psychiatry, 46*, 667–686.

Ingram, R. E., Miranda, J., & Segal, Z. V. (1998). *Cognitive vulnerability to depression*. New York, NY: Guilford Press.

International Telecommunications Union (2013). *The world in 2013 – ICT facts and figures*. Telecommunication Development Bureau. Retrieved from: http://www.itu.int/en/ITU-D/Statistics/Pages/facts/default.aspx.

Irwin, M., Artin, K., & Oxman, M. N. (1999). Screening for depression in the older adult. *Archives of Internal Medicine, 159*, 1701–1704.

Jacobs, R. H., Reinecke, M. A., Gollan, J. K., & Kane, P. (2008). Empirical evidence of cognitive vulnerability for depression among children and adolescents: A cognitive science and developmental perspective. *Clinical Psychology Review, 28*, 759–782.

Jenkins, S. R., Goodness, K., & Buhrmester, D. (2002). Gender differences in early adolescents' relationship qualities, self-efficacy, and depression symptoms. *Journal of Early Adolescence, 22*, 277–309.

Joiner, T. E., Jr., Steer, R. A., Abramson, L. Y., Alloy, L. B., Metalsky, G. I., & Schmidt, N. B. (2001). Hopelessness depression as a distinct dimension of depressive symptoms among clinical and non-clinical samples. *Behavior Research and Therapy, 39*, 523–536.

Joormann, J. (2004). Attentional bias in dysphoria: The role of inhibitory processes. *Cognition & Emotion, 18*, 125–147.

Joormann, J., Gilbert, K., & Gotlib, I. H. (2010). Emotion identification in girls at high risk for depression. *Journal of Child Psychology and Psychiatry, 51*, 575–582.

Joormann, J., & Gotlib, I. H. (2006). Is this happiness I see? Biases in the identification of emotional facial expressions in depression and social phobia. *Journal of Abnormal Psychology, 115*, 705–714.

Joormann, J., & Gotlib, I. H. (2007). Selective attention to emotional faces following recovery from depression. *Journal of Abnormal Psychology, 116*, 80–85.

Joormann, J., & Gotlib, I. H. (2008). Updating the contents of working memory in depression: interference from irrelevant negative material. *Journal of Abnormal Psychology, 117*, 182–192.

Joormann, J., & Gotlib, I. H. (2010). Emotion regulation in depression: Relation to cognitive inhibition. *Cognition and Emotion, 24*, 281–298.

Joormann, J., Talbot, L., & Gotlib, I. H. (2007). Biased processing of emotional information in girls at risk for depression. *Journal of Abnormal Psychology, 116*, 135–143.

Jungbluth, N. J., & Shirk, S. R. (2013). Promoting homework adherence in cognitive-behavioral therapy for adolescent depression. *Journal of Clinical Child and Adolescent Psychology, 42*(4), 545–553.

Kabat-Zinn, J. (1990). *Full catastrophe living: Using the wisdom of your mind and body to face stress, pain, and illness.* New York: Delacorte.

Kabat-Zinn, J. (1994). *Wherever you go, there you are: Mindfulness meditation in everyday life.* New York: Hyperion.

Kahneman, D. (2011). *Thinking, fast and slow.* New York, NY: Farrar, Straus and Giroux.

Kaufman, J., Birmaher, B., Brent, D., Rao, U., & Ryan, N. (1996). *The schedule for affective disorders and schizophrenia for school-age children.* Pittsburgh: University of Pittsburgh Medical Center.

Kavanagh, D. J., & Bower, G. H. (1985). Mood and self-efficacy: Impact of joy and sadness on perceived capabilities. *Cognitive Therapy and Research, 9*, 507–525.

Kavanagh, D. J., & Wilson, P. H. (1989). Prediction of outcome with group cognitive therapy for depression. *Behavior Research and Therapy, 27*, 333–343.

Kendall, P. C., & Beidas, R. S. (2007). Smoothing the trail for dissemination of evidence-based practices for youth: Flexibility within fidelity. *Professional Psychology: Research and Practice, 38*, 13–20.

Kendler, K. S., Eaves, L. J., Walters, E. E., Neale, M. C., Heath, A. C., & Kessler, R. C. (1996). The identification and validation of distinct depressive syndromes in a population-based sample of female twins. *Archives of General Psychiatry, 53*, 391–399.

Kendler, K. S., Hettema, J. M., Butera, F., Gardner, C. O., & Prescott, C. A. (2003). Life event dimensions of loss, humiliation, entrapment, and danger in the prediction of onsets of major depression and generalized anxiety. *Archives of General Psychiatry, 60*, 789–796.

Kendler, K. S., Kuhn, J. W., & Prescott, C. A. (2004). Childhood sexual abuse, stressful life events and risk for major depression in women. *Psychological Medicine, 34*, 1475–1482.

Kendler, K. S., Thornton, L. M., & Gardner, C. O. (2000). Stressful life events and previous episodes in the etiology of major depression in women: An evaluation of the "kindling" hypothesis. *American Journal of Psychiatry, 157*, 1243–1251.

Kerfoot, M., Dyer, E., Harrington, V., Woodham, A., & Harrington, R. (1996). Correlates and short-term course of self-poisoning in adolescents. *British Journal of Psychiatry, 168*, 38–42.

Kessler, R. C. (2012). The costs of depression. *Psychiatric Clinics of North America, 35*(1), 1–14.

Kessler, R. C., Berglund, P., Borges, G., Nock, M., & Wang, P. S. (2005). Trends in suicide ideation, plans, gestures, and attempts in the United States, 1990–1992 to 2001–2003. *Journal of the American Medical Association, 293*, 2487–2495.

Kessler, R. C., Berglund, P., Demler, O., Jin, R., Koretz, D., Merikangas, K. R., . . . National Comorbidity Survey (2003). The epidemiology of major depressive disorder: results from the National Comorbidity Survey Replication (NCS-R). *JAMA, 289*(23), 3095–3105.

Khan, A., Faucett, J., Lichtenberg, P., Kirsch, I., & Brown, W. A. (2012). A systematic review of comparative efficacy of treatments and controls for depression. *PLoS One, 7*, e41778.

Khoury, B., Lecomte, T., Fortin, G., Masse, M., Therien, P., Bouchard, V., . . . & Hofmann, S. G. (2013). Mindfulness-based therapy: A comprehensive meta-analysis. *Clinical Psychology Review, 33*(6), 763–771.

Killingsworth, M. A., & Gilbert, D. T. (2010). A wandering mind is an unhappy mind. *Science, 330*(6006), 932.

Kircanski, K., Joormann, J., & Gotlib, I. H. (2012). Cognitive aspects of depression. *Wiley Interdisciplinary Reviews: Cognitive Science, 3*, 301–313.

Klein, J. B., Jacobs, R. H., & Reinecke, M. A. (2007). Cognitive-behavioral therapy for adolescent depression: A meta-analytic investigation of changes in effect-size estimates. *Journal of the American Academy of Child and Adolescent Psychiatry, 46*(11), 1403–1413.

Kramer, G. M., Mishkind, M. C., Luxton, D. D., & Shore, J. H. (2012). Managing risk and protecting privacy in telemental health: An overview of legal, regulatory and risk-management issues. In K. Myers & C. L. Turvey (Eds.), *Telemental health: Clinical, technical and administrative foundations for evidence-based practice* (pp. 83–107). Waltham, MA: Elsevier.

Kroenke, K., Spitzer, R. L., & Williams, J. B. W. (2001). The PHQ-9: Validity of a brief depression severity measure. *Journal of General Internal Medicine, 16*, 606–613.

Kujawa, A. J., Torpey, D., Kim, J., Hajcak, G., Rose, S., Gotlib, I. H., & Klein, D. N. (2011). Attentional biases for emotional faces in young children of mothers with chronic or recurrent depression. *Journal of Abnormal Child Psychology, 39*, 125–135.

Kuyken, W., & Dalgleish, T. (2011). Overgeneral autobiographical memory in adolescents at risk for depression. *Memory, 19*, 241–250.

Kuyken, W., Howell, R., & Dalgleish, T. (2006). Overgeneral autobiographical memory in depressed adolescents with, versus without, a reported history of trauma. *Journal of Abnormal Psychology, 115*, 387–396.

Kuyken, W., Padesky, C. A., & Dudley, R. (2009). *Collaborative case conceptualization: Working effectively with clients in cognitive-behavioral therapy*. New York, NY: Guilford Press.

La Greca, A. M., & Harrison, H. M. (2005). Adolescent peer relations, friendships, and romantic relationships: Do they predict social anxiety and depression?. *Journal of Clinical Child and Adolescent Psychology, 34*, 49–61.

Lambert, M. J., Harmon, C., Slade, K., Whipple, J. L., & Hawkins, E. J. (2005). Providing feedback to psychotherapists on their patients' progress: Clinical results and practice suggestions. *Journal of Clinical Psychology, 61*(2), 165–174.

Lambert, M. J., Whipple, J. L., Hawkins, E. J., Vermeersch, D. A., Nielsen, S. L., & Smart, D. W. (2003). Is it time for clinicians to routinely track patient outcome? A meta-analysis. *Clinical Psychology: Science and Practice, 10*(3), 288–301.

LeMoult, J., Joormann, J., Sherdell, L., Wright, Y., & Gotlib, I. H. (2009). Identification of emotional facial expressions following recovery from depression. *Journal of Abnormal Psychology, 118*, 828–833.

Leppanen, J. M., Milders, M., Bell, J. S., Terriere, E., & Hietanen, J. K. (2004). Depression biases the recognition of emotionally neutral faces. *Psychiatry Research, 128*, 123–133.

Lerner, J., Safren, S. A., Henin, A., Warman, M., Heimberg, R. G., & Kendall, P. C. (1999). Differentiating anxious and depressive self-statements in youth: Factor structure of the Negative Affect Self-Statement Questionnaire among youth referred to an anxiety disorders clinic. *Journal of Clinical Child and Adolescent Psychology, 28*, 82–93.

Lewinsohn, P. M. (1974). A behavioral approach to depression. In R. M. Friedman & M. M. Katz (Eds.), *The psychology of depression: Contemporary theory and research* (pp. 157–185). New York, NY: Wiley.

Lewinsohn, P. M., Joiner, T. E., & Rohde, P. (2001). Evaluation of cognitive diathesis-stress models in predicting major depressive disorder in adolescents. *Journal of Abnormal Psychology, 110*, 203–215.

Lewinsohn, P. M., Roberts, R. E., Seeley, J. R., Rohde, P., Gotlib, I. H., & Hops, H. (1994). Adolescent psychopathology: II. Psychosocial risk factors for depression. *Journal of Abnormal Psychology, 103*, 302–315.

Linehan, M. M., Goodstein, J. L., Nielsen, S. L., & Chiles, J. A. (1983). Reasons for staying alive when you are thinking of killing yourself: The Reasons for Living Inventory. *Journal of Consulting and Clinical Psychology, 51*, 276–286.

Liu, R. T., & Miller, I. (2014). Life events and suicidal ideation and behavior: A systematic review. *Clinical Psychology Review, 34*, 181–192.

Loas, G. (1996). Vulnerability to depression: a model centered on anhedonia. *Journal of Affective Disorders, 41*(1), 39–53.

Lumley, M. N., & Harkness, K. L. (2007). Specificity in the relations among childhood adversity, early maladaptive schemas, and symptom profiles in adolescent depression. *Cognitive Therapy and Research, 31*, 639–657.

Ma, S. H., & Teasdale, J. D. (2004). Mindfulness-based cognitive therapy for depression: Replication and exploration of differential relapse prevention effects. *Journal of Consulting and Clinical Psychology, 72*(1), 31.

Manber, R., Edinger, J. D., Gress, J. L., San Pedro-Salcedo, M. G., Kuo, T. F., & Kalista, T. (2008). Cognitive behavioral therapy for insomnia enhances depression outcome in patients with comorbid major depressive disorder and insomnia. *Sleep, 31*, 489–495.

Mandal, M. K., & Palchoudhury, S. (1985a). Perceptual skill in decoding facial affect. *Perceptual and Motor Skills, 60*, 96–98.

Mandal, M. K., & Palchoudhury, S. (1985b). Responses to facial expression of emotion in depression. *Psychological Reports, 56*, 653–654.

March, J., Silva, S., Petrycki, S., Curry, J., Wells, K., Fairbank, J., . . . Treatment for Adolescents With Depression Study (2004). Fluoxetine, cognitive-behavioral therapy, and their combination for adolescents with depression: Treatment for Adolescents With Depression Study (TADS) randomized controlled trial. *Journal of the American Medical Association, 292*, 807–820.

March, J. S., Silva, S., Petrycki, S., Curry, J., Wells, K., Fairbank, J., . . . & Severe, J. (2007). The Treatment for Adolescents with Depression Study (TADS): Long-term effectiveness and safety outcomes. *Archives of General Psychiatry, 64*, 1132–1143.

Marcotte, D., Lévesque, N., & Fortin, L. (2006). Variations of cognitive distortions and school performance in depressed and non-depressed high school adolescents: A two-year longitudinal study. *Cognitive Therapy and Research, 30,* 211–225.

Martell, C. R., Dimidjian, S., & Herman-Dunn, R. (2013). *Behavioral activation for depression: A clinician's guide.* New York, NY: Guilford Press.

McCauley, E., Mitchell, J. R., Burke, P. M., & Moss, S. J. (1988). Cognitive attributes of depression in children and adolescents. *Journal of Consulting and Clinical Psychology, 56,* 903–908.

McClure, E. B., & Pine, D. S. (2007). Social stress, affect, and neural function in adolescence. In D. Romer & E. Walker (Eds.), *Adolescent psychopathology and the developing brain: Integrating brain and prevention science* (pp. 219–244). New York, NY: Oxford University Press.

McKinley, J. C., & Hathaway, S. R. (1944). A multiphasic personality schedule (Minnesota): V. Hysteria, hypomania, and psychopathic deviate. *Journal of Applied Psychology, 28,* 153–174.

Merikangas, K. R., & Knight, E. (2009). The epidemiology of depression in adolescents. In S. Nolen-Hoeksema & L. M. Hilt (Eds.), *Handbook of depression in adolescents* (pp. 53–74). New York, NY: Routledge/Taylor & Francis.

Messer, S. C., Angold, A., Costello, E. J., Loeber, R., Van Kammen, W., & Stouthamer-Loeber, M. (1995). Development of a short questionnaire for use in epidemiological studies of depression in children and adolescents: Factor composition and structure across development. *International Journal of Methods in Psychiatric Research, 5,* 251–262.

Meyer, I. H. (2003). Prejudice, social stress, and mental health in lesbian, gay, and bisexual populations: Conceptual issues and research evidence. *Psychological Bulletin, 129,* 674–697.

Mezulis, A., Simonson, J., McCauley, E., & Vander Stoep, A. (2011). The association between temperament and depressive symptoms in adolescence: Brooding and reflection as potential mediators. *Cognition and Emotion, 25,* 1460–1470.

Miller, A. B., Esposito-Smythers, C., Weismoore, J. T., & Renshaw, K. D. (2013). The relation between child maltreatment and adolescent suicidal behavior: A systematic review and critical examination of the literature. *Clinical Child and Family Psychology Review 16,* 146–172.

Miller, A. L., Rathus, J. H., & Linehan, M. M. (2006). *Dialectical behavior therapy with suicidal adolescents.* New York: Guilford Press.

Miller, W. R. (1983). Motivational interviewing with problem drinkers. *Behavioural Psychotherapy, 11,* 147–172.

Miller, W. R. (2008). It all depends. *Addiction, 11,* 1819–1820.

Miller, W. R., & Rollnick, S. (2002). *Motivational interviewing: Preparing people for change* (2nd ed.). New York: Guilford Press.

Miller, W. R., & Rollnick, S. (2012). *Motivational interviewing: Helping people change.* New York, NY: Guilford Press.

Miller, W. R., & Rose, G. S. (2009). Toward a theory of motivational interviewing. *American Psychologist, 64,* 527–537.

Mishna, F., Newman, P. A., Daley, A., & Solomon, S. (2009). Bullying of lesbian and gay youth: A qualitative investigation. *British Journal of Social Work, 39,* 1598–1614.

Moberly, N. J., & Watkins, E. R. (2008). Ruminative self-focus and negative affect: an experience sampling study. *Journal of Abnormal Psychology, 117,* 314–323.

Mohr, D. C., Burns, M. N., Schueller, S. M., Clarke, G., & Klinkman, M. (2013). Behavioral intervention technologies: Evidence review and recommendations for future research in mental health. *General Hospital Psychiatry, 35*(4), 332–338.

Mohr, D. C., Cuijpers, P., & Lehman, K. (2011). Supportive accountability: A model for providing human support to enhance adherence to eHealth interventions. *Journal of Medical Internet Research, 13*, e30.

Monroe, S. M., & Harkness, K. L. (2005). Life stress, the "kindling" hypothesis, and the recurrence of depression: considerations from a life stress perspective. *Psychological Review, 112*(2), 417.

Monroe, S. M., & Harkness, K. L. (2011). Recurrence in major depression: A conceptual analysis. *Psychological Review, 118*(4), 655.

Monroe, S. M., Harkness, K., Simons, A. D., & Thase, M. E. (2001). Life stress and the symptoms of major depression. *Journal of Nervous and Mental Disease, 189*, 168–175.

Monroe, S. M., Slavich, G. M., Torres, L. D., & Gotlib, I. H. (2007). Major life events and major chronic difficulties are differentially associated with history of major depressive episodes. *Journal of Abnormal Psychology, 116*, 116–124.

Morin, C. M. (2010). Chronic insomnia: Recent advances and innovations in treatment developments and dissemination. *Canadian Psychology, 51*, 31–39.

Morris, R. R., Schueller, S. M., & Picard, R. W. (2015). Efficacy of a web-based, crowdsourced peer-to-peer cognitive reappraisal platform for depression: Randomized controlled trial. *Journal of Medical Internet Research, 17*(3).

Moulds, M. L., Kandris, E., Starr, S., & Wong, A. C. (2007). The relationship between rumination, avoidance and depression in a non-clinical sample. *Behavior Research and Therapy, 45*, 251–261.

Muris, P. (2002). Relationships between self-efficacy and symptoms of anxiety disorders and depression in a normal adolescent sample. *Personality and Individual Differences, 32*, 337–348.

Muscatell, K. A., Slavich, G. M., Monroe, S. M., & Gotlib, I. H. (2009). Stressful life events, chronic difficulties, and the symptoms of clinical depression. *Journal of Nervous and Mental Disease, 197*, 154–160.

Naar-King, S., & Suarez, M. (2011). *Motivational interviewing with adolescents and young adults.* New York, NY: Guilford Press.

Nelson, E. L., & Duncan, A. B. (2015). Cognitive behavioral therapy using televideo. *Cognitive and Behavioral Practice.*

Nezu, A. M. (2005). Problem solving and behavior therapy revisited. *Behavior Therapy, 35*, 1–33.

Nezu, A. M., Nezu, C. M., Friedman, J., & Lee, M. (2009). Assessment of depression. In I. H. Gotlib & C. L. Hammen (Eds.), *Handbook of Depression* (pp. 44–68). New York: Guilford Press.

Nielsen (2013, October 29). *Ring the bells: More smartphones in students' hands ahead of back-to-school season.* Retrieved from http://www.nielsen.com/us/en/insights/news/2013/ring-the-bells-more-smartphones-in-students-hands-ahead-of-back.html.

Nock, M. K. (2009). Why do people hurt themselves? New insights into the nature and functions of self-injury. *Current Directions in Psychological Science, 18*, 78–83.

Nock, M. K., Goldman, J. L., Wang, Y., & Albano, A. M. (2004). From science to practice: The flexible use of evidence-based treatments in clinical settings. *Journal of the American Academy of Child and Adolescent Psychiatry, 43*, 777–780.

Nock, M. K., Green, J. G., Hwang, I., McLaughlin, K. A., Sampson, N. A., Zaslavsky, A. M., & Kessler, R. C. (2013). Prevalence, correlates, and treatment of lifetime suicidal behavior among adolescents: results from the National Comorbidity Survey Replication Adolescent Supplement. *JAMA Psychiatry, 70*(3), 300–310.

Nock, M. K., Holmberg, E. B., Photos, V. I., & Michel, B. D. (2007). Self-injurious thoughts and behaviors interview: Development, reliability, and validity in an adolescent sample. *Psychological Assessment, 19*(3), 309–317.

Nock, M. K., & Kazdin, A. E. (2002). Examination of affective, cognitive, and behavioral factors and suicide-related outcomes in children and young adolescents. *Journal of Clinical Child and Adolescent Psychology, 31*(1), 48–58.

Nolen-Hoeksema, S. (1991). Responses to depression and their effects on the duration of depressive episodes. *Journal of Abnormal Psychology, 100*, 569–582.

Nolen-Hoeksema, S. (2004). Gender differences in risk factors and consequences for alcohol use and problems. *Clinical Psychology Review, 24*, 981–1010.

Nolen-Hoeksema, S., & Davis, C. G. (1999). "Thanks for sharing that": Ruminators and their social support networks. *Journal of Personality and Social Psychology, 77*, 801–814.

Nolen-Hoeksema, S., Stice, E., Wade, E., & Bohon, C. (2007). Reciprocal relations between rumination and bulimic, substance abuse, and depressive symptoms in female adolescents. *Journal of Abnormal Psychology, 116*, 198–207.

Nolen-Hoeksema, S., Wisco, B. E., & Lyubomirsky, S. (2008). Rethinking rumination. *Perspectives on Psychological Science, 3*, 400–424.

Osman, A., Jones, & Osman, J. R. (1991). The Reasons for Living Inventory: Psychometric properties. *Psychological Reports, 69*, 271–278.

Ottenbreit, N. D., & Dobson, K. S. (2004). Avoidance and depression: The construction of the cognitive-behavioral avoidance scale. *Behavior Research and Therapy, 42*, 293–313.

Ottenbreit, N. D., Dobson, K. S., & Quigley, L. (2014). An examination of avoidance in major depression in comparison to social anxiety disorder. *Behavior Research and Therapy, 56*, 82–90.

Overholser, J. C. (2011). Collaborative empiricism, guided discovery, and the Socratic method: Core processes for effective cognitive therapy. *Clinical Psychology: Science and Practice, 18*(1), 62–66.

Pantalone, D. W., Iwamasa, G. Y., & Martell, C. R. (2009). Cognitive-behavioral therapy with diverse populations. In K. S. Dobson (Ed.), *Handbook of cognitive-behavioral therapies* (pp. 445–464). New York, NY: Guilford Press.

Paredes, P. P., & Zumalde, E. C. (2014). A test of the vulnerability–stress model with brooding and reflection to explain depressive symptoms in adolescence. *Journal of Youth and Adolescence*, 1–10.

Park, R. J., Goodyer, I. M., & Teasdale, J. D. (2002). Categoric overgeneral autobiographical memory in adolescents with major depressive disorder. *Psychological Medicine, 32*, 267–276.

Park, R. J., Goodyer, I. M., & Teasdale, J. D. (2004). Effects of induced rumination and distraction on mood and overgeneral autobiographical memory in adolescent major depressive disorder and controls. *Journal of Child Psychology and Psychiatry, 45*, 996–1006.

Pearlstein, T., & Stone, A. B. (1998). Premenstrual syndrome. *Psychiatric Clinics of North America, 21*(3), 577–590.

Peckham, A. D., McHugh, R. K., & Otto, M. W. (2010). A meta-analysis of the magnitude of biased attention in depression. *Depression and Anxiety, 27*, 1135–1142.

Perini, S., Titov, N., & Andrews, G. (2008). The Climate Sadness program: An open trial of internet-based treatment for depression. *E-journal of Applied Psychology, 4*(2), 18–24.

Perlis, R. H., Fraguas, R., Fava, M., Trivedi, M. H., Luther, J. F., Wisniewski, S. R., & Rush, A. J. (2005). Prevalence and clinical correlates of irritability in major depressive disorder: A preliminary report from the Sequenced Treatment Alternatives to Relieve Depression study. *Journal of Clinical Psychiatry, 66*(2), 159–166.

Perloe, A., Esposito-Smythers, C., Curby, T. W., & Renshaw, K. D. (2014). Concurrent trajectories of change in adolescent and maternal depressive symptoms in the TORDIA study. *Journal of Youth and Adolescence, 43*(4), 612–628.

Persons, J. B., Davidson, J., & Tompkins, M. A. (2001). *Essential components of cognitive-behavior therapy for depression*. Washington, DC: American Psychological Association.

Persons, J. B. & Tompkins, M. A. (2011). Cognitive-behavioral case formulation. In T. D. Eells (Ed.), *Handbook of psychotherapy case formulation* (pp. 290–316). New York, NY: Guilford Press.

Phillips, W. J., Hine, D. W., & Thorsteinsson, E. B. (2010). Implicit cognition and depression: A meta-analysis. *Clinical Psychology Review, 30*, 691–709.

Posner, K., Brent, D., Lucas, C., Gould, M., Stanley, B., Brown, G., . . . & Mann, J. (2008). *Columbia-Suicide Severity Rating Scale (C-SSRS)*. New York: Columbia University Medical Center.

Pope, A., & West, A. S. (2014). *Essay on criticism*. Cambridge: Cambridge University Press.

Post, R. M. (1992). Transduction of psychosocial stress into the neurobiology of recurrent affective disorder. *American Journal of Psychiatry, 149*, 999–1010.

Pretorius, W. M. (2006). Cognitive behavioural therapy supervision: Recommended practice. *Behavioural and Cognitive Psychotherapy, 34*(4), 413–420.

Prochaska, J. O., & DiClemente, C. C. (1984). *The thranstheoretical approach: Crossing traditional boundariesof therapy*. Homewood, IL: Dow/Jones Irwin.

Proudfoot, J., Ryden, C., Everitt, B., Goldberg, D., Tylee, A., Gray, J. A., et al. (2004). Clinical efficacy of computerised cognitive-behavioural therapy for anxiety and depression in primary care: Randomised controlled trial. *British Journal of Psychiatry, 185*(1), 46–54.

Pumariega, A. J., Rothe, E., Mian, A., Carlisle, L., Toppelberg, C., Harris, T., . . . & Adolescent Psychiatry Committee on Quality (2013). Practice parameter for cultural competence in child and adolescent psychiatric practice. *Journal of the American Academy of Child and Adolescent Psychiatry, 52*, 1101–1115.

Qin, P., & Nordentoft, M. (2005). Suicide risk in relation to psychiatric hospitalization: Evidence based on longitudinal registers. *Archives of General Psychiatry, 62*, 427–432.

Rao, U., Dahl, R. E., Ryan, N. D., Birmaher, B., Williamson, D. E., Giles, D. E., . . . & Nelson, B. (1996). The relationship between longitudinal clinical course and sleep and cortisol changes in adolescent depression. *Biological Psychiatry, 40*(6), 474–484.

Radloff, L. S. (1977). The CES-D Scale: A self-report depression scale for research in the general population. *Applied Psychological Measurement, 1,* 385–401.

Richards, D., & Richardson, T. (2012). Computer-based psychological treatments for depression: a systematic review and meta-analysis. *Clinical Psychology Review, 32*(4), 329–342.

Riso, L. P., du Toit, P. L., Stein, D. J., & Young, J. E. (Eds.) (2007). *Cognitive schemas and core beliefs in psychological problems: A scientist-practitioner guide.* Washington, DC: APA Books.

Roberts, J. E., Gilboa, E., & Gotlib, I. H. (1998). Ruminative response style and vulnerability to episodes of dysphoria: Gender, neuroticism, and episode duration. *Cognitive Therapy and Research, 22,* 401–423.

Robinson, M. S., & Alloy, L. B. (2003). Negative cognitive styles and stress-reactive rumination interact to predict depression: A prospective study. *Cognitive Therapy and Research, 27,* 275–291.

Rohde, P., Waldron, H. B., Turner, C. W., Brody, J., & Jorgensen, J. (2014). Sequenced versus coordinated treatment for adolescents with comorbid depressive and substance use disorders. *Journal of Consulting and Clinical Psychology, 82,* 342–348.

Rossello, J., & Bernal, G. (1999). The efficacy of cognitive-behavioral and interpersonal treatments for depression in Puerto Rican adolescents. *Journal of Consulting and Clinical Psychology, 67,* 734–745.

Rotter, J. B. (1966). Generalized expectancies for internal versus external control of reinforcement. *Psychological Monographs,* 80 (whole no. 609).

Rudd, M. D., Joiner, T. E., & Rajab, H. (1996). Relationships among suicide ideators, attempters, and multiple attempters in a young adults sample. *Journal of Abnormal Psychology, 105,* 541–550.

Rudolph, K. D. (2008). Developmental influences on interpersonal stress generation in depressed youth. *Journal of Abnormal Psychology, 117*(3), 673–679.

Rudolph, K. D., & Flynn, M. (2007). Childhood adversity and youth depression: influence of gender and pubertal status. *Developmental Psychopathology, 19,* 497–521.

Rudolph, K. D., & Hammen, C. (1999). Age and gender as determinants of stress exposure, generation, and reactions in youngsters: a transactional perspective. *Child Development, 70,* 660–677.

Rudolph, K. D., Hammen, C., Burge, D., Lindberg, N., Herzberg, D., & Daley, S. E. (2000). Toward an interpersonal life-stress model of depression: the developmental context of stress generation. *Developmental Psychopathology, 12,* 215–234.

Rutter, M., Kim-Cohen, J., & Maughan, B. (2006). Continuities and discontinuities in psychopathology between childhood and adult life. *Journal of Child Psychology and Psychiatry, 47*(3–4), 276–295.

Ryan, R. M., Lynch, M. F., Vansteenkiste, M., & Deci, E. L. (2011). Motivation and autonomy in counseling, psychotherapy, and behavior change: A look at theory and practice. *Counseling Psychologist, 1,* 1–68.

Saewyc, E., Poon, C., Wang, N., Homma, Y., Smith, A., & the McCreary Centre Society (2007). *Not yet equal: The health of lesbian, gay, and bisexual youth in BC.* Vancouver, BC: McCreary Centre Society.

Safer, D. J., & Zito, J. M. (2006). Treatment-emergent adverse events from selective serotonin reuptake inhibitors by age group: Children versus adolescents. *Journal of Child and Adolescent Psychopharmacology, 16,* 159–169.

Sebastian, C., Viding, E., Williams, K. D., & Blakemore, S. J. (2010). Social brain development and the affective consequences of ostracism in adolescence. *Brain and Cognition, 72,* 134–145.

Segal, Z. V., Williams, J. M. G., & Teasdale, J. D. (2012). *Mindfulness-based cognitive therapy for depression.* New York: Guilford Press.

Shaffer, D., Gould, M. S., Fisher, PL, Trautman, P., Moreau, D., Kleiman, M., et al. (1996). Psychiatric diagnosis in child and adolescent suicide. *Archives of General Psychiatry, 53,* 339–348.

Shapiro, S. L., Carlson, L. E., Astin, J. A., & Freedman, B. (2006). Mechanisms of mindfulness. *Journal of Clinical Psychology, 62*(3), 373–386.

Sheehan, D. V., Sheehan, K. H., Shytle, R. D., Janavs, J., Bannon, Y., Rogers, J. E., ... & Wilkinson, B. (2010). Reliability and validity of the Mini International Neuropsychiatric Interview for Children and Adolescents (MINI-KID). *Journal of Clinical Psychiatry, 71*(3), 313–326.

Shiffman, S., Stone, A. A., & Hufford, M. R. (2008). Ecological momentary assessment. *Annual Review of Clinical Psychology, 4,* 1–32.

Shih, J. H., Eberhart, N. K., Hammen, C. L., & Brennan, P. A. (2006). Differential exposure and reactivity to interpersonal stress predict sex differences in adolescent depression. *Journal of Clinical Child and Adolescent Psychology, 35,* 103–115.

Shore, J. H. (2013). Telepsychiatry: Videoconferencing in the delivery of psychiatric care. *American Journal of Psychiatry, 170*(3), 256–262.

Simon, T. R., Swann, A. C., Powerll, K. E., Potter, L. B., Kresnow, M., & O'Carroll, P. W. (2001). Characteristics of impulsive suicide attempts and attempters. *Suicide and Life-Threatening Behavior, 32,* 49–59.

Skinner, B. F. (1957). *Verbal behavior.* New York, NY: Appleton-Century-Crofts.

Slavich, G. M., & Epel, E. S. (2010). *The Stress and Adversity Inventory (STRAIN): An automated system for assessing cumulative stress exposure.* Los Angeles, CA: University of California, Los Angeles.

Slavich, G. M., Monroe, S. M., & Gotlib, I. H. (2011). Early parental loss and depression history: associations with recent life stress in major depressive disorder. *Journal of Psychiatry Research, 45,* 1146–1152.

Slavich, G. M., Thornton, T., Torres, L. D., Monroe, S. M., & Gotlib, I. H. (2009). Targeted rejection predicts hastened onset of major depression. *Journal of Social and Clinical Psychology, 28,* 223–243.

Smith, J. (2007). *The Beginner's Guide to Zen Buddhism.* New York: Harmony.

Somerville, L. H. (2013). Special issue on the teenage brain: Sensitivity to social evaluation. *Current Directions in Psychological Science, 22,* 121–127.

Spek, V., Nyklíček, I., Smits, N., Cuijpers, P. I. M., Riper, H., Keyzer, J., & Pop, V. (2007). Internet-based cognitive behavioural therapy for subthreshold depression in people over 50 years old: A randomized controlled clinical trial. *Psychological Medicine, 37*(12), 1797–1806.

Spence, S. H., & Reinecke, M. A. (2003). Cognitive approaches to understanding, preventing, and treating child and adolescent depression. *Cognitive Therapy Across the Lifespan: Evidence and Practice*, 358–395.

Spielmans, G. I., & Gerwig, K. (2014). The efficacy of antidepressants on overall well-being and self-reported depression symptom severity in youth: A meta-analysis. *Psychotherapy and Psychosomatics, 83*, 158–164.

Spielmans, G. I., Pasek, L. F., & McFall, J. P. (2007). What are the active ingredients in cognitive and behavioral psychotherapy for anxious and depressed children? A meta-analytic review. *Clinical Psychology Review, 27*(5), 642–654.

Spirito, A., Esposito-Smythers, C., Wolff, J., & Uhl, K. (2011). Cognitive-behavioral therapy for adolescent depression and suicidality. *Child and Adolescent Psychiatric Clinics of North America, 20*(2), 191–204.

Stange, J. P., Hamlat, E. J., Hamilton, J. L., Abramson, L. Y., & Alloy, L. B. (2013). Overgeneral autobiographical memory, emotional maltreatment, and depressive symptoms in adolescence: Evidence of a cognitive vulnerability-stress interaction. *Journal of Adolescence, 36*, 201–208.

Stark, K. D., Streusand, W., Krumholz, L. S., & Patel, P. (2010). Cognitive-behavioral therapy for depression: The ACTION treatment program for girls. In J. R. Weisz & A. E. Kazdin (Eds.), *Evidence-based psychotherapies for children and adolescents* (2nd ed.) (pp. 93–109). New York, NY: Guilford Press.

Stasiak, K., Hatcher, S., Frampton, C., & Merry, S. N. (2012). A pilot double blind randomized placebo controlled trial of a prototype computer-based cognitive behavioural therapy program for adolescents with symptoms of depression. *Behavioural and Cognitive Psychotherapy, 20*, 1–17.

Steer, R. A., Kumar, G., & Beck, A. T. (1993). Self-reported suicidal ideation in adolescent psychiatric inpatients. *Journal of Consulting and Clinical Psychology, 61*(6), 1096.

Stewart, J. G., & Harkness, K. L. (2012). Symptom specificity in the acute treatment of major depressive disorder: A re-analysis of the treatment of depression collaborative research program. *Journal of Affective Disorders, 137*(1), 87–97.

Stewart, J. G., Kim, J.C., Esposito, E. C., Gold, J., Nock, M. K., & Auerbach, R. P. (2015). Predicting suicide attempts in depressed adolescents: Clarifying the role of disinhibition and child sexual abuse. *Journal of Affective Disorders, 187*, 27–34.

Stroud, C. B., Davila, J., Hammen, C., & Vrshek-Schallhorn, S. (2011). Severe and nonsevere events in first onsets versus recurrences of depression: Evidence for stress sensitization. *Journal of Abnormal Psychology, 120*, 142–154.

Stroud, L. R., Foster, E., Papandonatos, G. D., Handwerger, K., Granger, D. A., Kivlighan, K. T., & Niaura, R. (2009). Stress response and the adolescent transition: Performance versus peer rejection stressors. *Developmental Psychopathology, 21*, 47–68.

Strunk, D. R., & Adler, A. D. (2009). Cognitive biases in three prediction tasks: A test of the cognitive model of depression. *Behaviour Research and Therapy, 47*(1), 34–40.

Strunk, D. R., DeRubeis, R. J., Chiu, A. W., & Alvarez, J. (2007). Patients' competence in and performance of cognitive therapy skills: Relation to the reduction of relapse risk following treatment for depression. *Journal of Consulting and Clinical Psychology, 75*(4), 523.

Strunk, D. R., Lopez, H., & DeRubeis, R. J. (2006). Depressive symptoms are associated with unrealistic negative predictions of future life events. *Behaviour Research and Therapy, 44*(6), 861–882.

Sue, S., Zane, N., Nagayama Hall, G. C., & Berger, L. K. (2009). The case for cultural competency in psychotherapeutic interventions. *Annual Review of Psychology, 60,* 525–548.

Sumner, J. A., Griffith, J. W., Mineka, S., Rekart, K. N., Zinbarg, R. E., & Craske, M. G. (2011). Overgeneral autobiographical memory and chronic interpersonal stress as predictors of the course of depression in adolescents. *Cognition and Emotion, 25,* 183–192.

Sveindottir, H., & Backstrom, T. (2000). Prevalence of menstrual cycle symptom cyclicity and premenstrual dysphoric disorder in a random sample of women using and not using oral contraceptives. *Acta Obstetricia et Gynecologica Scandinavica, 79*(5), 405–413.

Sweeney, M., Robins, M., Ruberu, M., & Jones, J. (2005). African-American and Latino families in TADS: Recruitment and treatment considerations. *Cognitive and Behavioral Practice, 12,* 221–229.

Tang, T. Z., & DeRubeis, R. J. (1999). Sudden gains and critical sessions in cognitive-behavioral therapy for depression. *Journal of Consulting and Clinical Psychology, 67*(6), 894–904.

Tang, T. Z., DeRubeis, R. J., Beberman, R., & Pham, T. (2005). Cognitive changes, critical sessions, and sudden gains in cognitive-behavioral therapy for depression. *Journal of Consulting and Clinical Psychology, 73*(1), 168–172.

Taurines, R., Gerlach, M., Warnke, A., Thome, J., & Wewetzer, C. (2011). Pharmacotherapy in depressed children and adolescents. *World Journal of Biological Psychiatry, 12,* S11–S15.

Teasdale, J. D., Segal, Z. V., Williams, J. M. G., Ridgeway, V. A., Soulsby, J. M., & Lau, M. A. (2000). Prevention of relapse/recurrence in major depression by mindfulness-based cognitive therapy. *Journal of Consulting and Clinical Psychology, 68,* 615–623.

Technow, J. R., Hazel, N. A., Abela, J. R., & Hankin, B. L. (2015). Stress sensitivity interacts with depression history to predict depressive symptoms among youth: Prospective changes following first depression onset. *Journal of Abnormal Child Psychology, 43,* 489–501.

Tee, J., & Kazantzis, N. (2011). Collaborative empiricism in cognitive therapy: A definition and theory for the relationship construct. *Clinical Psychology: Science and Practice, 18*(1), 47–61.

Titov, N., Andrews, G., Davies, M., McIntyre, K., Robinson, E., & Solley, K. (2010). Internet treatment for depression: A randomized controlled trial comparing clinician vs. technician assistance. *PloS One, 5*(6), e10939.

Torous, J., Staples, P., Shanahan, M., Lin, C., Peck, P., Keshavan, M., & Onnela, J. P. (2015). Utilizing a personal smartphone custom app to assess the Patient Health Questionnaire-9 (PHQ-9) depressive symptoms in patients with major depressive disorder. *JMIR Mental Health, 2*(1), e8.

Trepper, T. (1991). Senior editor's comments. In M. Worden (Ed.), *Adolescents and their families: An introduction to assessment and intervention.* New York: Haworth Press.

Treynor, W., Gonzalez, R., & Nolen-Hoeksema, S. (2003). Rumination reconsidered: A psychometric analysis. *Cognitive Therapy and Research, 27*, 247–259.

Tsapakis, E. M., Soldani, F., Tondo, L., & Baldessarini, R. J. (2008). Efficacy of antidepressants in juvenile depression: Meta-analysis. *British Journal of Psychiatry, 193*, 10–17.

Tseng, W. S., & Streltzer, J. (2008). *Cultural competence in health care: A guide for professionals.* New York, NY: Springer Science and Business Media.

Twenge, J. M., & Nolen-Hoeksema, S. (2002). Age, gender, race, socioeconomic status, and birth cohort differences on the children's depression inventory: A meta-analysis. *Journal of Abnormal Psychology, 111*(4), 578–588.

Van Ryn, M. (2002). Research on the provider contribution to race/ethnicity disparities in medical care. *Medical Care, 40*, 140–151.

Wagner, B., Horn, A. B., & Maercker, A. (2014). Internet-based versus face-to-face cognitive-behavioral intervention for depression: A randomized controlled non-inferiority trial. *Journal of Affective Disorders, 152*, 113–121.

Wagner, S., Muller, C., Helmreich, I., Huss, M., & Tadic, A. (2015). A meta-analysis of cognitive functions in children and adolescents with major depressive disorder. *European Child and Adolescent Psychiatry, 24*, 5–19.

Webb, C. A., Auerbach, R. P., & DeRubeis, R. J. (2012). Processes of change in CBT of adolescent depression: Review and recommendations. *Journal of Clinical Child and Adolescent Psychology, 41*(5), 654–665.

Webb, C. A., Beard, C., Auerbach, R. P., Menninger, E., & Bjorgvinsson, T. (2014). The therapeutic alliance in a naturalistic psychiatric setting: Temporal relations with depressive symptom change. *Behavior Research and Therapy, 61*, 70–77.

Webb, C. A. & Pizzagalli, D. A. (in press). Sadness and Depression. In M. Lewis, J. M. Haviland-Jones, & L. F. Barrett (Eds.), *The handbook of emotion* (4th ed.). New York: Guilford.

Weersing, V. R., & Gonzalez, A. (2009). Effectiveness of interventions for adolescent depression: Reason for hope or cause for concern? In S. Nolen-Hoeksema & L. M. Hilt (Eds.), *Handbook of depression in adolescents.* New York: Routledge.

Weissman, A. N., & Beck, A. T. (1978). Development and validation of the Dysfunctional Attitude Scale: A preliminary investigation. Paper presented at the annual meeting of the American Educational Research Association, Toronto, Ontario, Canada.

Weisz, J. R., McCarty, C. A., & Valeri, S. M. (2006). Effects of psychotherapy for depression in children and adolescents: A meta-analysis. *Psychological Bulletin, 132*, 132–149.

Williams, J. M., Barnhofer, T., Crane, C., Herman, D., Raes, F., Watkins, E., & Dalgleish, T. (2007). Autobiographical memory specificity and emotional disorder. *Psychological Bulletin, 133*, 122–148.

Williams, J. M., & Broadbent, K. (1986). Autobiographical memory in suicide attempters. *Journal of Abnormal Psychology, 95*, 144–149.

Williamson, D. E., Birmaher, B., Frank, E., Anderson, B. P., Matty, M. K., & Kupfer, D. J. (1998). Nature of life events and difficulties in depressed adolescents. *Journal of the American Academy of Child and Adolescent Psychiatry, 37*, 1049–1057.

Wing, R. R., & Phelan, S. (2005). Long-term weight loss maintenance. *American Journal of Clinical Nutrition, 82*(1), 222S–225S.

Young, J. E., Klosko, J. S., & Weishaar, M. E. (2003). *Schema therapy: A practitioner's guide.* New York: Guilford Press.

Young, J. F., Mufson, L., & Davies, M. (2006). Impact of comorbid anxiety in an effectiveness study of interpersonal psychotherapy for depressed adolescents. *Journal of the American Academy of Child and Adolescent Psychiatry, 45,* 904–912.

Zettle, R. D., Rains, J. C., & Hayes, S. C. (2011). Processes of change in acceptance and commitment therapy and cognitive therapy for depression: A mediation reanalysis of Zettle and Rains. *Behavior Modification, 35*(3), 265–283.

Zinbarg, R. E., Craske, M. G., & Barlow, D. H. (2006). *Mastery of your anxiety and worry: Therapist guide.* New York, NY: Oxford University Press.

Zung, W. W. (1965). A self-rating depression scale. *Archives of General Psychiatry, 12*(1), 63–70.

Index

abbreviated thought records 100, 101
Abela, John 22–23
Abramson, L. Y. 22
abuse 14, 69–70, 163, 189
Acceptance and Commitment Therapy (ACT) 104n3, 148
acculturation 174
Achenbach, T. M. 38
ACT *see* Acceptance and Commitment Therapy
ACTION treatment program 124
activating situations 70, 75
activity logs 86–92, 93, 94, 99–100
activity monitoring 83, 86–92, 99–100
activity scheduling 76, 78, 90, 92–95, 211
ADAA *see* Anxiety and Depression Association of America
ADDRESSING acronym 169
affirmations 63
agenda setting 79–80, 85, 106
aggression 190–191
aggressive communication 118–120
alcohol 33, 176, 179, 184, 196–197
all-or-nothing thinking 109, 111, 213
alliance-interfering behaviors 55–59
alternative thoughts 109, 110
ambivalence 63–64
American Psychological Association (APA) 164, 166n14
AMT *see* Autobiographical Memory Task
anger: aggressive communication 120; cognitive themes 101, 102; interpersonal exchanges 77; mindfulness training 149–150; negative automatic thoughts 6; suicidality 190
anhedonia 4, 138; attentional bias 26; behavioral activation 86; residual symptoms 139–140; suicide risk 190
antidepressants 5, 123, 175, 185–187
anxiety: additional treatment for 142; cognitive distortions 183; cognitive themes 101, 102; comorbidity 2, 178, 179–180, 181–182; iCBT 210; K-SADS-PL 35; mindfulness 146, 147, 150; negative automatic thoughts 6; problem list 74; schemas 21; suicidality 190, 191; targeted rejection 13; treatment plan 76
Anxiety and Depression Association of America (ADAA) 212n22, 213
APA *see* American Psychological Association
apologies 57
appetite disturbance 4
apps 211, 212–215
Armstrong, T. 25–26
Artin, K. 37
assertive communication 120–122
assessment 30–42; cultural considerations 167–169; diagnostic interviews 32–35; family involvement 173–174; goals of 30–32; observational methods 37–38; self-report questionnaires 35–37, 139, 208, 212; suicidality 39–41, 188–199, 203; third-party reports 38–39

assets 70–71, 76
assignments 48–49, 51, 112–113; *see also* homework
assumptions 77, 78, 114–115
Astin, J. A. 147
attention 146–147, 148, 154, 158
attentional biases 25–26, 105, 115
attitudes 114
attributional style 21–22, 23
Auerbach, R. P. 26
Autobiographical Memory Task (AMT) 27
autonomy 60–61, 84, 106, 161, 164, 197
avoidance 16–17, 67, 75, 102; activity scheduling 94; anxiety disorders 181; problem list 74; treatment plan 76

Bandura, A. 18–19
Barbaranelli, C. 18–19
BDI-II *see* Beck Depression Inventory
Beating the Blues (BTB) 206
Beck, A. T. 20–21, 69, 157
Beck Depression Inventory (BDI-II) 32n, 36, 47, 139, 212
Beck Scale for Suicide Ideation (BSI) 40
behavioral activation (BA) 6, 85, 86–95, 134, 135, 181; *see also* activity monitoring; activity scheduling
behavioral experiments 77, 111–112, 175, 178, 185
behavioral models 10, 16–18
behaviors: activity scheduling 93–94; CBT triangle 6; goals 72; introducing CBT to the patient 82–83; observational methods 37; problem list 74; reinforcement 16; suicidality 201–202
beliefs: anxiety disorders 181; barriers to problem solving 126–127; behavioral experiments 77; case conceptualization 69; core 48, 77, 103, 113–116; cultural considerations 172, 173; intermediate 69, 113, 114–115, 162, 178; LRFL Inventory 41; negative cognitive triad 20; self-efficacy 18; sleep problems 178; substance use disorders 184–185; *see also* negative automatic thoughts
Berman, A. L. 188, 192, 194
Bishop, S. R. 146–147
Blazer, D. G. 5
bodily sensations 146, 148, 149, 153–154, 183
body scan meditation 153–154
booster sessions 144–145
Bordin, E. S. 50
boundaries 55, 160–162
Brahm, Ajahn 128
brain processes 13, 28
brainstorming 83, 106, 112, 125, 127–128, 138, 203, 211
breathing exercises 145, 148, 150, 151–153, 177, 182
Brent, David 123, 189
brooding 22, 24
Brown, George 11
BSI *see* Beck Scale for Suicide Ideation
Buddhism 120, 128, 145–146, 157–158
Buhrmester, D. 19
bullying 74, 75, 172, 191
buy-in 52, 78, 108, 198

caffeine 176
Caporino, N. E. 179–180
Caprara, G. V. 18–19
Carlson, L. E. 147
Carter, J. S. 12
case conceptualization 68–71, 74–77, 78, 81, 86, 115, 141, 171–172
catastrophizing 109, 111, 183, 213
CBCL *see* Child Behavior Checklist
CBT *see* cognitive behavior therapy
Center for Epidemiological Studies Depression Scale (CES-D) 36–37
chain analysis 98–99, 137, 140, 144–145
change 59, 60, 61, 62
Child Behavior Checklist (CBCL) 39
Child Response Styles Questionnaire (CRSQ) 23n1
cognitive behavior therapy (CBT) 5–7, 8; collaborative empiricism 48, 49,

105–106, 108; comorbidity 178–185; early sessions 66–95; first session structure 79, 81–83; insomnia 175–178; mindfulness 157–158, 159; post-treatment competency in CBT skills 134–137; problem solving 123–124, 129; psychoeducation 46–47; stressful life events 15; suicidality 200; technological developments 205–216; therapeutic alliance 49–55; time-limited nature of 73, 131–132
cognitive case conceptualization 68–71, 74–77, 78, 81, 86, 115, 141, 171–172
Cognitive Conceptualization Diagram 113, 114
cognitive control 28–29
cognitive distancing 104, 157–158
cognitive distortions 6, 82, 109–111; anxiety disorders 183; guided-intervention apps 213; Socratic method 106
cognitive flexibility 129
cognitive models 10, 19–24
cognitive restructuring 77, 96, 104–105, 123, 162; anxiety disorders 182, 183; cognitive flexibility 129; cultural considerations 172–173; guided-intervention apps 213; iCBT 210
cognitive rigidity 190, 194
cognitive themes 101–102
Cognitive Theory (Beck) 20–21, 69
collaboration 61–62, 105
collaborative empiricism 48, 49, 65, 105–106, 108, 167
Columbia Suicide Severity Rating Scale 40, 41
communication: communication styles 116–122; cultural considerations 171; interpersonal skills 202–203; with parents 161–162
comorbidity 2, 141, 178–185; K-SADS-PL 35; sequential treatment 178–180; simultaneous treatment 180–185
compensatory strategies 69, 75
computer-based programs 205–206

concentration difficulties 3, 22, 38, 191
conduct disorder 2, 189
confidence 52
confidentiality 43–44, 142
confirmation bias 113
consequences 16
consequential thinking 125
contingencies 16, 68
coping cards 77
coping strategies: anxiety disorders 183; Personal Relapse Prevention Plan 137; Social Cognitive Theory 18; suicidality 191, 200, 201
coping toolboxes 184
core beliefs 48, 77, 103, 113–116
crisis survival skills 184
CRSQ *see* Child Response Styles Questionnaire
cultural considerations 164–174; assessment of cultural factors 167–169; case conceptualization 171–172; cognitive restructuring 172–173; communication 171; family involvement 173–174; heterogeneity within cultural groups 169–170; self-evaluation 165–166; self-guided education 166–167
Cummings, C. M. 179–180

DBT *see* Dialectical Behavior Therapy
Deci, E. L. 59
dependency 22
dependent events 12, 13, 14
developmental appropriateness 78–79
Diagnostic and Statistical Manual of Mental Disorders (DSM-5) 3–5, 141
diagnostic interviews 32–35
Dialectical Behavior Therapy (DBT) 148
diathesis-stress models 14, 19–22, 27, 29, 70, 137
didactic approach 107, 171
diet 176
digestible bites 127
discrimination 172
distraction 24
distress reduction 50, 51–52
divorce 14–15

Dobson, Keith 16–17
dot-probe task 25
downward arrow technique 102–104, 113, 173
Dozois, David 21
drug use *see* substance use
DSM-5 *see Diagnostic and Statistical Manual of Mental Disorders*
Dudley, R. 66
dysfunctional attitudes 20–21, 75
dysphoria 23–24

early sessions 66–95; activity monitoring 86–92; activity scheduling 92–95; case conceptualization 68–71, 74–77, 81, 86; first session structure 79–84; general structure 84–86; identification of presenting issues 66–68; setting goals 71–73; treatment plans 76, 77–79
early-warning signs 136, 138, 184, 200, 201
Ebert, D. D. 210
Ecological Momentary Assessment (EMA) 145n10, 212, 214
education 33
Eliot, George 95
EMA *see* Ecological Momentary Assessment
emotions: activity logs 99; anxiety disorders 183; attentional biases 25; Beck's Cognitive Model 21; CBT triangle 6; core beliefs 115; emotion-processing biases 27–28; emotional regulation 52, 134; HEADS-ED 33; introducing CBT to the patient 82–83; mindfulness 147, 148, 149, 157; NATs and 96–97; positive 71; problem list 74; suicidality 201; themes 101–102; thought records 101, 110
empathy 29, 50, 51
ending treatment 131–132
epidemiology 1–3
episodes 3, 29, 70, 141
ethnicity 2, 164–165, 168, 169–170; *see also* cultural considerations

evidence 107, 108–109, 112, 115–116, 127
evocation 62
exercise 176
expectations of therapy 43–44, 46–47
exposure activation 181

facial expressions 27–28
family 142, 160–164; cultural considerations 173–174; HEADS-ED 33; parental depression 142–144; suicidality 189, 194–195, 199, 200; *see also* parents
fatigue 3, 4, 38, 138, 139, 140
feedback 50, 53–55, 85; assignments 113; from colleagues 58; first session 79, 84
Ferster, C. B. 16, 17
5 Ps 124–126
fluoxetine 185
Fournier, J. C. 5
Freedman, B. 147
Friedman, J. 42
friendships 17, 75
Frost, R. 55
full remission 3
functional analysis 17
functional impairment 179

Garber, J. 11, 12
Gardner, E. A. 36
gender 2
Gilbert, K. 28
goals: assessment 30–32; booster sessions 145; first session 79, 81; goal list 81, 83, 86; patient involvement 106; Personal Relapse Prevention Plan 135, 136; post-treatment 133–134; problem solving 124; reassessing 132–133; setting 71–73; short-, medium-, and long-term 73; therapeutic alliance 50, 52; treatment plans 76, 78
Goldston, D. 40
Goodness, K. 19
Gotlib, Ian 14, 28, 29
guided discovery 48–49, 57, 65, 182
guided-intervention apps 213

guilt 3, 190; aggressive communication 120; cognitive themes 102; melancholia 4

Hammen, C. L. 11
Harkness, Kate 5, 11, 14
Harvey, A. G. 177
Hays, P. 169
HEADS-ED 33–34
helplessness 113
home environment 142
homework 112–113, 134; first session 79, 83; iCBT 206, 208; non-compliance 68; patient involvement 106; reviewing 85, 91; smartphones 211; thought records 100, 109–110; *see also* assignments
hopelessness 4, 6, 21–23, 181; barriers to problem solving 126; suicide risk 189, 190, 192, 194, 195
hospitalization 196, 197, 198, 199, 200
"hot" cognitions 97

iCBT *see* internet-delivered cognitive behavior therapy
identification of problems 66–68
identity, cultural 170, 171, 172–173
impulse control 149–150, 190–191, 194, 196
inattention 4
indecision 4
independent events 12, 13, 14
information-processing biases 6, 10, 24–29, 70, 105
inhibition 28–29
injustice 6, 119
insomnia 3, 22, 132, 138, 139, 174–178; *see also* sleep problems
intermediate beliefs 69, 113, 114–115, 162, 178
internet-delivered cognitive behavior therapy (iCBT) 205–210, 216
interpersonal skills 202–203
interviews 32–35
invalidating environments 56–57
irritability 4, 118; alcohol use 184; cognitive themes 101, 102; early-warning signs 138; medication side effects 186; mindfulness training 150; negative automatic thoughts 119; psychoeducation 45
Irwin, M. 37
isolation 6, 76, 134, 194, 195

Jenkins, S. R. 19
Joormann, Jutta 28, 29
judgmentalism 56

Kabat-Zinn, Jon 146, 157
Keiley, M. K. 11
Kendall, P. C. 179–180
Kessler, R. C. 5
Kiddie Schedule for Affective Disorders and Schizophrenia for School Age Children Present and Lifetime Version (K-SADS-PL) 34–35
Koko 206–207
Kuyken, W. 66, 68, 171–172

Lee, M. 42
length of therapy 132
Lewinsohn, P. M. 17
life stress 5, 10–15, 22, 96, 129, 137, 189; *see also* stress
life-threatening symptoms 179
Linehan's Reasons for Living (LRFL) Inventory 40, 41
locus of control (LOC) 19, 106, 191

Martin, C. 11
mastery 85, 90, 92, 93, 125, 134
MBCT *see* Mindfulness-Based Cognitive Therapy
medication 5, 123, 142, 175, 185–187, 196
meditation 150, 153–154, 182
melancholia 4
memory biases 26–27, 105, 212
mental health disorders 189
mental status 188, 190–191, 196
metacognitive awareness 96, 104, 148
MI *see* motivational interviewing
Miller, W. R. 59, 64
mind reading 109

mindfulness 104n3, 145–158, 159; benefits of 147–148; definition of 146–147; in everyday life 156–157; metaphors 154–156; mind wandering 145–146, 152, 156–157; mindfulness of the breath exercise 151–153; therapeutic insights 158

Mindfulness-Based Cognitive Therapy (MBCT) 104n3, 148–149, 159

Mini International Neuropsychiatric Interview for Children and Adolescents (MINI-KID) 35

Minnesota Multiphasic Personality Inventory for Depression 36

mistakes 57–58

mobile depression interventions 210–215

Mobilyze! 214

Monroe, S. M. 14

mood: activating situations 70; activity monitoring 89, 90–91, 92, 99; activity scheduling 93; introducing CBT to the patient 82; melancholia 4; mind wandering 145–146; mood disorders 189; observational methods 37; passive data collection 214; Personal Relapse Prevention Plan 136; premenstrual mood disorder 5; rating 51, 79, 80, 84, 85, 95; smartphone apps 211; substance use disorders 184; targeted rejection 13; tracking 51, 52, 83, 213

Mood and Feelings Questionnaire 37

MoodGym 206

motivational interviewing (MI) 59–65, 198

Muris, P. 19

Naar-King, S. 62, 63

National Comorbidity Study – Adolescent (NCS-A) Supplement 1–3

National Depression Screening Day (NDSD) 42

National Health Service (NHS) 208

negative automatic thoughts (NATs) 6, 47, 51, 63, 147–148; assessment of CBT skills 135;

case conceptualization 68; challenging 71, 105–112, 127; cognitive restructuring 77; collaborative empiricism 48; cultural considerations 167, 173; ending treatment 132; family involvement 162; guided-intervention apps 213; iCBT 206–207; identification of 77, 85, 92, 96–97, 104–105, 127, 135; in-session 100; introducing CBT to the patient 82–83; medication 186; mindfulness 146, 148–149, 153, 156, 157; passive style 120; problem solving 126, 127; residual symptoms 140; schemas 69; sleep 178; strategies to elicit 97–104; therapist's own 143; unfairness 119

negative cognitive triad 6, 20

negative reinforcement 16

neglect 14, 69–70

Nezu, A. M. 42

Nezu, C. M. 42

NHS *see* National Health Service

nicotine 176

Nolen-Hoeksema, S. 2, 23

non-judgmentalism 56–57, 65, 89, 146–147, 148, 183–184

non-suicidal self injury (NSSI) 40, 41, 140; *see also* self-harm

OARS 62–65

observational methods 37–38

obstacles to treatment 77, 78

Olatunji, B. O. 25–26

open-ended questions 54, 63, 66, 97–98, 106–108, 170

oppositional defiant disorder 2

over-general memories (OGMs) 27

over-reaches 64

Oxman, M. N. 37

Padesky, C. A. 66

Panoply 206–207

parents 74, 160–164; Child Behavior Checklist 39; cultural considerations 173–174; HEADS-ED 33; iCBT 210; initial contact with 43–44; loss of 14–15; parental depression 142–144;

problem list 74; suicidality 194–195, 198–199, 200; treatment plan 76; triangulating 58–59; *see also* family
partial remission 3
passive-aggressive communication 118
passive communication 117–118, 120
passive data collection 214–215
passive thinking 23
Pastorelli, C. 18–19
PDD *see* persistent depressive disorder
PDST *see* Psychological Distancing and Scaling Task
Pearlstein, T. 5
peer relationships 11, 33
Perlis, R. H. 4
persistent depressive disorder (PDD) 4
Personal Relapse Prevention Plan 134–135, 136, 137, 138, 209
personality disorders 141–142
personality traits 189
pharmacotherapy 77, 182, 185–187; *see also* medication
placebos 185
pleasure 47, 90, 92, 93–94, 138, 140
PMD *see* premenstrual mood disorder
positive events 150
positive problem orientation 129
practice 112, 137
precipitating factors 70, 75; cultural considerations 172; suicidality 188, 189–190; *see also* triggers
predisposing factors 69–70, 75; cultural considerations 172; suicidality 188, 189; *see also* vulnerability
premenstrual mood disorder (PMD) 4–5
prevalence of depression 1–2
priming 26, 29, 128
privacy 161
proactive approach 137–138
probability overestimation 183
problem list 66–67, 68–69, 74, 79, 81, 83, 86
problem solving 23n1, 24, 123–129, 162, 163
Problem-Solving Therapy (PST) 123, 124
problems, identification of 66–68

psychoeducation 8, 29, 44–47; anxiety disorders 181; first session 80–1; guided-intervention apps 213; iCBT 206, 208, 210; mindfulness 148, 151; parental depression 144; sleep hygiene 175; substance use disorders 184
Psychological Distancing and Scaling Task (PDST) 21
psychomotor agitation 3, 4, 37–38
psychomotor retardation 3, 4, 22, 37–38, 140
Pumariega, A. J. 173

questionnaires 35–37, 139, 208, 212
questions 54, 63, 66; cultural considerations 168, 170; negative automatic thoughts 97–98; Socratic method 106–108

race 2, 164–165, 168, 169–170; *see also* cultural considerations
rapport 98, 161, 163, 183; diagnostic interviews 32, 34; early sessions 79, 84, 85; motivational interviewing 59
recovery 3
recurrence 3–4, 129, 131, 138
reflection 24
reflections, therapist's 63–64
reframing 116, 207
reinforcement 10, 16, 17, 92–93
rejection 12–13, 189
relapse 3–4, 129, 131, 158–159; additional treatment to prevent 142; booster sessions 144–145; family involvement 174; iCBT 208–209; mindfulness training 148–150; Personal Relapse Prevention Plan 134–135, 136, 137, 138, 209; post-treatment competency in CBT skills 134–137; post-treatment goals 133; residual symptoms 138–139; vulnerability factors 141–142
relaxation 177, 181–182, 211
remission 3, 129, 141, 142, 175
residual symptoms 138–141, 174–175
resilience 172
resistance 51, 60, 62

250   Index

Response Styles Theory (RST) 23–24
righting reflex 62
risk assessment 188–189, 191–199
role play 100, 112, 121–122, 125, 162, 202–203
Rollnick, S. 64
Rose, G. S. 59
Rotter, J. B. 19
RST *see* Response Styles Theory
Rudolph, K. D. 11
rules 114
rumination 18, 23–24, 147–148; anxiety disorders 181; early-warning signs 138; insomnia 177; pros and cons 111
Rush, A. J. 157
Ryan, R. M. 59

SAD *see* seasonal affective disorder
sadness 4, 22, 76; cognitive themes 102; facial expressions 27–28; negative automatic thoughts 6; problem list 74; psychoeducation 45; suicidality 190; treatment plan 76
Sadness Program 206
safety 68, 182, 183, 196
safety plans 200–202, 215
Schedule for Affective Disorders and Schizophrenia for School Age Children Present and Lifetime Version (K-SADS-PL) 34–35
scheduling 57
schemas 20, 21, 48, 75; case conceptualization 69; childhood abuse 69–70; cultural considerations 173; schema change methods 77
school 10–11, 76, 142; booster sessions 144; problem list 74; treatment plan 76
SCT *see* Social Cognitive Theory
seasonal affective disorder (SAD) 4–5
seat/feet mindfulness 150
selective serotonin reuptake inhibitors (SSRIs) 185–186, 187
self-criticism 22
self-determination theory 59
self-disclosure 50, 55
self-efficacy 10, 18–19, 62, 118, 191

self-esteem 22, 191
self-evaluation 126, 165–166
self-harm 6, 140; assessment 30, 39–41; identification of 68; non-judgmentalism 56–57
Self-Injurious Thoughts and Behaviors Interview 40, 41
self-monitoring apps 212–213
Self-Referential Encoding Task (SRET) 26
self-regulation 84, 146–147
self-report questionnaires 35–37, 139, 208, 212
self-worth 4, 18, 47, 173; *see also* worthlessness
separation, parental 14–15
serotonin and norepinephrine inhibitors (SNRIs) 186
sexual abuse 14, 189
sexual assault 75
sexual orientation 168–169, 172, 173
shame 102, 190
Shapiro, S. L. 147
skills 52, 53, 65; booster sessions 145; crisis survival 184; iCBT 208–209; interpersonal 202–203; metacognitive awareness 96; mood rating 80; post-treatment competency 134–137; problem-solving 129; social 17, 77
Slavich, G. M. 14
sleep problems 3, 4, 22, 174–178; early-warning signs 138; medication side effects 186; sleep hygiene 175–178; sleep management apps 214–215; suicidality 191; *see also* insomnia
SMART goals 71–73
smartphones 89, 94, 112, 145n10, 154, 176, 205, 210–215, 216
SNRIs *see* serotonin and norepinephrine inhibitors
social cognitive learning models 10, 18–19
Social Cognitive Theory (SCT) 18
social feedback 13
social skills 17, 77
social support 11, 18, 183, 191, 200–201, 203, 207

socioeconomic status (SES) 2
Socratic method 106–108
specifiers 4–5
SRET *see* Self-Referential Encoding Task
SSRIs *see* selective serotonin reuptake inhibitors
Stewart, J. G. 5
stimulus control 175–177
Stone, A. B. 5
STRAIN *see* Stress and Adversity Inventory
strengths 70–71, 76, 172
stress 5, 51–52, 84, 123, 129, 147; cultural minorities 172; diathesis-stress models 14, 19–22, 27, 29, 70, 137; hopelessness 22; precipitating factors 70; proactive approach 137–138; residual symptoms 138–139; school 142; stress sensitization 13–15, 149; stressful life events 11–15; suicide risk 189, 192
Stress and Adversity Inventory (STRAIN) 34
Suarez, M. 62, 63
substance use 2, 178, 179, 182–185; HEADS-ED 33; suicidality 189, 194, 196
sudden gains 47
suicidality 188–204; assessment 30, 39–41, 188–199, 203; comorbidity 179; contraindications 191; family involvement 163; HEADS-ED 33; iCBT 208; imminent suicide risk 198–199; medication 186–187; mental status 190–191; precipitating factors 189–190; predisposing factors 189; prevalence 3; risk assessment 188–189, 191–199; sleep disturbance as risk factor 175; substance use disorders 182; suicidal ideation 15, 22, 40, 140, 188, 190, 192–194, 197, 203, 208; treatment 199–203
summaries 64, 70, 75–76, 79, 84, 85
Sumner, J. A. 27
supervision 58, 166
Swartz, M. S. 5

symptoms 3, 5; Beck Depression Inventory 36; changes in 47, 72; early-warning signs 138; family involvement 163; functional impairment 179; hopelessness 22; K-SADS-PL 35; life-threatening 179; medication side effects 186; Mood and Feelings Questionnaire 37; observational methods 37–38; psychoeducation 45–46, 81; reassessing treatment goals 132; residual 138–141, 174–175; tracking 31, 32, 139, 212, 213

targeted rejection 12–13, 189
tasks 50
Teacher's Report Form (TRF) 39
team approach 199–200
technology 205–216; iCBT 205–210, 216; smartphones 89, 94, 112, 145n10, 154, 176, 205, 210–215, 216; videoconferencing 215–216
termination of treatment 131–132, 174
therapeutic alliance 49–55, 65, 77; activity scheduling 93; cultural considerations 165; downward arrow technique 104; family involvement 162; substance use disorders 183; videoconferencing 215
thinking biases 105
thinking traps *see* cognitive distortions
third-party reports 38–39
thought records 109–110, 112, 129, 211; abbreviated 100, 101; sleep problems 178
thoughts: alternative 109, 110; anxiety disorders 181, 182, 183; CBT triangle 6; introducing CBT to the patient 82–83; mindfulness 146, 147, 148–149, 157–158; observational methods 37; problem list 74; suicidality 201; *see also* negative automatic thoughts
time sampling 89
Track Your Happiness 213
transtheoretical model of change (TTM) 59
treatment plans 76, 77–79

Trepper, T. 59
TRF *see* Teacher's Report Form
triangulation 58–59
triggers 69, 70, 137–138; booster sessions 145; Personal Relapse Prevention Plan 135, 136; suicidality 188, 189–190, 200, 201; *see also* precipitating factors
trust 52, 77, 79, 161, 163
TTM *see* transtheoretical model of change
Twenge, J. M. 2

unfairness 119
unlovability 6, 69, 75, 77, 103, 113, 115
unsolicited advice 62

validation 50, 51, 61, 63
videoconferencing 215–216

vulnerability: anxiety disorders 183; cognitive 19–20, 21, 22–23; models of depression 10; rumination 24; suicidality 188, 189; underlying factors 141–142; *see also* predisposing factors

walking meditation 150, 153–154
"weakest link" approach 22–23
weight change 3, 38
weight loss 131
wellness visits 42
Williamson, D. E. 11
withdrawal 102, 134
word completion tasks 26
worry 22, 177, 178
worthlessness 3, 6, 113, 115

Youth Self-Report (YSR) 39

Zung Self-Rating Depression Scale 36